SELLING IT

Information technology (IT) is an essential core of the economy today. Corporations and governments worldwide rely on it to drive their core strategy and develop and execute business models. Amounting to over 3.7 trillion US dollars of worldwide spending, the growing significance of the IT industry in the global economy is now well established. Hence, it is crucial to understand the marketplace within which it exists, and this book presents a systematic analysis of the processes, techniques, and methods involved in IT sales and marketing.

In *Selling IT*, the book:

- Integrates a large IT provider's selling process with the enterprise user's IT buying process to highlight the nuances of selling, marketing, and developing IT solutions that create value for customers.
- Discusses various key concepts such as value-based IT selling, business case for IT acquisition, vendor evaluation and management, account and customer relationship management, customer segmentation, and techniques for customer acquisition and retention.
- Analyses the challenges and opportunities involved in selling digital IT and examines the evolution of jobs and careers based on the changed IT landscape.
- Includes lesson plans, case studies, and chapter-wise practice questions to support teaching and learning.

The book boasts a robust theoretical foundation supported by a clear exposition of concepts and management theories. It will be of benefit to professionals using organisation-mandated selling processes. Young executives with a technology background looking for a sales and marketing career in the IT industry can also effectively use this book. It will also be an essential read for scholars and researchers in B2B marketing, IT consulting, technology sales, and digital transformation.

Sandip Mukhopadhyay is an associate professor at the Institute of Management Technology, Ghaziabad, India. His research interests include digital platforms and ecosystems, social media analytics and selling technology, and IT solutions. He has published widely in different international journals and authored multiple case studies. Before academia, he worked for IBM, Ericsson, Reliance, and Siemens for about twenty years, focusing on selling and deploying technology solutions. He received his PhD from MDI Gurgaon, India, specialising in business models for digital platforms. Prior to that, he received his PGDM (MBA) from IIM-Calcutta and studied engineering at IIEST, Calcutta, India.

Srinivas Pingali has close to 30 years of varied experience in product development and innovation and sales and marketing in multinationals and entrepreneurial companies. He is currently a professor of practice at the Indian Institute of Management, Udaipur, India. His areas of expertise include strategy, digital transformation, entrepreneurship, and innovation. He is a chemical engineer for Osmania University, College of Technology, India, and holds an MBA degree in marketing from the University of Illinois at Champaign–Urbana, USA. He is an executive fellow in management (doctoral equivalent) at the Indian School of Business.

Amitabh Satyam is chairman of Smart Transformations and a former managing partner of SAP. A graduate of IIT Kanpur with an MBA from Fisher College of Business, USA, he led Global Telecom Consulting at IBM, where he also set up the global IoT practice. His earlier roles include managing director at MobiApps, vice president at Siemens, national head of operations at Reliance Infocomm, and financial advisor at Morgan Stanley Smith Barney. His book, *The Smart City Transformations* (2017), is an established global reference book on the topic. In the United States, he taught for four years at Ohio State University and Rider University.

SELLING IT

The Science of Selling, Buying, and Deal-Making

Sandip Mukhopadhyay, Srinivas Pingali, and Amitabh Satyam

LONDON AND NEW YORK

First published 2022
by Routledge
2 Park Square, Milton Park, Abingdon, Oxon OX14 4RN

and by Routledge
605 Third Avenue, New York, NY 10158

Routledge is an imprint of the Taylor & Francis Group, an Informa business

© 2022 Sandip Mukhopadhyay, Srinivas Pingali and Amitabh Satyam

The right of Sandip Mukhopadhyay, Srinivas Pingali and Amitabh Satyam to be identified as authors of this work has been asserted by them in accordance with sections 77 and 78 of the Copyright, Designs and Patents Act 1988.

All rights reserved. No part of this book may be reprinted or reproduced or utilised in any form or by any electronic, mechanical, or other means, now known or hereafter invented, including photocopying and recording, or in any information storage or retrieval system, without permission in writing from the publishers.

Trademark notice: Product or corporate names may be trademarks or registered trademarks, and are used only for identification and explanation without intent to infringe.

British Library Cataloguing-in-Publication Data
A catalogue record for this book is available from the British Library

Library of Congress Cataloging-in-Publication Data
Names: Mukhopadhyay, Sandip, author. | Pingali, Srinivas, author. |
    Satyam, Amitabh, author.
Title: Selling IT: the science of selling, buying and deal-making/
    Sandip Mukhopadhyay, Srinivas Pingali and Amitabh Satyam.
Description: New York, NY: Routledge, 2022. | Includes
    bibliographical references and index.
Identifiers: LCCN 2021016106 (print) | LCCN 2021016107 (ebook) |
    ISBN 9780367694999 (hbk) | ISBN 9780367725747 (pbk) |
    ISBN 9781003155270 (ebk)
Subjects: LCSH: Information Technology—Marketing. | Information
    Technology—Vocational guidance.
Classification: LCC HF5439.I47 M85 2022 (print) |
    LCC HF5439.I47 (ebook) | DDC 004.068/8—dc23
LC record available at https://lccn.loc.gov/2021016106
LC ebook record available at https://lccn.loc.gov/2021016107

ISBN: 978-0-367-69499-9 (hbk)
ISBN: 978-0-367-72574-7 (pbk)
ISBN: 978-1-003-15527-0 (ebk)

DOI: 10.4324/9781003155270

Typeset in Sabon
by Apex CoVantage, LLC

All three authors would like to dedicate this book to their wonderful colleagues in the IT industry.

. . . .

Sandip Mukhopadhyay dedicates this book to his mother, Smt. Rekha Mukherjee; his wife, Barnali; and his children Soham and Aahana.

Srinivas Pingali dedicates this book to his mother, Dr Sunanda Rao Pingali.

Amitabh Satyam dedicates his book to his mother, Smt Pratibha Sinha, an educationist and social activist.

CONTENTS

List of figures	*viii*
List of tables	*x*
Introduction	1
1 Understanding the IT market	5
2 Business value of IT	27
3 IT project management essentials	50
4 Sales and bid management process	79
5 Buying IT	108
6 Client and account management	132
7 Marketing and sales enablement	157
8 Leading with digital	180
9 Selling cloud to enterprises	203
10 Careers in IT: today and tomorrow	223
Razorpay: providing payment convenience to disruptors	*237*
Index	*261*

FIGURES

1.1	Constructs of buyer–seller relationship in business markets	9
2.1	Drivers of IT investment	29
2.2	Worldwide IT service spending	34
2.3	The rising importance of technology firms in the global economy	35
3.1	Phases in the traditional waterfall software development method	53
3.2	Contrasting visibility	55
3.3	Comparing change management ability	56
3.4	Agile scrum framework and ceremonies	57
3.5	Risk exposure matrix	67
3.6	Typical IT project management schedule	75
4.1	Value-based IT sales management process	80
4.2	Mapping between customer and opportunity types	81
4.3	Possible outcomes of the opportunity assessment process	94
4.4	Bid management team composition	94
4.5	Developing winning value propositions	96
5.1	IT vendor management process	110
6.1	Customer portfolio management matrix	136
6.2	Sample key account	137
6.3	Mapping the state of client relationship	139
6.4	Loyalty ladder	140
6.5	Mapping future services using an Ansoff matrix	140
6.6	Customer service loop	144
6.7	Sample governance matrix	149
6.8	Sample escalation matrix	152
7.1	Ansoff matrix	161
7.2	Sample target profile	161
7.3	Roles in buyer organisations	163
7.4	Illustrative pipeline	164
7.5	Sources of demand	164
7.6	Benefits and uses of social media platforms	165

FIGURES

7.7	Sample telemarketing campaign	169
7.8	Marketing plan activities	171
7.9	Role of marketing along the buying process	171
7.10	Porter's Five Forces (adapted)	174
8.1	Structuring the field of digital technologies	183
8.2	Benefits of blockchain	189
8.3	Ecosystem leader in multi-sided platforms	196
8.4	Design thinking process	199
9.1	Three primary cloud service models	214
9.2	Market size of different types of public cloud	215
9.3	Hybrid cloud (co-existence of traditional and cloud IT)	216
9.4	Benefits of hybrid and multi-cloud	218
10.1	Emergence of new roles as per the WEF study	234

TABLES

1.1	B2B vs. B2C markets	6
1.2	Categories of IT	11
1.3	Products vs. services vs. platforms	14
1.4	Advantages and disadvantages of various engagement models	16
1.5	Use of contracts by project type	17
1.6	Roles of stakeholders in a buyer organisation	20
1.7	Mapping of customer and vendor teams	20
2.1	Multiple stakeholders and their contrasting priorities in the buying process	39
2.2	Multiple ways to develop value proposition	40
2.3	Facts and assumptions about Mphone	43
2.4	Value-based business case preparation	45
3.1	Contrasting risk and non-risk events	64
3.2	Risk response strategies	68
3.3	Resource estimation using the waterfall method	72
3.4	Level of accuracies in estimation	73
4.1	Proactive vs. reactive selling	82
4.2	Stakeholder management plan	89
4.3	Structured opportunity assessment	91
4.4	Value proposition with KPI	98
4.5	Multiple types of cost-reimbursable contracts	100
4.6	Estimating contract value	103
5.1	Framework suggesting a make decision	112
5.2	Factors affecting single/multi-sourcing decisions	115
5.3	Transaction vs. relationship-oriented buying behaviour	117
5.4	Information that impacts the vendor selection process	123
5.5	An empirical approach for vendor selection	123
6.1	Information elements in a CRM platform	134
6.2	Information for creating an account plan	138
6.3	Touchpoints for capturing feedback	144
6.4	Client service metrics	146
6.5	Sample communication plan	150

TABLES

6.6	Client–vendor relationship mapping	153
7.1	Components of a sales toolkit	173
8.1	Types of blockchain	190
9.1	Conversation starters in cloud selling	219
9.2	Key decision-makers and their priorities in cloud buying	220
10.1	Roles in IT development	226
10.2	Infrastructure and operations roles	227
10.3	Marketing and pre-sales roles	228
10.4	Account management roles	228
10.5	Business analytics and data management roles	229
10.6	General management roles	229
10.7	Consulting roles	231
10.8	New-age roles in the IT industry	233

INTRODUCTION

In this book on "Selling IT", we synthesise our own corporate and research experiences with the existing body of knowledge scattered in multiple business and technical disciplines. Besides understanding the sales and marketing aspects, a good seller also needs to understand the buying process and buyer characteristics. The book provides a broader perspective by integrating a large IT provider's selling process with the enterprise user's IT buying process. The value-based IT selling defined in the book can create value for multiple stakeholders within the organisation of the customer and the IT provider, as well as for the managers involved in the selling and buying process.

Though the book has used the IT industry as the context, sellers working in any technological organisation would find it useful. The book can be effectively used by MBA students with some IT experience or young IT executives looking for a sales and marketing career in the same industry. An MBA or final-year engineering student with no work experience would also benefit from this book, as it will provide them an understanding of the nuances of selling, marketing, and developing an IT solution that creates value for the customer. The book does not assume prior experience in the IT industry, though readers with some amount of IT experience would find it easier to relate to.

The book also takes into account two characteristics of the IT industry that increase the sales and marketing challenges in the IT domain. Primary among them is the highly innovative nature of the field; new technologies appear in waves—rising and falling. Presently we are witnessing the transformational impact of digital technologies such as artificial intelligence, machine learning, blockchain, digital platform, and others. The rapid progress in IT-enabled technologies has made IT the core component of corporate strategy and source of competitiveness. However, it is also making the existing sales and marketing processes and offerings of IT providers obsolete. Similarly, IT professionals face enormous challenges in reskilling and adopting newer technologies and business models. The second challenge arises from the fact that IT sales is an interdisciplinary subject that draws

DOI: 10.4324/9781003155270-1

INTRODUCTION

from diverse knowledge areas such as IT, B2B marketing, services sales, relationship marketing, international marketing, consulting, and innovation management. In addition, the subject might require knowledge of contract drafting, labour laws, tariffs such as duties on imports, and non-tariff subjects relating to visas and work permits.

While the instructors in management schools do not have a suitable textbook or reference book that addresses these challenges, working professionals also do not have a guide that helps them on the job. They learn the subject through on-the-job training and often in-house training while working for large organisations. We have endeavoured to develop a book that directly matches the learning needs of the students as well as professionals. Besides covering the processes, techniques, and methods used in industry, the book also provides a robust theoretical foundation with key concepts and management theories. The professionals who are using the organisation-mandated selling processes every day are usually unaware of the profound management theories behind the methods. This conceptual foundation also helps the students and the professionals generalise the concepts they learn and use them across a wide variety of situations they come across. We have also included a number of case studies and real-life examples to enhance the reader's understanding of the topics.

The book can be logically divided into four sections, representing the major areas within IT sales and marketing.

1   **Value-Based Selling Process:** This section introduces the basic characteristics of the IT industry and the key differences of IT selling compared to other types of B2B sales. As value-based selling is the cornerstone of this book, we introduce the concept of value, methods of developing compelling value propositions, and articulating and measuring value from existing B2B marketing literature. The book adopts those theories and concepts to suit the IT industry. The section provides details of the activities done in a four-step value-based selling process, which aims to take the sales out of the selling process (Terho, Haas, Eggert, and Ulaga, 2012). The section also educates readers on developing winning proposals based on the client's context and provider's capability.

2   **IT Capability Acquisition:** We start by discussing the significance of a coherent strategy for IT capability acquisition instead of tactical IT acquisition primarily focused on cost savings. We describe the key objectives and activities in different stages of the vendor management process. The sellers should be able to identify multiple stakeholders involved in the buying decisions and also their conflicting priorities based on their roles. We introduce an empirical framework that the learner can use for vendor selection, incorporating multiple commercial and technical criteria with different importance.

INTRODUCTION

3 **Account Management and Relationship Management:** As IT vendors are focused on a limited number of enterprise buyers, it is imperative for them to retain and nurture these accounts. A dissatisfied customer can potentially become a negative reference affecting future sales to other buyers. This section emphasises the value of the long-term relationship and the concept of co-creation of value. We explain the different methods of customer segmentation and the importance of identifying and nurturing key accounts which are of strategic importance to sellers. We introduce the concept of account planning, drivers of success in a relationship, and methodologies to track the progress in the key accounts. The methods and processes of strategic governance of large accounts in addition to the ongoing program and operation management are also included.

   In addition, we have covered the marketing activities practised in the IT industry for customer acquisition and customer retention. We describe the role of organisation-wide collaborative processes and tools such as knowledge management, a project repository, and customer relationship management (CRM) in the context of increasing efficiency in the sales process.

4 **Evolution of Technology and IT Careers:** While organisations have been using IT as a business enabler for decades, the recent renewed focus on IT is due to the high pace of innovation in IT and its adjacent areas. In this chapter, we study a few of those unique technological advances that are making IT even more strategic to business users. We also discuss the nuances and additional challenges and opportunities of selling digital IT. The last part of the book describes the evolution of jobs and careers based on the changed IT landscape. We focus on jobs and career options in the IT marketplace today, primarily focusing on business, consulting, and sales/marketing roles.

We want to thank several people, many of whom are our colleagues in the IT industry and academia, for supporting the conceptualisation and development of this book. We thank and appreciate Professor Asit Barma and Professor Rajesh Kumar for conceptualising an elective for MBA students focusing on IT sales and marketing in IMT, Ghaziabad, India, which raised our interest in this topic. We thank Ms Shoma Choudhury and Ms Anvitaa Bajaj for supporting this book's project from the publisher's side. We are also grateful to the reviewers of the different chapters of the book, who dedicated much time and effort to provide suggestions for improvement.

We hope all of the readers would enjoy reading the book and benefit by achieving their career objectives. We request all of the readers to send us their feedback and connect to us for any discussions.

INTRODUCTION

Gurgaon, India
Hyderabad, India
Bangalore, India
March 2021

Sandip Mukhopadhyay
Srinivas Pingali
Amitabh Satyam

Reference

Terho, H., Haas, A., Eggert, A., and Ulaga, W. (2012). "It's almost like taking the sales out of selling"—towards a conceptualization of value-based selling in business markets. *Industrial Marketing Management*, *41*(1), 174–185.

1

UNDERSTANDING THE IT MARKET

1.1 Learning objectives

This chapter provides an overview of the information technology (IT) industry within the framework of a larger B2B sales concept. The reader will learn the following:

- The unique features of business-to-business (B2B) markets and its contrast to business-to-consumer (B2C) markets
- The IT industry landscape and the players in the industry
- Engagement models of the players prevalent in the industry
- An introduction to the concept of IT selling
- The roles of key actors involved in buying and selling of IT.

1.2 Introduction

IT is critical for running today's businesses. Most companies use IT to drive their core strategy, develop and execute business models, and run business processes. For these companies, information technology is much more than a backend activity. One cannot imagine Walmart, Reliance Jio, and Amazon's businesses without appreciating their technology infrastructure. In addition, corporations, governments, and social organisations effectively use IT to provide services to citizens, provide assistance to the under-privileged, and create an enabling environment for businesses and entrepreneurs. Many macroeconomic studies have shown that countries that lead the global race for technology innovations enjoy a competitive edge over other nations. The United States, China, and India are some examples. We have discussed the importance of IT in business, economy, and government in more details in Chapter 2.

With the growing significance of the IT industry in the global economy, it is essential to understand the marketplace within which it exists.

The IT services industry mainly falls within the context of B2B markets. We therefore begin the book and this chapter by defining B2B markets and how they are both similar and different from B2C markets.

DOI: 10.4324/9781003155270-2

The second part of the chapter introduces the IT industry landscape, the types of IT products and services, and the prevailing and emerging engagement models in the IT industry. The chapter provides an overview of the IT services sales process, the competencies required for successful selling, and profiles of typical customers and vendors.

1.3 B2B markets

If a business sells a product or service directly to another business, government entity, or a social organisation rather than to an individual customer, the transaction is referred to as B2B (Anderson, Narus, Narayandas, and Seshadri, 2011). Businesses acquire these goods or services either for their own use, or to incorporate into their products and services, or for selling to their customers (Anderson et al., 2011). Sales of input material for manufacturing an automobile or steel for constructing a factory are all examples of B2B markets. Most IT sales fall under B2B transactions, with IT vendors selling services and products to IT customers. Table 1.1 provides an overview of the significant differences between B2C and B2B markets.

From Table 1.1, it can be inferred that customers in B2B markets focus on the impact of the solution that they purchase on their businesses. The impact could be in the form of increase in sales, profitability, and customer satisfaction. In contrast, in the consumer market, the focus remains on aesthetics, usability, and price.

Table 1.1 B2B vs. B2C markets

Attribute	Business-to-Consumer (B2C)	Business-to-Business (B2B)
No. of buyers	Large numbers; highly fragmented	Relatively fewer
No. of sellers	Relatively larger	Relatively fewer
Products	Mass-produced	Customised
Pricing	Fixed price	Negotiated
Transaction value	Relatively lower and one-time	High-value and likelihood of repeat purchase
Pre-sales process	Unaided and impacted by advertisement	Detailed evaluation
Sales process	Brief and focussed on one transaction	Lengthy and complex
Decision-makers	Individual or family	Multiple decision-makers
Influencers	Media, family, friends	Company internal personnel, consultants, reference customers
Value	Price, perception, usability, experience	Business impact
Demand	Derived	Direct/media-stimulated

UNDERSTANDING THE IT MARKET

In B2B markets, sellers develop solutions that provide business value, effectively communicate it to customers, measure the value created, and gain an adequate return (Anderson et al., 2011). The concept of value and its application in IT sales is explained further in Chapters 2 and 4.

Customer–supplier relationships in IT, like other B2B markets, operate at two levels; they are organisation-to-organisation relationships and people-to-people relationships. We discuss organisation-to-organisation partnerships in greater detail in later chapters.

Other than the business relationship between two or multiple organisations, people-to-people relationships down to the level of the salesforce handling the transaction play an important role in B2B transactions. Some of the concepts that have been studied in the academic literature on this subject include customer-oriented selling and adaptive selling. Customer-oriented selling is putting the customer at the centre of the sales process. In this paradigm, salespersons empathise with their customer by putting themselves in the shoes of the customer and working closely with them to develop a solution. This is against selling pre-packaged or standardised solutions. Adaptive selling is about a salesperson altering the sales behaviour and process based on new information received during the sales process. Another approach to selling is value-based selling. This approach has three key dimensions (Terho, Haas, Eggert, and Ulaga, 2012). The first step is for a salesperson to get a better understanding of a customer's business context. Once this is understood, the second step is to craft a value proposition. Value for the customer is derived from the benefits of consuming the service or product characteristics, both tangible and intangible. The final step is communicating the value to the customer. We have described this in detail in Chapter 4.

Another construct used to describe the selling process is consultative selling. In consultative selling, salespersons are "value advisors", where they provide information to customers to help them take actions that will add value to their business (Liu and Leach, 2001). In value advising, rather than promoting specific products or services, salespersons focus on working with their clients to understand the specific issues they are trying to solve and advise them on solutions leveraging their own market information and knowledge. As an example, in traditional IT sales, a supplier responds to a request for proposals (RFP). RFPs are structured documents that state the challenge being faced by a customer and the specific solutions they are seeking. Suppliers responding to RFPs do not have much flexibility in crafting creative solutions. Even the process of asking questions is highly structured and time bound. As against this approach, in consultative selling, suppliers have the opportunity to present industry and market trends and suggest solutions on how a customer can manage or cope with these trends. The next step is to develop specific solutions in conjunction with customers. This form of selling also enhances the trust and interpersonal bonds between the client and supplier personnel. A client is happy that a supplier is tracking the customer's business and proactively providing solutions rather than waiting for an RFP. From a supplier perspective, this form of selling has the added benefit of ensuring that there is no competitive bidding (via an RFP process) for the engagement.

Relationships are not static and transition through various states. These include the positive states of exploration, endowment, and recovery and negative states of neglect and betrayal (Zhang, Watson IV, Palmatier, and Dant, 2016). Both buyers and sellers need to be aware of these states and deploy strategies to move to higher positive states and avoid negative ones.

As increasing elements of the sales and marketing processes move to digital technologies, it is even more essential for companies and individual sales personnel to appreciate the importance of relationships in the sales process and ensure that the essential human element of relationship-building is not lost.

Several frameworks have been used in academic literature to describe the construct of a buyer–seller relationship in business markets. Figure 1.1 is a comprehensive model first developed in the late 1990s (Cannon and Perreault, 1999).

The model (Figure 1.1) describes the relationship between three groups.

Market and Situational Determinants: These are external to the relationship of buyers and sellers and are dependent on the number of vendors, the dynamics between these vendors, and the substitutability of vendors. Market determinants also account for environmental uncertainty and characteristics of the service being bought. However, these constructs are relatively uniform across vendors and therefore are not differentiators.

Relational Constructs: The authors identify a set of constructs that are key to the relationship and differentiate one vendor from another:

Information Exchange: Willingness of both vendors and customers to share information. In the context of IT, this could include customers sharing a business strategy, technology plans, and project schedules with the vendors. From a vendor's perspective, the information can extend to areas such as growth plans, new products and services, and mergers and acquisitions. Openness to sharing information is an indicator of trust. On the contrary, the lack of information sharing and communication will lead to a relationship breakdown.

Operational Linkages: Operational linkages capture the extent to which customers' and vendors' processes and systems are integrated. These linkages help in the seamless delivery of operations. For example, if a project is being developed partly by a vendor and partly by an in-house team of the customer, then the linking of systems and delivery mechanisms becomes critical in delivering the project. Operational linkages also extend to individuals. An example is vendor representatives being deeply linked to the planning process of the customer organisation.

UNDERSTANDING THE IT MARKET

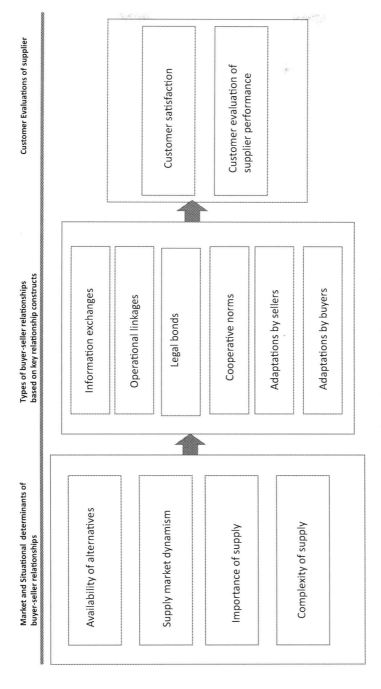

Figure 1.1 Constructs of buyer–seller relationship in business markets

Legal Bonds: Legal bonds are contractual agreements. These documents specify the obligations and roles of both parties in the relationship. While it can be debated if legal documents help maintain a relationship, there is no doubt of them being a hygiene factor in any customer–vendor relationship.

Cooperative Norms: Many vendor–customer relationships are not "win-win". The customer has a constant upper hand and dictates the relationship. Cooperative norms reflect customers and vendors working together to achieve mutual and individual goals jointly. Such norms ensure the longevity of a relationship that is mutually beneficial.

Adaptations by Seller and Buyer: This is a one-way connector and is defined as the relationship-specific investments made in the process, product, or procedures specific to meet the needs of the other party. One example is a vendor investing in a new technology that will be useful for the customer even though it may not be profitable in the short run. Similarly, a customer could support its vendor in building new capabilities that the vendor could offer to other customers.

Consequences of the Relational Constructs: The deeper the relational constructs, the stronger the customer and vendors' relationship. For the customer, this means a long-term partner who is willing to invest and grow with them. For the vendors, it is a long-term relationship that will generate value.

1.3.1 B2B2C markets

Another way to conceptualise B2B markets is B2B2C, where businesses sell their products to an intermediary business, who in turn sells the products to end consumers. In the past, the original business was disconnected from the end customer. From their perspective, the transaction was B2B. However, as businesses realise the value of connecting with the final user and receiving customer data and feedback, they are building connections with the end customer without disturbing their relationship with the intermediary business. An example of this is a pharmaceutical company (primary business) who sells its products to hospitals, doctors, or pharmacies (intermediary business), who in turn sell the products to a patient (consumer). Businesses who sell their products to e-commerce platforms, who in turn sell products to consumers is another example. In both these cases, the original producer was traditionally disconnected from the end consumer. However, newer technologies are enabling the original producer to obtain data and feedback from the end consumer.

1.4 The IT industry landscape

The technologies associated with IT are continuously evolving, creating a big challenge for management. McAfee (2006) argued that to make the

UNDERSTANDING THE IT MARKET

Table 1.2 Categories of IT

Categories	Description	Examples
Functional IT	IT that helps in executing discreet tasks	MS Office, design software
Collaborative IT	IT that facilitates interactions	Email, blogs, messaging tools
Enterprise IT	IT that manages business processes	CRM, SCM, ERP
Insight IT	IT that provides insight related to customers and business	MIS, analytics

most productive use of IT, managers should stop treating IT merely as a technological initiative and develop a comprehensive model of what IT can achieve for their organisations. McAfee (2006) conceptualised three categories of IT, which the authors have extended to four categories (Table 1.2).

1.5 IT customers and service providers

In this section, the categories of customers and IT service providers are outlined.

1.5.1 Buyers of IT services

Like any B2B market, the IT industry has multiple sets of buyers and vendors. In this chapter and the rest of this book, buyers are referred to as customers or clients and sellers as vendors or suppliers.

IT customers are classified by several parameters, including the geographic location, industry segment, and size.

Geography: Typically, customers are classified into domestic and international. The United States (~60%), United Kingdom (~17%), and Europe (~13%) account for the largest proportion of global IT business. In the last decade, IT vendors try to de-risk their business by diversifying to newer markets such as Australia, Asia Pacific, and Africa.

Industry Segments: Some of the key industry segments for the IT industry include:

Banking, Financial Services, and Insurance (BFSI): This segment includes retail and commercial banking, capital markets, life, and general insurance. BFSI is the largest segment for most IT companies.

Healthcare and Life Sciences: Healthcare includes both providers (hospitals) and payers (health insurance companies). Life sciences covers pharmaceutical and biotech companies.

Retail and Fast-Moving Consumer Goods (FMCG): Retail and e-commerce is one of the fastest-growing segments for the IT industry.

Telecom and Media: The traditional telecom and media business has been on a decline over the last decade but has been replaced by newer companies. The distinction between these newer media companies and the technology segment is very blurred. (For example, is Facebook a media or technology customer?)

High-Tech: Most electronic and chip manufacturers are classified as high-tech companies. Some vendors classify customers such as Microsoft and Facebook as high-tech as well.

Manufacturing: Traditional manufacturing customers include those in the chemicals, oil and gas, and processing industries.

Government: Government business is vast but requires companies to pass stringent selection criteria.

Utilities: Utilities includes electricity, water, power, etc. Contracts in this industry are typically long-term but of low margin.

Most large IT vendors are organised by customer segments. They also de-risk their business by targeting multiple segments. Smaller vendors often focus on a single segment and position themselves as experts in these segments.

1.5.2 Sellers of IT services

The IT vendor market is also fragmented, but their business models can be broadly classified into three categories.

Services companies

As mentioned in the previous section, IT services vendors are either multi-services organisations or niche players. Full-service vendors target multiple customer industries and offer a range of both specialised and horizontal services. These horizontal services include digital, enterprise software, testing, and product development, among others. The United States and India have the largest revenue share of outsourced services vendors. Examples of global services companies include Accenture and IBM, while Indian services companies include TCS, Infosys, and Wipro.

Product companies

These are companies that offer software products such as enterprise resource planning (ERP), customer relationship management (CRM), and payments. Product companies generally perform higher value-added activities and develop intellectual property. Microsoft and SAP are examples of software product companies. The business model for product companies is usually license or subscription-based, while service companies price based on time and materials.

Software product selling is a combination of B2B and B2C methods. For example, companies such as Microsoft and Norton sell their products to corporate customers as well as directly to end consumers. The products, business models, and channels vary for these two segments. Product companies have separate teams and strategies to handle each of these segments.

In B2B sales, most large software product companies follow a multi-channel approach. For large or corporate customers, they use a direct salesforce. For smaller customers, they employ digital marketing or value-added resellers (VARs). These VARs, also referred to as system integrators (SI) or partners, are trained in selling, implementing, and supporting software products and work on behalf of the parent company. Using a VAR strategy provides software companies with a broader geographic and segment reach.

In B2C sales, software companies either use a channel sales strategy that consists of distributors and retailers or multiple e-commerce platforms to sell to end customers.

Platform companies

Some IT companies are moving towards platform-based business models. In this model, the IT provider develops the core capabilities and products and allows its varied partners to create and offer multiple services and add-on products. The external sourcing of innovation ensures that the platform leader does not need to invest huge amounts and carry the risk of a commercially unsuccessful innovation. Companies such as Amazon, and Google have successfully used platforms. Their platforms have enabled many apps and services to be available to their customers. This model's primary challenge is to attract innovative partners (complementors) in large numbers until the platform attracts a significant base of interested users. The platform providers also need to avoid competition with complementors and enforce fair benefit-sharing mechanisms to encourage investment in innovation. At the same time, the platform leaders work towards ensuring that the vision, integrity and the reputation of the platform are not impacted by the contribution made by the complementors (Mukhopadhyay and Bouwman, 2019).

Some key differences between products, services, and platforms are given in Table 1.3.

As evident from Table 1.3, each type requires different sales strategies and skills.

Until a decade ago, software products were sold mainly for a one-time license fee. However, this model had several disadvantages. First, the revenue was based on the number of licenses sold and therefore did not result in a steady revenue stream throughout the year. Second, once a software product was sold and implemented, there was a discontinuity in the vendor's

UNDERSTANDING THE IT MARKET

Table 1.3 Products vs. services vs. platforms

	Software Products	*Software Services*	*Platforms*
Scope	Usually limited to one process or area	Varied and multi-functional	Varied and multi-functional
Payment model	One-time fee or license + annual maintenance fee (AMC)	Negotiated based on the scope of the work	Revenue share
Intellectual property (IP)	Belongs to the developer/vendor	Belongs to the customer	Platform IP belongs to the platform owner. Partner IP belongs to partners.
Level of customisation	Low Limited customisation based on customer needs	High Delivered to customer specifications	Base platform is standard. Partners must conform to platform standards, while developing their extensions.
Domain knowledge required by the vendors	High, onus of innovation with vendors	Low	Domain knowledge required by partners
Gestation period for development	High gestation period and investments	Low initial investment and project-based	Lower ongoing investment from partners; higher initial investment from platform providers
Sales model	One-time and need-based	Incremental and relationship-based	Platform providers drive the sales using marketplaces and traditional sales force

relationship with the customer. Third, the lack of an ongoing relationship led to the disuse of the product over time. As a result, most product suppliers have migrated to a subscription-based model that allows for an ongoing relationship with a customer.

1.6 Engagement models

In the information technology world, the term engagement model is used describe the framework that defines the collaboration between customers and their suppliers. The supplier can be a third-party outsourcing company or an insourcing shared services arm of the company.

Several contractual frameworks and pricing models exist in the industry to govern the relationship between a customer and the outsourced or insourced supplier.

Scope-based delivery: This is the most common type of engagement where a company sources parts of its development and maintenance from a vendor. This type of arrangement can be both long- and short-term, where the services are delivered based on the scope of the project and service level agreements (SLAs). The pricing mechanism for scope-based delivery is usually based on time and material or a fixed price. The details of different contract types used in the IT industry are explained in Chapter 4.

- **Time and material** is among the oldest pricing model in the industry and is mostly used in new customer–vendor relationships. The administration of the model requires robust processes for timekeeping. In this model, the vendor is not motivated to optimise resource efficiency. However, the model is useful when the project scope cannot be well defined.
- **A fixed price** provides certainty to the customer on the overall cost of a project. In this scenario, the vendor estimates the total cost of a statement of work (SoW) and provides a fixed price for the project. The vendor retains any efficiency gains.

Dedicated teams: Customers that have a continuous need for resources prefer dedicated teams. This provides for better resource continuity and allows the customer to manage the utilisation of the teams directly.

Captive unit: A captive unit is wholly owned and managed by a customer. Outsourced vendors do not have a role in captive centres. However, in some cases, vendors help set up captive centres through a build–operate–transfer (BOT) or a joint venture (JV) model. This model is more common in locations where a customer does not have any presence or capabilities.

Offshore development centre (ODC): An extension of the dedicated teams model is setting up an ODC. An ODC replicates a customer's office space within an outsourcer's environment. It includes dedicated teams, dedicated and secure space, supervisors from the customer organisation, and implementing customer policies. The vendor's organisation has limited control and role in an ODC, and the customer decides the teams' priorities. Essentially, an ODC is a hybrid captive.

The advantages and disadvantages of the models are discussed in Table 1.4.

Many global customers choose hybrid models. They outsource part of their IT requirements and manage the "higher-end," or intellectual property (IP)–based processes, internally. As a corollary, software product companies tend to set up captive units compared to other companies for whom IT is a backend operation.

Table 1.4 Advantages and disadvantages of various engagement models

Model	Advantages	Disadvantages
Scope-based delivery (time and material)	Flexible Fast to implement Highly scalable	Limited control Vendors not incentivised to complete on time Price escalation
Scope-based delivery (fixed price)	Flexible Fast to implement No risk of price escalation Scalable	No ability to increase the scope Efficiency gains to vendor's benefit Need to be able to scope the project entirely, up-front
Dedicated teams	Greater control Continuity of resources Scalable	Less flexible Fixed people cost
ODC	A high degree of control of the customer Direct supervision Support services provided by the vendors	Less flexible Fixed people cost Fixed infrastructure costs Long-term commitment
Captive	Complete control by the customer Increased security for intellectual property Ability to replicate company culture Increased customer connection with development teams Less scalable	Fixed costs No flexibility Extended lead time to set up Long-term commitment

Types of contracts

Most customer–vendor engagements operate under an overarching master services agreement (MSA). The MSA is a legal document and provides an umbrella agreement for all the work performed by a vendor. The typical sections include contracting parties, relationship governance, jurisdiction, liabilities, and warranties. An MSA does not have details of specific projects, as these are covered separately in individual SoWs. MSAs are signed for upwards of one year, but usually in the range of three to five years.

SoWs contain specific details relating to each project. The details include project scope, pricing, team size, timelines, project governance, etc. In case of any conflict, the terms of an MSA prevail over those of an SOW.

Table 1.5 outlines the types of contracts that are relevant in multiple scenarios.

UNDERSTANDING THE IT MARKET

Table 1.5 Use of contracts by project type

		Project	
Customer		Old	New
	Old	SoW Extension	New SoW
	New	NA	New MSA and SoW

1.7 Location of service delivery

IT suppliers can deliver the work to a customer from multiple locations.

Onsite: Work that is outsourced to an external vendor but delivered from the customer's location. The reasons for onsite delivery include the following:

- Part of a complete outsourcing engagement that is required to be performed in a customer location
- The vendor has taken over crucial customer personnel as part of the engagement
- Services like deskside technical support needs to be performed at customer locations
- The vendor's staff are onsite to complete the knowledge transfer process, especially during the initial phase of the engagement.

Onshore: Work delivered from vendor sites that are in the same country as the customer. Onshore is used for work that:

- Requires end-customer connect
- Is physical work, for example, logistics
- Is restricted from being moved offshore due to regulatory and compliance issues
- Requires skills that are not available offshore.

Nearshore: Work that is delivered from a country in close physical proximity to the customer country. Typically work that needs to be in the same time zone or requires language capabilities that are not available in offshore locations is delivered from lower-cost countries in close geographic proximity. Central American countries like Costa Rica for the United States and Estonia and Poland for Europe are illustrative nearshore locations.

Offshore: Work that is delivered from offshore locations. A large proportion of IT outsourcing is delivered from offshore locations such as India, Poland, and the Philippines. These locations are more economical and have a large pool of qualified workforce.

17

UNDERSTANDING THE IT MARKET

Offshore Onsite: Work that is delivered from the customer's captive offshore sites. Many large companies have captive locations globally. These companies also co-locate some of their vendors in these locations. For example, companies such as Google and Microsoft have their IT services vendors co-located on their campuses in India.

1.8 Types of IT services

IT companies provide a range of services. Their offerings can be broadly classified into three buckets:

Consulting: This includes business strategy development, digital strategies, technology road-mapping, business process maturity assessment, industry benchmarking, and talent management. Consulting is the highest level of the value addition provided by the IT services company. Among larger vendors, consulting is a significant revenue stream. For smaller vendors, it is considered a hook to get new business.

Application Development and Maintenance (ADM): This is a core offering of all IT services companies. These services include software development, maintenance and enhancement, and operation of the installed software. Specific activities under ADM may consist of business requirement gathering, design, coding, system integration, testing, deployment, and ongoing software operation. Developing a new application is considered a higher value-adding activity. The maintenance and ongoing management of software are high-volume, stable, but usually low-margin businesses.

Prime System Integration: Large-scale IT implementations require a range of hardware, software, and platform solutions. No single company has the breadth of capabilities to meet all these needs. However, many customers want one vendor to manage the entire implementation and coordinate with various vendors. System integrators perform this role. Most large IT services companies are also system integrators. They help their customers develop an overall solution and identify the multiple elements required to implement the solution. They also assist in identifying suitable vendors and manage programs and project implementations. Large-scale implementations also have a concept of a lead system integrator that drives other subordinate system integrators.

Customers select vendors for programs and projects based on specific skills and criteria. Therefore, it is not uncommon for a vendor to be a solution provider on one project, systems integrator for another, and lead systems integrator for a third.

Outsourcing: Outsourcing creates value through a strategic relationship with a vendor, who assumes responsibility for portions of the information technology environment and certain business process operations. For large IT vendors, outsourcing represents one of the most important business opportunities and accounts for a significant amount of their revenues.

Outsourcing is beneficial for customers, as it frees them from the burden of managing and expanding the IT infrastructure. They can use the additional management bandwidth on improving customer relationships and innovation.

Digitalisation Services: Digital technologies are leading the next wave of IT development. Most global companies have begun large-scale digital transformations and are outsourcing the entire process. The digital transformation process involves mapping the customer journey, design thinking, digital roadmap development, and digital implementation using agile development. The development of digital platforms is an important part of a customer's digital roadmap.

Many leading companies are developing their own B2B and B2C platforms and reshaping their business models. Platforms provide two significant advantages. First, the marginal costs post-development are lower, and second, they offer network effects. The term "network effect" is used to describe a scenario where the value of a product or service increases with the number of users. These two advantages allow platform companies to grow faster and at minimal incremental cost into newer markets. For example, once Uber or Airbnb built their platforms, it took less effort to expand to newer geographies. As the number of users on these platforms grew, it attracted a larger number of providers. This, in turn, fuelled even greater growth in users.

IT services companies are rapidly re-tooling their internal workforces to support customers in their transformation journeys. At a technology layer, artificial intelligence (AI), blockchain, Internet of Things (IoT), the cloud, robotics, and analytics related skills have become more critical. Customers expect their vendors to support them in customer journey mapping, business model transformation, and change management at a business layer. While legacy development and maintenance will continue, IT vendors must lead their marketing efforts with digital transformation.

1.9 Characteristics of IT selling

This section discusses some of the characteristics of a typical IT sales process. Each of these areas are discussed in greater detail in subsequent chapters.

1.9.1 Team-based process

The sales process in IT sales is team-based. Buyers typically have a team to evaluate and select a vendor. A sample team composition and the roles they play are outlined in Table 1.6.

Similarly, on the supplier side, an entire team is involved with the sales process. This includes personnel from the pre-sales team who generated the lead, the sales team, key account managers, the head of delivery (if it is an

Table 1.6 Roles of stakeholders in a buyer organisation

Team Member	Activities	Role Played in the Sales Process
Procurement	Run the formal procurement process as per corporate guidelines, including the RFQ/RFP process	Gatekeepers
Vendor management	Work with the procurement team to help select the final vendor. The vendor management team then carries the relationship forward.	Influencers
Finance and legal	Work with the procurement and vendor teams to negotiate and finalise the contracts	Gatekeepers
Operations/business unit team	The owners of the process for which the vendors are being selected	Users/recommenders
Leadership team	Provide strategic guidance and are involved in the final decision	Deciders

Table 1.7 Mapping of customer and vendor teams

Customer Team Member	Vendors Team Member
Procurement	Sales Team
Vendor Management	Sales Team
Finance and Legal	Sales Team
Operations/Business Unit Team	Key Account Managers, Delivery, and Domain Experts
Leadership Team	Leadership

existing customer), domain experts, and the vendor's leadership. In a complex sale, each team member is mapped against a corresponding member of the customer team.

An illustrative mapping is provided in Table 1.7.

This mapping ensures that the vendors remain connected with every decision-making point in the customer organisation, and there is focussed communication at each level.

In large and complex deals, supplier sales teams also use the help of internal and external sales coaches. These coaches are experts who have

UNDERSTANDING THE IT MARKET

successfully led deals similar in size and scope. Sales coaches help in sharing best practices and in scenario planning. They also provide unbiased feedback on the sales process. In large deals, suppliers also configure their team based on the competition involved. For example, if a vendor finds that their competition is weak in a specific domain area, they will play up their strength by involving more domain experts in that area. They may also bring in external partners to strengthen this area.

1.9.2 Long sales cycles

The sales cycle is the time from when the first contact is made for a new sales opportunity to the time a contract is signed. A typical IT sales cycle varies from a few months to a few years. Some factors that impact the sales cycle are:

Relationship with the customer: With an existing customer, the trust is already established and an MSA and working governance process are in place. A sale cycle to a current customer is therefore relatively shorter than that for a new customer. However, if the customer has multiple approved vendors, they may still go through a proposal process.

New project vs. extension: Project extensions generally have a short lead time. For example, if a vendor implements an ERP in one geography, extending this contract to newer geographies is relatively easier.

Size and complexity of the project: Smaller projects take shorter lead times and are usually awarded to existing vendors. Larger and more complex projects go through a formal RFP process irrespective of the existence of approved vendors. In many cases, this requirement is driven by corporate governance guidelines.

Exclusive vs. competitive: Sole-source or exclusive deals take a shorter time to close. All vendors try to create opportunities proactively, so the sales process is exclusive to them. Reactive selling is almost invariably competitive and is RFP based.

A longer pre-sales cycle and significant pre-sales investment indicate that the seller needs to identify better opportunities and move away from opportunities that are less likely to be successful. While a larger deal size is good for IT providers, it also exposes the vendor to a greater risk caused by project failure or the customer's inability to pay.

1.9.3 High dependency on resources

In the IT services industry, revenue is generally a function of the number and skills of resources deployed. So, when a company acquires a large deal, it needs to plan for adequate skilled resources. Most large suppliers are trying to overcome the linear growth model by using automation, workflows, and robotics.

1.9.4 Susceptible to non-tariff barriers

A large proportion of the IT services is exported, which requires the movement of resources with different skills across boundaries. As a result, the IT industry is highly impacted by work permits, visas, language, and cultural issues. Large IT providers have adopted multiple strategies to overcome these challenges, including recruiting resources in the host countries.

1.10 Evolving profile of customer personnel

As mentioned earlier in the chapter, IT customers are also diverse in terms of geography, industry segment, and outsourcing maturity. As a result, "a one size fits all" approach to selling is not effective. Vendors need to tailor their sales process according to a customer's needs.

Over the last few decades, the profile and expectations of buyers have evolved.

Knowledgeable and Experienced: Buyers are knowledgeable about outsourcing, offshoring, and vendors. They are usually well-networked among their peers and, in many cases, have worked across multiple companies. They are aware of most large vendors' strengths and weaknesses and keep in touch with the industry through conferences and reports like the Gartner Magic Quadrant reports. Unlike in the past, customers know most of the vendors participating in a bidding process. While this should not stop vendors from showcasing their strengths, sales messages need to be focused and highlight recent developments and capabilities rather than historical achievements.

Culturally Diverse: IT services outsourcing has always involved people from multiple geographies and cultures. Traditionally, customers were based in Europe and North America, and vendors were from lower-cost countries such as India. In the early days of outsourcing and offshoring, cross-country transactions posed several cultural and time zone-related challenges. It was not uncommon for personnel within the customer and vendors' organisations to not know much about each other's country or culture. With the industry maturing, many of these challenges have diminished.

Vendors, especially from offshore locations, have frontend sales and relationship personnel from the customer's country. Similarly, many large customers have onboarded vendor managers who are from the vendors' country. Buyer personnel have travelled extensively to offshoring locations and are familiar with these countries' geography and culture. While the academic literature has not focused much on the impact of cultural gaps in IT outsourcing, it forms a critical component of a customer's decision-making process.

Need for Value Addition: In the past, most marketing efforts, especially from offshore vendors, were based on providing services cheaper, faster, and better. With the increased number of vendors and ease of communication in the digital age, customers are bombarded with information from potential vendors. Customers are therefore less likely to meet vendors with standard products anymore. They expect the vendors to have researched their organisation and developed prescriptive solutions right from the first meeting. The solutions must be focused on how the vendor can support the customer in becoming more competitive rather than cutting costs.

Healthy Scepticism: While customer personnel seek value addition from newer vendors, they are also sceptical about their ability to deliver. This scepticism might have grown out of dealing with vendors who over-promised and under-delivered. It is therefore vital for vendors to back their pitches with a robust delivery plan. This plan can be based on successful prior implementations or customer referrals. If an idea is new and untested, customers expect vendors to outline up-front the potential risks and mitigation strategies.

1.11 Competencies of sales personnel

Like any B2B sales, IT sales is also highly dependent on the relationship between customer and vendor personnel. The key attributes that are used by human resources departments to evaluate key customer management personnel can be summarised into four categories (adapted from Zunk, 2013).

Emotional Competence: Emotional competence refers to a person's ability to deal effectively with people in real situations. Emotional competence has also been shown to have a high correlation with empathy, the ability to tolerate stress, increased flexibility, and the ability to deal with change. Emotional competence allows an individual to communicate transparently with others. This is a critical personality trait in dealing with project hurdles in complex IT implementations.

Personal Competence: Personal competence is related to attitudes, value systems, and beliefs that individuals carry. Personal competencies include self-awareness, self-management, social awareness, relationship skills, and responsible decision-making. Some personal competence characteristics include having a realistic self-image, acting according to one's own convictions, and being socially responsible. This competency helps in building trust.

Professional Competence: Professional competence comprises skills and knowledge to perform the job. For example, a key account manager possesses skills such as industry knowledge, program management, and value delivery.

Methodological Competence: Methods and procedures drive the IT industry. Methodological competence refers to having the knowledge, skills, and tools to determine the right path for any issue and having the ability to follow the path to completion. For key account managers, an example of methodological competence is escalation management.

1.12 Keeping pace with technology changes

The technology industry is changing rapidly, and this is impacting both customers and vendors. Increased processing speeds, cheaper storage, and faster transmission speeds have resulted in the rapid proliferation of digital technologies. Customers are scrambling to put together their digital roadmaps while managing their current legacy business. As described in Section 1.8, vendors are re-skilling their workforce with digital technologies, including AI, IoT, analytics, and blockchain. These changes have a significant impact on the IT sales process.

Multiple Decision Makers: The CTO/CIO organization made all IT decisions in the past. Digital transformation is strategy-led and backed by technology. New roles such as chief digital officer (CDO) have emerged. Many CDOs are from a business background and do not have extensive technical skills. For a vendor, this means building relationships with a new set of customer personnel. It also requires learning to sell with the strategy in focus, rather than technology.

Consulting Led Sales: Digital is a new concept for most customers. There is considerable ambiguity on the right business models for the future and the technologies required to implement these business models. Customers expect that vendors help them map this journey and provide direction in making the right decisions.

Blending New and Old Technologies: Two-speed IT has become the norm. This includes a fast-tracked, customer-centric frontend running alongside a slower-speed, transaction-focused legacy backend. Vendors are expected to support both tracks and provide the temporary hooks to keep the two tracks synchronised.

New Engagement Models: Software products channel partners that now need to move away from a one-time license-based sale to annuity sales. This implies that they need to build skills in recurring billing and ongoing customer management. E-commerce has also reduced its influence in the sale process.

Competing with Niche Vendors: Start-ups and newer companies are at the forefront of technology innovation. Vendors need to keep track of these smaller companies and develop partnerships to bring these technologies to their customers.

Impact on Sale Process: Digital technologies have also impacted the backend of sales processes. There is greater use of social media such as LinkedIn and Facebook in branding and lead-generation efforts. CRM and Salesforce optimisation tools are being used to make sales efforts more efficient. Analytics and AI are being implemented to help create targeted sales campaigns

UNDERSTANDING THE IT MARKET

and reduce the time to sell. Mobile technologies are across the sales process, from salesforce tracking and collaboration to capturing meeting notes and conducting product demos.

1.13 Chapter highlights

- This introductory chapter provides an overview of the IT industry as a subset of B2B markets.
- The chapter defines critical terms used in the industry. Buyers are known as customers or clients, while sellers are referred to as vendors or suppliers.
- Vendors classify customers based on geography and industry segments.
- Some of the broader industry segments include financial services, technology, and healthcare.
- Vendors are broadly classified into IT services, products, and infrastructure companies. However, most large vendors offer a mix of all three services.
- Several engagement models exist in the industry—from a simple "time and materials" to outcome-based pricing. Each of the engagement models has certain advantages and risks. Customers and vendors need to find the appropriate engagement model that is a "win-win" for both parties. This ensures the longevity of the contract.
- The IT industry is very rapidly evolving into new business models. "As a Service" models across the entire stack (infrastructure, platforms, software, and business processes) are becoming the new norm. Vendors must reassess their operations to cater to these new needs.
- Customer–vendor relationships are very complex and operate at multiple levels. At a transactional level, they are based on contracts and processes. They are based on factors such as trust, communication, and cultural connection at a relationship level.

1.14 Questions for discussion

1. How are B2B and B2C markets different? Provide three key differences and illustrate with examples from the IT industry. What are the key differences between a seller working in the FMCG industry and in IT industry?
2. What are the reasons many IT buyers are moving away from one-time license fees to subscription-based services?
3. Could you find similarities and dissimilarities between the business model of TCS and Microsoft?
4. What engagement models do IT product companies and platform companies prefer?

5   What are digitisation services? Why are more and more suppliers focusing on these services?

6   How are technology changes impacting the IT selling and buying process? Provide three ways the industry is being forced to adapt.

1.15 References

Anderson, J. C., Narus, J. A., Narayandas, D., and Seshadri, D. V. R. (2011). *Business market management (B2B): Understanding, creating, and delivering value*. Pearson Education.

Cannon, J. P., and Perreault, W. D. (1999). Buyer—seller relationships in business markets. *Journal of Marketing Research*, 36(4), 439–460.

Liu, A. H., and Leach, M. P. (2001). Developing loyal customers with a value-adding sales force: Examining customer satisfaction and the perceived credibility of consultative salespeople. *Journal of Personal Selling & Sales Management*, 21(2), 147–156.

McAfee, A. (2006). Mastering the three worlds of information technology. *Harvard Business Review*, 84(11), 141.

Mukhopadhyay, S., and Bouwman, H. (2019). Orchestration and governance in digital platform ecosystems: A literature review and trends. *Digital Policy, Regulation and Governance*, 21(4).

Terho, H., Haas, A., Eggert, A., and Ulaga, W. (2012). "It's almost like taking the sales out of selling"—towards a conceptualisation of value-based selling in business markets. *Industrial Marketing Management*, 41(1), 174–185.

Zhang, J. Z., Watson IV, G. F., Palmatier, R. W., and Dant, R. P. (2016). Dynamic relationship marketing. *Journal of Marketing*, 80(5), 53–75.

Zunk, B. M. (2013). Ideal-typical competence profile of industrial buyer-seller relationship controllers in technology firms—empirical evidence from Austria. *Environments*, 3(4), 5.

2

BUSINESS VALUE OF IT

Learning Objectives:

- The reader will appreciate the importance of IT in different aspects of business: business process automation and optimisation, customer experience management, data-driven insight, and a source of competitive advantages.
- Provide exposure to two competing debates, while the resource-based view (RBV) explains how IT capabilities can create sustainable competitive advantages. The other approach views IT as an infrastructure which is essential for conducting business, but it does not generally provide competitive advantages.
- Understand the concept of value and value proposition in an IT context.
- Understand different methods for creating value propositions.
- Use financial management techniques like net present value (NPV) and internal rate of return (IRR) to create business cases to demonstrate value.

2.1 Changing role of IT

As discussed in the last chapter, enterprises buy IT solutions, as IT creates value for their organisations. As a result, one of the most important tasks of a sales engagement is to establish and communicate the value proposition to the relevant stakeholders of the buyer organisation. To do so, we need to first understand the role of IT in today's business. It is evident that the role of IT has gone through significant changes over time.

Many of the older definitions link information technology to multiple technologies that organisations use to collect, pre-process, store, and transmit digital information. This definition primarily focuses on multiple types of physical equipment such as computers, network equipment, and storage devices and highlights that IT primarily is used for bulk data processing activities. Since 1990, organisations started using IT in other strategic

DOI: 10.4324/9781003155270-3

areas as well, i.e. optimising, integrating, and automating their key business processes. The deployment of IT also helped to replace human beings for monotonous day-to-day work, allowing employees to concentrate on more strategic and innovative works. Business process streamlining and automation provided much-needed financial savings to justify further investment in IT.

Other than the obvious reasons of efficiency and cost savings, there was another reason which forced businesses to take an interest in IT. As IT systems were increasingly being used to store and process data for the organisations, they also started developing different types of performance reports, popularly known as management information systems (MIS) reports. The reports were used by organisations to review performances of the entire organisation, various departments, employees, and product lines. While MIS and other regular reports still exist in most organisations, technologically advanced firms use the concepts and methods of Big Data, machine learning, and visualisation techniques to develop real-time, actionable insights. With the rapidly increasing importance of technology, IT is also being deployed to provide more advanced functionalities, such as providing a better and more personalised experience to customers and using insights to develop new avenues of revenue. In essence, information technology has moved beyond the "backend activities" and "batch processing" of its initial days. Today most firms cannot function without IT, as even their core business processes today are IT-enabled. Besides, some of the firms use IT as part of their core strategy and the driver of their business model. As mentioned before, we cannot imagine the business of Facebook, Flipkart, and Amazon without appreciating their technology infrastructure.

Due to the rapid pace of innovation, business and technology are becoming deeply intertwined. Due to the technological development in the field of mobile communication and Web 2.0, human- and machine-generated data are experiencing an exponential growth. The number of users and applications on social media platforms and the number of devices on Internet of Things (IoT) platforms are growing rapidly. Social media users are not just passive consumers of information—they actively generate a large volume of data with multiple varieties. Firms can hardly afford to ignore the conversations on social media, and similarly, they cannot afford to miss out on the new opportunities offered by IoT. As a result, while cost optimisation remains a big driver of IT investment, other priorities are rapidly taking centre stage.

A recent survey by Frost & Sullivan to identify the top 3 drivers for IT investment brings interesting insight. Figure 2.1 shows that a large number of executives are ready to use IT to improve their online presence and collaboration among employees and partners.

Based on the earlier discussion on the changing role of IT, we can define information technology (IT) as an integrated collection of 1) hardware,

BUSINESS VALUE OF IT

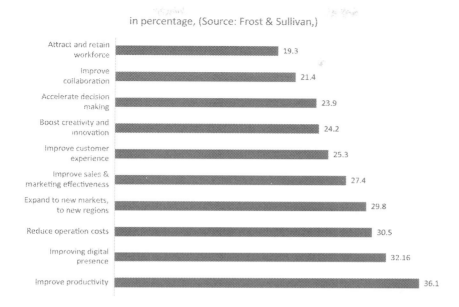

Figure 2.1 Drivers of IT investment
Source: Frost & Sullivan

covering computer, network, storage and other telecommunication devices; 2) software; and 3) services covering consulting, application development, and maintenance that help an organisation deliver business value through a combination of activities in the following forms:

1 Business process automation, integration, and optimisation leading to cost reduction
2 Developing new revenue streams or new markets
3 Delivering an improved customer experience
4 Developing a competitive advantage in the marketplace.

In the next section, we have provided two real-life examples of information technology delivering value in one of these forms for enterprises and governments.

2.2 Information technology delivering value: some examples

2.2.1 Amazon's recommendation system

Recommendation systems are software tools providing suggestions for items to prospective buyers or users. The suggestions are related to various decision-making processes, such as the choice of products to buy, the type of music to listen to, or the item of online news to read. Recommendation systems are primarily directed towards individuals who lack sufficient personal experience or competence to evaluate the potentially overwhelming number of alternative items that an online marketplace or website, for example, may offer. Nowadays all online marketplaces such as Amazon and Alibaba and news aggregators and producers like NDTV. com and Yahoo News depend heavily on their recommender engines for increasing sales or usage of their product. Amazon has integrated recommender systems on every part of the user's purchase process—from product discovery to checkout. As per an analysis in Fortune magazine (Mangalindan, 2012), a well-designed and popular recommender system allowed the company to achieve a 29% immediate increase in sale compared to the year before.

2.2.2 Government of India's Aadhaar platform

Governments in many countries are increasingly using information technology to improve the services provided by the governments, as well as the public-sector organisations. In developing countries like India, governments have additional challenges to serve a large poor population, which demands a very scalable IT infrastructure. Poor people in India were unable to participate in the formal economy or use commercially available essential government or private services such as access to banking, mobile telephony, or acquiring a driving license, due to a lack of verifiable and acceptable identity. As the magazine *The Economist* (2012) explained: "Poverty has many causes and no simple cure. But one massive problem in India is that few poor people can prove who they are". The government of India launched the nationwide unique identification project of UIDAI, or Aadhaar program, in early 2009 with the aim of providing identification to all residents of India. As opposed to other offline identification documents, the Aadhaar identity can be verified and authenticated in an online, cost-effective way. Aadhaar also addresses the challenge of duplicates and fake identities. The success of the project and the social impact can be gauged from the fact that by mid-2017, 1.17 billion Indian residents were enrolled in the database, which covered 99% of all Indian adults. According to *Economic Times* (2017), the total number of Aadhaar-authenticated transactions (verification of online identity) until July 2017 was 8.5 billion, and it processed a total of 900 million transactions in July 2017.

With proper regulatory support, Aadhaar can be used by mobile, banking, and financial institutions for online authentication of their customers, reducing customer acquisition expenses and onboarding time (Mukhopadhyay, Bouwman, and Jaiswal, 2019). The government of India also used Aadhaar to directly transfer subsidies and other benefits to the poor, in the process reducing transaction cost and leakage, as well as minimizing wrong targeting of the beneficiary.

2.3 Contrasting perspectives on IT's role in business

In spite of IT's increasing importance in business, many researchers and managers have divergent views on IT's actual contribution to the success of a business. We will study two contrasting viewpoints in this regard. A section of researchers view capabilities related to IT, such as data-driven decision-making enabled by state-of the-art analytics infrastructure, as a source of competitive advantage which guarantees superior business performance. The RBV is used to link these types of capabilities and assets with competitive advantage. There is also an equally large number of researchers who view IT as an infrastructure for running business, as well as a tool to achieve operational efficiency. The operational efficiencies, however, are diffused across the industry, as best practices and individual firms cannot command any strategic advantage (Porter, 1996). We will discuss both these perspectives, as each contains many valid arguments.

Resource-based view: viewing IT as a combination of organisational resources and capability

The RBV propagated by (Barney, 1991; Penrose, 1959; Wernerfelt, 1984) states that a firm's differentiated performance and the associated competitive advantage can be explained based on organisational resources controlled or owned by an organization. Though researchers have varying opinions on the definition of resources, we have further categorised resources into assets and capabilities. Assets can be either tangible or intangible inputs required for the production of products and services for a market. Examples of resources in the context of IT would be hardware, software, network, intellectual property rights (IPRs) such as patents, and human resources such as developers and architects. Capabilities originate from the maturity of an organisation and allow the same inputs to be converted to an output of higher worth (Wade and Hulland, 2004). Examples of capabilities are data-driven organisational culture, matured software development processes, and an effective partnership between IT and business.

Firms would have a competitive advantage once they are able to acquire resources that are valuable for their businesses and are rare and sticky, i.e. resources that cannot be easily transferred or copied from one firm to another. While access to many of the basic assets is available to everybody, developing intangible capabilities, including an organisational work culture, cannot be easily imitated by competitors. IT capabilities are neither easy to create nor easy to copy because they involve a system of practices. While copying any one piece of capabilities might be straightforward, an isolated capability without the organisational systems necessary for its functioning would not provide any real benefit.

As a result, organisations can use these types of resources to create a competitive advantage and superior business performance. If we review the business models of successful digital platforms like Facebook and Amazon, it becomes clear that they have acquired a massive volume of data on their consumers, markets, and products. These types of resources are owned by a small number of firms and cannot be easily acquired by competitors. In line with RBV, these firms enjoy a superior competitive advantage and continue to dominate their industry. New entrants might find it difficult to dislodge these firms due to the network externality (large network of partners, customers, and related datasets) these incumbents have created.

While information technology resources are becoming increasingly critical, in many cases, IT resources alone cannot provide competitive advantages. Rather, they work in synergy and through complementary relationships with other assets and capabilities of the firm. That's why, unlike some resources such as brand equity or financial assets, IT resources many times may not directly contribute to creating a sustained competitive advantage. Instead, they form part of a complex chain of assets and capabilities that may lead to sustained performance. To get the maximum benefit out of IT resources, it is important to have an effective partnership in the form of integration and alignment between the multiple business functions and the IT function of the organisation.

Opposing view: IT does not provide a competitive advantage

In 2003, Nicholas Carr (2003) published an article in *Harvard Business Review* (HBR) titled, "IT Does Not Matter" that attracted considerable attention and created an uproar. Many took the title of the article at face value without going into the structure of the arguments, either to support or oppose the theme that information technology as a whole is no longer important.

Carr's primary assertion was that in the initial phase of new technology, only a limited number of organisations have access to the technology. Due to its rarity, the firms having access to information technology can enjoy a competitive advantage over their competitors. Over a period of time, technology becomes more powerful, but at the same time, its ubiquity also grows. Keeping in mind that the core functions of IT during Carr's time was data storage and data processing, capability for performing these functions became available, as well as affordable, to every organisation. As RBV points out, the scarcity of specific resources makes it strategic, and IT that is used for generic activity like data collection and processing can no longer be termed strategic resources, but rather should be treated as a commoditised resource. In that sense, IT can be equated with other infrastructure required for running businesses. This perspective treats IT as an essential capability for running a business, but inconsequential for the strategy.

Carr also observed that a new technology in its initial or build-up phase can impose a restriction on its accessibility, and hence can be a source of competitive advantage. The accessibility can be restricted through IPR, non-availability of skilled resources, higher usage cost, and the non-existence of standards. But it has been observed that technologies, particularly those that are initially sought after by the industry, diffuse quickly with time. As a result, this type of competitive advantage exists only for a limited period.

Carr also advised IT managers to avoid the trap set by IT sellers by investing in new features without being backed by solid business requirements. Until there is a strong business case, it is beneficial to be a follower of technology. While adopters of new technologies need to spend considerably in evolving technologies, followers can always access commoditised and matured technologies at much lower risk and at a lower cost.

There are important insights that one can derive from Carr's article without necessarily agreeing to all his views. For salespersons, it is essential to understand the customer's IT requirements, as well as its inclination for innovation. Organisations of all sizes would buy standard IT products to run businesses; some of them would acquire deeper insights in using this technology to improve cost structure, or would simplify business processes. A few technology-savvy organisations would develop a competitive advantage by using technology to engage with customers and partners, as well as by changing the rules of the competition. However, their ability to develop a competitive advantage using IT does not depend on IT alone, but rather on aligning IT resources and capabilities with multiple business capabilities.

This discussion highlights that organisations demonstrate differential information technology usage maturity levels and inclinations for innovative technology. In the next section, we will discuss the role of IT in the context of the global economy.

2.4 Importance of IT in the global economy

A macroeconomic analysis of the global economy over the last few decades has confirmed that countries that create and sustain a competitive advantage are generally adept at developing advanced technologies, as well as exploiting their full potential (Henry-Nickie, Frimpong, and Sun, 2019). The United States is an excellent example of a country that has led the global race for technology innovations post the Second World War and enjoys a competitive edge over other nations. An empirical study by Vincenzo Spiezia (2013) has confirmed that the growth rate in information and communication technology (ICT) investment can be used to explain the increase in gross domestic product (GDP) growth, as well as the global competitiveness of individual countries. The recent economic rise of China and India can also be attributed to their above-average spending on technology.

While reviewing the contribution of IT and technological innovations to the overall economy, we also need to include the spill-over effect of technology to other non-technology sectors of the economy. IT companies, being the supplier of technology capabilities to these industries, transfer the innovation and technology capabilities to multiple sectors of the economy. While this leads to innovations in other non-technology-intensive sectors as well as a rise in productivity, it opens a considerable business-to-business (B2B) market for IT vendors. A report by Business Wire (February 4, 2016) based on a study done by IDC estimated that worldwide IT spending was $2.46 trillion in 2015. As per Gartner's estimate, global IT spending was over $3.7 trillion in 2019 (Gartner, 2019). If we focus only on IT services, it was worth more than $1 trillion in 2019 (Holst, 2020). Figure 2.2 shows the increase in IT services spending by corporations over the year.

Because of the large value of the market, information technology companies have also become the most prolific job creators in our economy. As per data from the US Bureau of Labor Statistics, the IT industry has shown the maximum promise with respect to job creation between 2006 and 2016. Based on data from the same source regarding the projected employment in the year 2026, information technology sectors will account for the maximum, or almost 15% of the 11.5 million projected newly created American jobs.

While the IT industry's role in creating a large number of jobs is well-known, workers in the IT industry are also associated with higher productivity and higher-than-average earning. The data from the US Bureau of Economic Analysis for the time span of 2006 to 2018 found that the average GDP output per employee in IT and related industry was more than twice the average productivity of the total economy. IT employees are associated

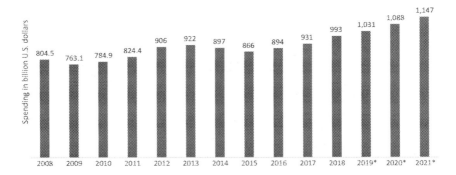

Figure 2.2 Worldwide IT service spending
Source: Statista, 2020

not only with higher GDP output but have also seen much higher GDP output growth during this period. In 2006, the contribution to annual GDP per employee in the US information technology sector was $321,659, which increased to $408,129 in 2016. The same statistics for the entire economy were only $120,876 in 2006, which marginally increased to $132,873 in 2016 (Henry-Nickie et al., 2019).

The Indian IT services industry, being a nascent industry in 1990, has emerged as one of the main pillars of India's success in the last two decades. In 2014, it constituted 8% of India's overall GDP with an annual revenue of 120 billion US dollars (Asher, 2020). In 2020, IT sector continue to contribute around 8% of Indian GDP. Out of this figure, 98 billion is achieved through exports, making India the world's largest IT services exporter. In terms of employment opportunity, in India 4 million people are directly employed (Balaji, 2017) while providing indirect employment to another 10 million workers.

Another way to look at the rising importance of technology and IT service providers is to analyse their performance in the stock market. Technology-focused companies who primarily use technology to conduct business or are a supplier of technology to a multitude of other firms are valued highly by investors. In 2018, six technology companies figured among the ten most valuable companies in the world (Statista, 2020), while in 2007 this number was only one (Figure 2.3). This information clearly explains the rising importance of technology focused firms in our economy.

Lastly, the importance of technology would increase even more with the rapid proliferation of mobile and computing technologies, abundance of

Figure 2.3 The rising importance of technology firms in the global economy

data, and the focus of firms and governments on technological leadership. As a result, firms would continue to spend more on information technology, and technology would take centre stage in business functions. Managers who can appreciate technology and develop business cases linking technology to superior firm performance would be highly valued.

The discussions so far have established the importance of the IT industry and its influence on the enterprises, as well as in the overall economy. The sales managers in IT organisations can reinforce the rising importance of IT by effectively communicating and demonstrating business value in any IT initiative. The concept of value discussed here will work as a foundational block for the consecutive chapters.

2.5 Value in the context of IT solutions

Anderson, Narus, Narayandas, and Seshadri (2011) assert that value is the cornerstone of the B2B market. The sales and marketing processes in IT markets, like other B2B markets, are value-driven. IT is a specific type of B2B market, and we will describe and define the concept of value in this context. In the case of an IT solution or initiative, value is defined by the real and perceived benefits derived from an IT solution or offering. Even in the early stages of the sale, a salesperson should have a fair understanding of the customer's explicit and implicit requirements and aspirations, as well as their business priorities, issues, and challenges. The sales team is aided by a group of business and technical pre-sales specialists, who would have a fair idea of the features their proposed solution is going to offer. The extended sales team should incorporate all these insights to identify the features of the IT solution that can be used in the customer organisation to create value. This value can be in the form of monetary or non-monetary benefits accrued to the buyer, keeping in mind the priorities and requirements of the customer.

Anderson et al. (2011) have classified these benefits into four categories: economic, technical, service, and social. For simplicity, the researchers have also classified benefits in two major categories: economic and non-economic. For solutions with non-economic benefit, the challenges lie in converting them to monetary values that are acceptable to both buyers and sellers. In many cases, buyers might need some additional investment to avail themselves of the benefits from the functionalities provided by the IT solution. The proposal developed by the seller should also include those additional costs. As a result, a minimum additional investment of time and financial resources would be required to reap benefit out of an implemented IT solution. For example, Reliance Jio in India has launched several apps for entertainment for their mobile subscribers; the leading apps are Jio Cinema and Jio Music. The IT and telecom infrastructure allows onboarding and authentication of customers, delivery of content and recommendations, and managing payments. But that may not be enough to successfully run the business. Jio needs to have arrangements with multiple content owners for using their content such as movies and songs. Therefore, in the case of a large IT provider, in order to develop a similar proposal for other competing telecom operators to enable selling entertainment content, the proposal should include the needed investment for content acquisition and processing.

When evaluating IT offerings, IT buyers look for key benefits in terms of three key outcomes: cost and risk reduction, enabling new revenue opportunity, and achieving strategic objectives. Strategic objectives can include compliance with regulatory requirements. It can be to focus on customer centricity in the form of enhanced customer satisfaction by collecting and processing more meaningful customer data. So, IT solution developers and sales professionals can support increasing value in one or more of the three fundamental categories without necessarily reducing the offering price. An IT offering can reduce its own downtime (i.e. unplanned service outage), thus allowing less disruption to the business and potential to generate more revenue. This proposal would increase the value of the IT offering despite the price remaining unchanged. Similarly, an IT offering can have the provision of easy integration with other systems, thus potentially reducing the cost for system integration. This is an example of the overall cost, or total cost of ownership (TCO) reduction, for the IT buyer without compromising the price. An IT offering can also be of strategic importance to the business when it collects significant information about its core customers without compromising privacy or impacting the customer experience. From this analysis, it becomes clear that the salesperson should be aware of customer-desired value (Flint, 2002) for a particular opportunity. This denotes a customer's perception of the scope of value and the expected outcome of the value creation and the metrics that would be used to measure the created value.

2.6 Value propositions

While a particular IT solution can offer values of different types, it is important for the seller to understand the priorities of the customer. During the purchase process, different stakeholders from multiple departments from the buyer side come together to evaluate competing products and to make the buying decision.

These sets of individuals who come together for the buying decision-making are known as organisational buying centres (OBC) or decision-making units (DMUs). The business functions that DMUs represent for specific initiatives can have conflicting priorities and interests, as well as a number of overlapping priorities.

The following is an example based on a technology-driven logistics organisation—let us assume its name is *Logicnet*. The short case study explains how different functional units within the same organisation can have different expectations from the same IT solution.

Logicnet provides shipping and logistics services primarily to large e-commerce companies like Flipkart and Amazon in India. *Logicnet* handles a large volume of inventory with specific agreed performance criteria and depends heavily on technology to execute its commitments. To achieve its objectives, *Logicnet* needs to work with a large number of transport service providers as well as drivers. These small transporters and drivers are paid a specific percentage of an agreed deal-value, based on achieving different milestones. These milestones can be 1) the event of the vehicles having loaded the goods or 2) the goods having reached specific locations or the warehouse. *Logicnet* also receives payments based on achieved milestones from its clients for different assignments; hence, payment collection, disbursement, and reconciliation are critical business capabilities. *Logicnet* wants the payment handling systems to have a high transaction success rate, low delay and downtime, and a lower bluff rate (i.e. false classification problem, classifying a failed payment as successful or vice versa). As the transport providers and drivers are smaller entities, any delay in releasing the payments to the transportation partners may delay the shipment, leading to customer dissatisfaction, as well as damage to the quality of the goods being shipped. Frequently, organisations such as *Logicnet* outsource payment functionalities to a B2B digital payment provider instead of developing these functionalities on their own.

The important functions of *Logicnet* are sales and marketing, IT, finance, and procurement and purchasing. The representatives from these functional areas would constitute the OBC. In the case of India, where *Logicnet* is located, the most important payment providers are Razorpay, Pay U, and Pay TM. For them, an effective sale engagement starts with identifying the key stakeholders who constitute the OBC and their priorities. A brief analysis of the OBC and their priorities in the context of *Logicnet* reveals the following information (Table 2.1).

Based on the understanding of the relative influence in the buying process of the customer's organisation (OBC) and the supplier's value creation capabilities, a consolidated stack of benefit or value proposition is developed for engaging and negotiating with the customer. Instead of a large list of isolated features and benefits, the value proposition expresses the consolidated and aligned packages of benefits designed specifically for a customer. The value proposition is also designed to convey the uniqueness of the seller's offering to deliver the desired business outcome, addressing the interests of each OBC. Configuring the benefits associated with the values plays a key role in communicating the credentials and capabilities of the providers, as well as demonstrating their ability to understand clients' context. A well-defined value proposition can be also used for measurement of value during the delivery phase, in addition to its importance during the sales phase.

Table 2.1 Multiple stakeholders and their contrasting priorities in the buying process

#	Functional Groups (OBC)	Priorities/Interests of the Groups
1	Sales and Marketing	• Better payment experience of the customers and partners • New innovations to increase sales
2	IT	• Ease of integration • Consolidated documentation for products and integration capabilities • Product performance meeting or exceeding specification • Convenient exception handling • Lower downtime or degradation of performance
3	Finance	• Reconciliation of payment received and outgoing payment • Meaningful and actionable reports generation
4	Procurement and purchasing	• Competitive pricing and payment terms • Better customer references • Adherence to regulations

Research by Anderson, Narus, and van Rossum (2006) has shown that organisations can take three distinct strategies in packaging the values or benefits into a consolidated value proposition. Those three value proposition definition strategies are described in Table 2.2.

While the importance of articulating an effective value proposition is well understood, sales leaders often fail to do the same. A few of the important reasons are:

- Inadequate competence in the area of business and technology, particularly in the areas of emerging technologies and business models such as analytics, cloud, and digital platforms.
- Not doing enough research using secondary information and, where required, not using primary business research techniques. The supplier of IT should also have adequate business and industry knowledge to provide recommendations to the buyer.
- Setting unrealistic customer expectations related to the capabilities of the solutions of the benefits of the offerings. This prevents meaningful discussions between the team of the supplier and the buyer.
- Lack of access to information that helps one gain knowledge about the customer business. In many instances, sellers do not have direct access to managers of the buyer's organisation responsible for marketing, sales, and finance. They have to interact with the IT team of the customer to

Table 2.2 Multiple ways to develop value proposition

Value Proposition Definition Strategy	Key Aspects in the Context of the IT Proposal
All benefits	• All benefits associated with an IT offering or proposals are highlighted. • This approach can be useful in the exploration phase, when the customer is not fully aware of its own priorities and objectives. • IT providers frequently use this strategy during the Request for Interest (RFI) phase. • Using this approach needs less understanding of the customer's business and technical context. • The supplier might end up highlighting points of irrelevance (POI) benefits. These are the benefits the proposed solution offers but those do not interest the customer.
Points of difference	• Points of difference (PODs) are the specific benefits that a market offering alone can offer relative to its immediate competitor. • This type of value proposition needs to be articulated when the buyer organisation shortlists a few of the IT service providers. For example, when IBM in 2019 won a five-year IT outsourcing contract from Vodafone-Idea in India for a value of $700 million, IBM had to convince the combined Vodafone-Idea entity about its unique value proposition compared to other competing vendors having similar capabilities. While highlighting PODs can be an effective strategy, it should be backed by important point of parity benefits as well. Point of parity benefits are important for the customer, though all competing sellers may be able to provide them.
Most important benefits	• The supplier needs to identify a limited set of benefits that would provide maximum value to the customer. The amount of value provided should be significant enough to motivate the customer to view the solution favourably. • As IT solutions are designed to offer multiple benefits, developing this type of value proposition can be very challenging. • This can be an effective strategy when the customer wants to achieve a specific objective and is not interested in other areas. For example, a mobile service provider facing high customer churn would prefer a solution that specifically helps to categorise and retain the dissatisfied customers. Similarly, a large bank facing higher non-performing assets (NPA) would prefer an analytical solution that provides multiple models to classify high-credit-risk customers.

BUSINESS VALUE OF IT

understand the expectations of managers of other functional groups, which are often not an accurate representation of their priorities.

- Customer feedback and discussions are not acted upon nor incorporated in the modified solutions or the proposals. This would mean that the delivered solution is not as per the customer's requirement, but based on the supplier's own interpretation of the problem.

Every offering has a consolidated value proposition and an associated price. In the case of the digital payment scenario, *Logicnet* has an option of buying similar payment processing offerings from multiple providers. Besides, large customers may consider the option of building their own payment gateway solution. While evaluating a make-or-buy decision or selecting from multiple alternatives, a firm would choose an offering that offers the best (Value – Total Cost of Ownership) differential. The higher the difference between these two concepts for a particular offering from a particular provider, the higher the customer's incentive to purchase.

Anderson et al. (2012) proposed the **fundamental value equation** as

$$(Value_{offr} - Price_{offr}) > (Value_{comp} - Price_{comp})$$

where $Value_{offr}$ and $Price_{offr}$ are the value and price of a particular IT seller's offering, whereas $Value_{comp}$ and $Price_{comp}$ depict the value and price of the next best offerings from its competitors. In the case of an IT solution, instead of the price paid, we focus on TCO. TCO not only includes the price paid to the supplier but also the related costs, such as the cost for maintaining and operating the IT solutions, the cost of space and power required for the hardware part of the solution, multiple types of hardware not included in the seller's proposal, costs of data and application migration, cost of training the users in the new application, and the future cost for version upgrades. The concept of TCO was initially popularized by the Gartner group in 1987 and henceforth is being used extensively in information technology services. The primary objective of TCO is to look beyond the price offered by the supplier and include all possible financial implications over the lifecycle of the proposed IT-driven initiative.

A customer's business case and its intention to purchase depend upon the difference between perceived value (expected value) and TCO. When selecting a strategic vendor in a large deal, it is quite common to use financial analysis techniques like NPV, IRR, and payback period. Decision-makers frequently use a combination of these techniques to select an offering and develop a business case of the proposed initiatives. The following caselet explains the estimation of business value for an IT initiative.

BUSINESS VALUE OF IT

Caselet 2.1: developing a value-based business case of an IT investment

This case study is centred around a fictional mobile telecom service provider, Mphone, in a small country. Telecom service providers often use average revenue per user (ARPU) as an important metric that indicates the health of their business. An increasing number of customers and an increasing trend of ARPU indicate an improving financial status of the service provider.

As Mphone is witnessing a trend of stagnant ARPU, it wishes to undertake an initiative to increase the ARPU and, as a result, the overall revenue. It has initiated discussions with a few large IT service providers for implementing a platform for launching mobile applications for its customers. Initially, it wants to launch entertainment-based applications. For sourcing the content for these applications, it plans to tie up with content owners by offering them a share of the revenue. One of the potential IT suppliers, ABM, is a globally established brand. It has an excellent existing relationship with Mphone and is keen to win this project.

The sales team of ABM has gathered significant information about the customer. They have also conducted secondary research on the company, its competitors, and the overall industry situation. Based on the same, they have developed an IT proposal and a cost–benefit model with the following assumptions:

1 Mphone has around 1,10,000 customers, and the annual growth rate of its customer base is 10%. So, at the end of year 3, it is expected to have 146,00 subscribers.

2 The management has a 3-year horizon to recoup the investment and earn profits from this venture. This is due to the fact that mobile telecommunication is a rapidly changing business. Technology and customer preferences in this domain change frequently.

The important facts of the buyer are summarized in Table 2.3.

In their proposal, other than describing the technical architecture, the consulting arm of ABM has also specified the following benefits and costs to the buyer:

1 In the first year, after the new system is ready, 5 new mobile apps would be launched. In the next 2 years, once the marketing and IT teams of the buyer become familiar with the platform and their partners, they can launch 10 apps per year. It is assumed that each mobile app would have a life of 2 years and the old apps would be retired after 2 years. Table 2.3 explains the schedule for app retirement in this scenario.

2 At present, 2% of the subscribers of Mphone are expected to subscribe to these applications. Due to the novelty of the applications and the

Table 2.3 Facts and assumptions about Mphone

Key Facts about Customer

	Year 0	Year 1	Year 2	Year 3
Subscriber Details				
Beginning Subscribers (000's)	110,000	110,000	121,000	133,100
Growth Rate		10%	10%	10%
Ending Subscribers (000's)	110,000	121,000	133,100	146,410
Average Subscribers in Period (000's)	110,000	115,500	127,050	139,755

CORE ASSUMPTIONS—PRODUCT MIX & VOLUME

Entertainment App	*Average Service Life*	*Year 1*	*Year 2*	*Year 3*
# of NEW Applications Launched each year		5	10	10
# of RETIRED Applications Removed from service at Year End	2 Years	0	2	5
NET Active Applications Offered each year		5	8	5
CUMULATIVE Active Applications available at Year End		5	13	18

increased customer satisfaction with the new platform, the purchase of an application is expected to rise by 1% every consecutive year.

3   Initially the subscription price for each app would be $1 per month/per subscriber. Due to the competition in the market and availability of many apps, this subscription price would reduce by 15% every year.

4   Mphone would pay 15% of the revenues collected from its customers to its content partner. The proposal includes the feature to calculate and automate the partner payment component.

5   Like any other large project, the major Capex of these expenses would be in year 0 and 1. There would be limited capital expenditure on Year 3.

6   The additional revenue from this IT investment would start accruing from year 1, based on the number of users who subscribe to the app, the initial price of the app, and the later reduction in its price. No revenue is expected in year 0, before the IT platform is made live. The yearly revenue increases sequentially as a larger number of apps are introduced each year and as their popularity increases.

7 The total additional economic value coming out of this investment would be in the form of incremental revenue, and the figure would be $551,345 for the three-year period.

8 The TCO of this IT initiative over this period would be $330,003. The TCO of any IT initiative is expected to be higher than the price asked by the seller. It is the duty of the buyer to develop the value of the TCO for competing IT solutions.

9 In this model, the TCO has two components: Capex and Opex. To summarise the costs: the capital expenditure would be paid to ABM for hardware, software, and IT development services. Opex would start from year 1, once the IT platform is made live. It is assumed that in year 0, there would not be any Opex, as systems are under development and implementation. The Opex includes costs for the maintenance of IT applications and associated hardware, any additional effort that would be required in the customer care group to support this new functionality, and royalty payments to the owners of the content.

10 Mphone considers 15% to be their cost of capital for a similar large project. If we use this cost of capital to calculate the discounted cash flow, then the NPV of the project would be $121,177. NPV indicates the net financial benefit after incorporating the time value of money.

11 The high-level calculation to calculate value; cost; and corresponding NPV, IRR, and payback criteria is shown in Table 2.4. The IT project is expected to have an IRR of 56% and a payback period of 2 years, 2 months.

The new IT application proposed by ABM can increase the overall revenue of the client, which is the primary objective of the buyer. A detailed empirical analysis with sufficient information demonstrates the seller's understanding of the client's business and the industry it operates in. It leads to deeper engagement from the different stakeholders of the buyers.

This analysis only includes the economic benefits in terms of additional revenue generated. To make the model more comprehensive, we can include other non-economic benefits. Those can be in the form of increased customer satisfaction and other propositions. A comprehensive business case and associated cost–benefit model would make the value propositions acceptable to multiple stakeholders of the buying organisation.

2.7 Multiple techniques for evaluating the financial attractiveness of IT solutions

The financial management discipline provides a host of techniques for appraisal of new projects (such as NPV, return on investment [ROI] and

BUSINESS VALUE OF IT

Table 2.4 Value-based business case preparation

Cash Flow Analysis and ROI

($ in thousands) Revenue Summary	0	YEAR 1	2	3
Projected Revenue from Entertainment App	$0	$59,388	$186,099	$305,858
Additional revenue (Economical Value)				
Cost Summary	Year 0	Year 1	Year 2	Year 3
Total CAPEX	$79,500	$99,375	$0	$31,260
Total OPEX	$0	$13,773	$41,434	$64,661
Other Costs	$0	$0	$0	$0
Total Annual Costs	$79,500	$113,148	$41,434	$95,921
Non-Discounted Cash Flows	Year 0	Year 1	Year 2	Year 3
Total Annual Revenue	$0	$59,388	$186,099	$305,858
Total Annual Costs	($79,500)	($113,148)	($41,434)	($95,921)
Net Non-Discounted Cash Flow	($79,500)	($53,760)	$144,665	$209,937
Cumulative Net Non-Discounted Cash Flow	($79,500)	($133,260)	$11,405	$221,343
Discounted Cash Flows	Year 0	Year 1	Year 2	Year 3
Discounted Annual Revenue	$0	$51,642	$140,718	$201,107
Discounted Annual Costs	($79,500)	($98,390)	($31,330)	($63,070)
Net Discounted Cash Flow	($79,500)	($46,748)	$109,388	$138,037
Cumulative Net Discounted Cash Flow	($79,500)	($126,248)	($16,860)	$121,177
ROI Measures	Year 0	Year 1	Year 2	Year 3
Return on Investment (ROI)	-100%	-71%	-8%	45%
Net Present Value (NPV)	$121,177			
Internal Rate of Return (IRR)	56%			
Payback (in years)	2 Years and 2 Months			

payback period). In most cases, more than one method would be used to compare the financial attractiveness of any proposal, or multiple solutions from different providers can be compared using those.

The readers can make use of any basic book on financial management to understand these concepts. Here a brief summary of the techniques is provided.

BUSINESS VALUE OF IT

2.7.1 Net present value

The key idea behind present value is that a dollar today is worth more than a dollar tomorrow. NPV analysis shows us the expected net monetary gain or loss from a project by discounting all expected future cash inflows and outflows to the present point in time. A positive NPV indicates that the project's return exceeds the cost of capital (the return available by investing the capital elsewhere). If solutions from multiple providers offer different NPVs for solving the same problem, we should choose the proposal which offers the highest NPV. Proposals with a negative or zero NPV are not selected for implementation.

It is intuitive that

- I would prefer to receive $100 today instead of $100 after one year
- The $100 today could be invested for the year
- The $100 received after one year has less purchasing power due to inflation.

How to calculate present value (PV)?

Present Value = Future Value / (1+ opportunity cost of capital)^n
where n = number of periods; in most cases, it would be in years.

- Cost of capital is 10%
- What would be the PV of $100 received in 1 year?

With this understanding, the PV of $100 would be $100 / 1.10 = $90.19.

So, please calculate the NPV of an IT deployment with the following details:

- Up-front investment = $ 5 million
- Additional revenue or incremental cash flow in 1st year = $5 million
- Additional revenue or incremental cash flow in 2nd year = $5 million
- Additional revenue or incremental cash flow in 3rd year = $5 million

PV of incremental cash flow would be: $12.5 million ($5M * 0.909 + $5M * 0.826 + $5M * 0.751).
The NPV of the IT project can be calculated by deducting the up-front investment from the total incremental cash flow.
In this case, it would be $12.5 million – $5 million = $7.5 million.

2.7.2 Return on investment

ROI can be calculated by subtracting the project cost from total project benefits and dividing it by costs. It can also be such that while the costs are incurred up-front, the benefits might come later.

So, it is better to consider total discounted cost and discounted benefits for the calculation. In that case, the calculation becomes (total discounted benefit − total discounted cost) / total discounted cost.

In the earlier scenario, ROI would be ($7.5 million) / $5 million = 150%. The ROI is reasonable, though it does not take into account the time it takes to achieve this much return.

2.7.3 Payback period

The payback period indicates the time it would take to recoup the total monetary investment in an IT initiative.

2.8 Chapter highlights

IT services are important for a variety of reasons for businesses, governments, and society at large.

- IT in organisations started for handling backend monotonous job in batch processing mode.
- IT today is used for business process automation and optimisation, providing justification for an organisation's investment in IT.
- Members of the leadership team started taking an interest in IT once IT systems were used to generate reports, helping them justify investment decisions, as well as evaluate the performance of multiple divisions of an organisation.
- IT, due to the rapid progress in technology, as well as an evolution of associated business models, is now used for strategic purposes, increasing customer centricity, and improving competitive positioning in the market.
- IT is also one of the main providers of higher-paying jobs. The importance of IT in the economy and business is expected to further rise.

IT services are primarily bought for the values they are expected to deliver:

- Value is defined by the real and perceived benefits derived from an IT solution or offering.
- The value can be monetary or non-monetary.
- The proposals or offers should include different types of benefits, as well as the costs required to avail oneself of these benefits or values.
- The buyer's propensity to opt for an IT solution depends on the differences between value and cost. The higher the difference, the higher the buyer's interest in buying.
- Instead of a large number of isolated value assessments, sellers can opt for showcasing a consolidated benefit stack or value proposition for communicating to the customer.

2.9 Questions for discussion

1 How do you define value in a B2B exchange? What are the possible approaches to creating a consolidated value proposition from a set of values? In IT selling, which approach of developing a value proposition is preferred?
2 While identifying value to a private enterprise may be easier, what are the possible values that governments might look for when acquiring IT capabilities?
3 IT procurements are driven by multiple departments within an organisation. How does that create additional complexity, and how do you suggest handling this type of situation?

2.10 References

Anderson, J. C., Narus, J. A., Narayandas, D., & Seshadri, D. V. R. (2011). *Business market management (B2B): Understanding, creating, and delivering value.* Pearson Education.

Anderson, J. C., Narus, J. A., and Van Rossum, W. (2006). Customer value propositions in business markets. *Harvard Business Review*, 84(3), 90.

Asher, V. (2020, July 29). IT industry in India—statistics & facts. *Statista*. Retrieved from www.statista.com/topics/2256/it-industry-in-india/

Balaji, S. (2017, July 31). New alternatives for India's growing number of retrenched IT employees. *Forbes*. Retrieved from www.forbes.com/sites/deloitte/2020/09/17/an-accelerated-future-for-tax-leaders/#3e0ab9a46516

Barney, J. B. (1991). Firm resource and sustained competitive advantage. *Journal of Management*, 17(1), 99–120.

Business Wire. (2016, February 4). *Worldwide IT spending will reach $2.8 trillion in 2019 with the strongest growth coming from the health care industry, according to IDC Business Wire.* Retrieved from www.businesswire.com/news/home/20160204005807/en/Worldwide-Spending-Reach-2.8-Trillion-2019-Strongest

Carr, N. G. (2003). IT doesn't matter. *Harvard Business Review*, 81(5), 41.

Economic Times. (2017, August 1). *Aadhaar authentications hit record high of 94 crore in July.* Retrieved from http://economictimes.indiatimes.com/news/economy/indicators/aadhaar-authentications-hit-record-high-of-94-crore-in-july/articleshow/59853131.cms

The Economist. (2012, January 14). *India's identity scheme – The magic number: A huge identity scheme promises to help India's poor – And to serve as a model for other countries.* Retrieved April 5, 2012, from http://www.economist.com/node/21542763/print

Flint, D. J. (2002). Compressing new product success-to-success cycle time: Deep customer value understanding and idea generation. *Industrial Marketing Management*, 31(4), 305–315.

Gartner (2019). Gartner says global IT spending to grow 3.7% in 2020. *Gartner.* Retrieved from www.gartner.com/en/newsroom/press-releases/2019-10-23-gartner-says-global-it-spending-to-grow-3point7-percent-in-2020

Henry-Nickie, M., Frimpong, K., and Sun, H. (2019, March 29). Trends in the information technology sector. *Brookings*. Retrieved from www.brookings.edu/research/trends-in-the-information-technology-sector/

Holst, A. (2020, August 20). Information technology (IT) services spending forecast worldwide from 2008 to 2021. *Statista*. Retrieved from www.statista.com/statistics/203291/global-it-services-spending-forecast/

Mangalindan, J. P. (2012, July 30). Amazon's recommendation secret. *Fortune*. Retrieved from https://fortune.com/2012/07/30/amazons-recommendation-secret/

Mukhopadhyay, S., Bouwman, H., and Jaiswal, M. P. (2019). An open platform-centric approach for scalable government service delivery to the poor: The Aadhaar case. *Government Information Quarterly*, 36(3).

Penrose, E. (1959). *The theory of the growth of the firm*. London: Basil Blackwell.

Porter, M. E. (1996). What is strategy? *Harvard Business Review*, 74(6), 61–78.

Spiezia, V. (2013). ICT investments and productivity: Measuring the contribution of ICTS to growth. *OECD Journal: Economic Studies*, 2012(1), 199–211.

Wade, M., and Hulland, J. (2004). The resource-based view and information systems research: Review, extension, and suggestions for future research. *MIS Quarterly*, 28(1), 107–142.

Wernerfelt, B. (1984). A resource-based view of the firm. *Strategic Management Journal*, 5(2), 171–180.

3

IT PROJECT MANAGEMENT ESSENTIALS

Learning Objectives

This chapter provides an overview of different software project management methodologies and key activities associated with them. By the end of this chapter, readers will be able to:

- Understand key features of plan-driven and agile software development methodologies
- Appreciate different techniques for capturing customer requirements, pain points, and business processes
- Understand different methods of estimation and understand what goes into making an estimate
- Develop an IT development and delivery schedule as part of the pre-sales process that the delivery team can use
- Develop a risk profile of the opportunity and identify the risk mitigation strategies.

3.1 Introduction

Organisations acquire new IT capabilities based on the business benefits committed in the sellers' proposal and their internal assessment. We have already discussed that IT capabilities alone cannot provide the desired business benefits or the competitive advantage. IT capabilities work with other organisational non-IT capabilities like sales and marketing, new product development, and others to achieve the same. While selling IT is a complex activity, IT providers might face greater challenges in delivering promised business benefits due to multiple reasons. Primary among them is the complexity involved in IT service delivery. The reasons for the complexity in IT service delivery are many. A few among them are listed here:

- Requirements are not communicated properly by the buyer or are misunderstood by the development team.
- Inadequate ongoing communication with the key stakeholders.

50   DOI: 10.4324/9781003155270-4

- Scope creep keeps moving the schedule and increasing the costs.
- Technical dependency with existing systems. The new system needs to integrate with existing systems. In many cases, the current systems need to be modified to accommodate a new system.
- Implementation of new IT capability would call for a change in existing business processes of the buyer.
- Travel restriction due to non-availability of the necessary documentation of engineers.
- Change in technology, regulation, and consumer preferences.

A successful relationship manager should have a fair understanding of the complexities associated with IT service delivery. A pre-sales professional has more reasons for understanding the IT service delivery methodology. A standard proposal always includes a brief description of the project management methodology, project plan, high-level estimation of efforts, communication plan, and risk management plan.

For IT service providers, it is imperative to develop competence in IT service delivery and project management. A troubled project can hurt IT vendors in multiple ways: 1) reduced profit or potential financial loss; 2) loss of reputation, harming its prospects in ongoing and future deals; 3) possible termination of other IT services contracts with the same buyer; and 4) not being considered for future opportunities for some time. In the next part of this section, we have introduced the concept of project management, types of project management methodologies, and a few of the IT project management activities that are critical for sales process.

The US-based Project Management Institute (PMI, www.pmi.org), which works to define and improve project management practices across domains, defines a project as a temporary endeavour undertaken to create a unique product or service. It highlights the temporary nature of the initiative. So, a project needs to be formally closed once objectives are achieved, or both parties (buyer and seller) decide so. In the context of IT services, a project can be defined as an endeavour for "achievement of a specific objective, which involves a series of activities and tasks which consume resources" (Munns and Bjeirmi, 1996, p. 81). It is in sync with our view that the project is a means to achieve the business objectives that was agreed to between buyers and sellers. A group of related projects catering to common strategic objectives and managed in a coordinated way can be called a program. Project management can be defined as "the process of controlling the achievement of the project objectives by applying a collection of tools and techniques" (Munns and Bjeirmi, 1996, p. 81). While a project can have a long-term tangible and intangible impact on the organisation, the project management methodology's effectiveness can be measured by achievements concerning the four constraints: time, cost, quality, and scope. In addition to these four constraints, IT project managers are evaluated based on customer satisfaction. There are scenarios where the project manager has managed the four constraints efficiently but faltered on relationship management, leading to loss of new business. Similarly, a good client relationship can allow the project manager to withstand the impact of limited slippage on these four fronts. In this next part, we have discussed the two dominant IT project management methodologies: 1) plan-driven waterfall model and 2) agile method.

3.2 Plan-driven software project management methodology

The large IT service providers often act as a system integrator (SI) or prime system integrator (PSI) in a multi-vendor scenario. In both these scenarios, the IT service provider is responsible for managing the cost, quality, timeline, and functionality of the components developed or provided by its multiple internal and external teams. The project management of complex software development programs includes coordination, integration, and testing of a large number of interoperating components produced by different groups or companies.

To manage the complexities of extensive system integration and application development activities, the plan-driven or predictive software development methodology was formalized in the 1970s, with the active involvement of the US Department of Defense and large technology companies like IBM, Siemens, and Hitachi (Boehm and Turner, 2003). The developments in the areas of quality and system engineering significantly influenced this methodology, with the prime intention of reducing chaos and increasing predictability.

A project management methodology is also tightly coupled with the lifecycle it follows. A project lifecycle is a collection of project phases. Breaking the project into phases enables the project work products to be produced logically and coherently. The project management team would be more comfortable implementing and controlling manageable pieces instead of a large, continuous work stream.

Predictive software development methodology follows the waterfall model with five project phases. The phases are:

- Requirement
- Design
- Construction
- Testing
- Deployment.

Once the code is deployed in the production infrastructure, the control of the IT systems moves to the operation team from the project team, and

IT PROJECT MANAGEMENT ESSENTIALS

Waterfall Model of SDLC

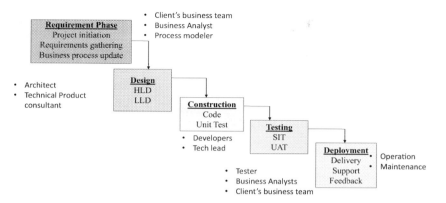

Figure 3.1 Phases in the traditional waterfall software development method

the project is formally closed. The waterfall method is sequential, and the team moves to the next phase only after the preceding phase is verified. This method provides much focus on documentation. The team creates and updates the detailed plan, workflow of activities, intermediate work products, roles, and responsibilities for team members. The lifecycle of the waterfall model, including the resources involved, is depicted in Figure 3.1.

The predictive waterfall method is the oldest software lifecycle model and easily understood by the senior managerial people. The method works well when requirements are well understood, the environment is stable, and uncertainty is low. The workflow is linear and sequential, and different job functions dominate these phases. Business analysts and process consultants drive the requirement phase. They collate, detail, and prioritize the requirements to be delivered by the project team. These new requirements might impact the existing business processes (such as customer onboarding or payment management processes of the client organisation). In some cases, it might call for the development of new business processes. Architects own design activities; they translate the business requirements to technical requirements to be delivered by the overall IT stack components. A good architecture ensures the scalability, fault tolerance, and easy maintenance of the systems; it also ensures that components are interoperable. The technical lead and software developers are involved in the construction phase, which involves developing the codes and associated basic level of testing. The testing phase is the longest and also consumes the maximum effort in a typical waterfall software development model, though organisations are increasingly automating these activities. The systems integration testing (SIT) involves exhaustive testing of the end-to-end flow, including the interfaces with both positive and negative scenarios. The SIT phase is driven by technical resources. A good SIT ensures that post go-live there would be fewer unexpected problems. The user acceptance test (UAT) is conducted by the actual users of the new systems in the buyer's organisation. The users primarily validate the systems from their usage point of view, keeping in mind the important functionalities, ease of use, and ability to get useful management reports. Based on these discussions, we can summarise that the waterfall model focuses on adhering to and improving engineering processes. Standardisation of processes can provide repeatability and becomes less dependent on the individuals. Organisations have tried to continuously improve their software development processes using an industry-standard roadmap like Capability Maturity Model Integration (CMMI). We also need to understand the limitations of this plan-driven approach and the emergence of agile methodologies, which would address many of these limitations.

3.3 Agile methodologies

The main issue with the plan-driven sequential methodology is its inability to accommodate changes, particularly when the changes emerge in the later phases. The methodology does not support iteration, so changes can cause confusion. Customers might find it very difficult to state all the requirements explicitly at the requirement phase. Besides, in today's continuously changing environments, market conditions change, new technologies emerge, and the end users' needs also evolve rapidly, so it is often becoming difficult to document how a computer application would evolve in the future (Pressman, 2005). A detailed definition and documentation of all requirements before the development part of the project starts are not realistic in today's rapidly evolving world. The second problem with this approach is the very low visibility of the working software until the final phase. The customer cannot experience and provide feedback on a working version of the software until the last phase. Organisations using software applications for competitive usage want the development team to provide new or enhanced applications on time, if not early (Turk, France, and Rumpe, 2014). This leads many to challenge the underlying philosophy of existing software engineering processes, which consider software development as a repeatable, predictable process (Sutherland, 2001).

The agile methodology was formalised in 2001 with the formulation of the Agile Alliance and the Agile Manifesto (Beck et al., 2001) with 12 core principles. Drawing inspiration from the manifesto, agile methodology focuses on iterative and evolutionary development, rapid and flexible response to changes, early development of code, and open communication in place of extensive documentation (Turk et al., 2014). One of the more important characteristics of agile is that it emphasises the rapid delivery of operational software instead of multiple intermediate work products and deliverables (Pressman, 2005). Two other important characteristics worth mentioning are 1) incorporation of the customer or its representative as part of the development team to get continuous feedback and 2) the underlying assumption that planning has its inherent limitations due to environmental uncertainty, and this calls for flexibility in response to changes (Mukhopadhyay and Gupta, 2019).

There are multiple implementations of agile methodology, such as scrum, lean, Kanban, extreme programming, crystal, dynamic software development method, and feature-driven development. All of the different implementations of agile possess a few common attributes (Boehm and Turner, 2003). They are:

1. Iterative development approach with multiple development cycles
2. Incremental approach: The team selects a few features for development in an iteration, and all features are not worked at in one iteration
3. Self-organising: Instead of the project manager dividing and allocating work, teams determine the best way to allocate and handle work
4. The emergence of processes suitable for the project during the project and less focus on adapting some well-defined processes and structures.

The plan-driven and agile methods can be contrasted with respect to their ability to handle changes and provide visibility of code readiness to the stakeholders (Figures 3.2 and 3.3). With regard to these parameters, agile methodology performs better than the all-at-once model of software

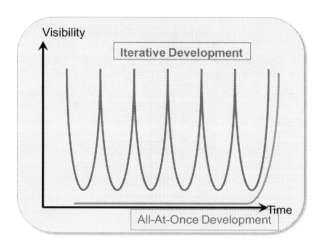

Figure 3.2 Contrasting visibility

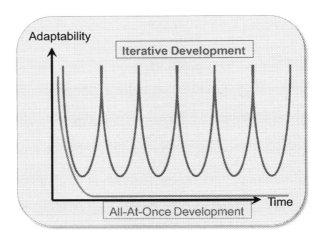

Figure 3.3 Comparing change management ability

development, but it fares poorly in handling complex, multi-vendor IT development. Agile methodology is more suited for a smaller team and when the developers have less dependence on external components. The traditional waterfall model still dominates large and complex systems development and integration projects.

Among the multiple agile implementations, scrum is most widely used in IT service delivery. Though scrum was initially developed for complex product development in an agile environment, it has the potential for being used for any complex, innovative work. Scrum allows the development team to deliver incremental software in multiple short-duration development cycles or sprints. At the end of each sprint, the team delivers potentially usable software for business users. The business team gets the opportunity to revise the requirement list and their priority at the beginning of each sprint, and at the same time can enjoy the benefits of incremental features delivered by the development team. The scrum process, with important meetings known as ceremonies, is depicted in Figure 3.4.

- Sprint planning is done at the beginning of a sprint for planning the scope and activities of a sprint.
- The daily stand-up is the most important meeting; it is a 15-minute face-to-face mini-meeting for the entire team to sync. To ensure the effectiveness of the meetings, each team member only shares three sets of information: what he did since the last meeting, what he is planning to do before the next meeting, and what obstacles he has?

IT PROJECT MANAGEMENT ESSENTIALS

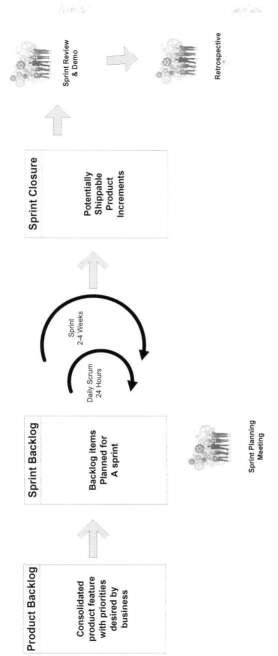

Figure 3.4 Agile scrum framework and ceremonies

- At the end of the sprint, the team demonstrates the newly developed features of the software in the sprint demo.
- The retrospective concludes a sprint. Here, the team collectively reviews what did and didn't go well in that sprint.

For a detailed understanding of IT project management, multiple textbooks are available. PMI is an excellent source of information related to project management methodologies and best practices.

In the remaining part of the chapter, we have provided a brief description of four critical functional areas related to IT project management. They are selected for discussion, as they play a critical role in the proposal phase. They are:

- Understanding the customer's pain points
- Risk management
- Estimation management
- Schedule management.

3.4 Understanding the customer's pain points

Developing a strong proposal and creating measurable value would need:

- In-depth knowledge of the customer's business, the market in which they operate, and their pain points impacting business performance
- A clear understanding of what the vendor (with its partners) can offer to help the customer in achieving its business objectives.

In most cases, the request for proposal/request for information (RFP/RFI) (or similar documents) shared by the customer does not adequately explain its pain points with the associated contexts. The vendors often need to collect additional information during the pre-sales phase and the project's requirement-gathering phase. IT vendors generally hire business analysts with MBA qualifications as well as experienced professionals with domain experience, for this type of work. This section has highlighted important sources of additional information and insight about the customer's context.

3.4.1 Secondary information

Most large and mature clients have documents explaining their business priorities, business processes covering key activities, architecture, interfaces, and functionalities of the existing IT systems. Most of these documents are readily available, and no additional data collection effort is required. Once the non-disclosure agreement (NDA) is signed, the vendor will have access to several of these documents. Besides, a vendor selected for delivering the project will have access to a more extensive set of company documents during the project initiation phase. This secondary information can be used to:

- Understand the problem stated by the customer
- Identify the requirement of additional information for developing a solution (the business case)
- Collect enough information to conduct possible interviews or workshop with important stakeholders
- Interpret primary data (the outcome of interviews, discussions, workshops) more insightfully
- Identify the modification required in the existing business processes or the need to introduce a new business process
- Conduct due diligence for complete IT functionality outsourcing.

3.4.2 Primary information

The gaps in secondary information can be addressed by collecting primary information. Primary information can also reinforce and expand existing knowledge about the customer. In-depth interviews or workshops are the most widely used methods for primary data collection.

In-depth interview

An in-depth interview can be thought of as a conversation with an individual with a purpose. The purpose is to obtain specific and useful information about the business and technical issues, priorities of different IT initiatives, and the attitudes of the influential persons. Interview styles can vary from unstructured (similar to conversations) to completely structured (where pre-defined questions are asked). In reality, a semi-structured interview style is most appropriate. In this scenario, an interview protocol with important queries is developed for facilitating the discussions. But at any time during the interview, the interviewees are allowed to divert and add any topic that they feel is important. In the corporate set-up, interviews are not generally recorded, but the facilitator should keep extensive notes of the discussions. In many cases, more than one person from the vendor's side participates in conducting the interview and taking notes of the important discussed issues. Two types of persons (from the buyer's organisation) are targeted for the interview:

- **Key informants:** They are the actual knowledgeable users, but they may not be very senior in the organisational hierarchy.
- **Decision-makers:** They have a more substantial influence in the organisation, so their opinions need to be incorporated. But many times, getting access to them for a longer duration remains a challenge.

59

IT PROJECT MANAGEMENT ESSENTIALS

The interview questions can be conceptually grouped into three categories:

- **Confirmatory questions:** The basic purpose is to validate the present understanding of the client's business issues, organisational structure, and as-is IT. This set of questions can also reveal discrepancies in the current information received from multiple sources, which should be probed further.

Example

- How many people are there in the IT department?
- Is the stability of the IT systems still a major issue?
- Does blockchain adoption remain the most important IT transformation agenda?

- **New information questions:** The vendor's team explores new but related areas on which not much information is available. These questions can also be used to gather specific and detailed information about some existing topics.

Example

- Is there any specific reason this thing has not been tried before?
- How does this IT initiative fit with the company's overall priorities?

- **Opinion questions:** Carefully executing these questions would allow us to understand the context and organisational dynamics relevant to the IT opportunity. These questions can be used to understand individual needs, desires, concerns, dynamics between multiple departments involved, and organisational values.

Example

- In your opinion, which functionality has the highest priority?
- What is the attitude of the operation team towards this new solution?

Generally, while discussing with the customer, business consultants should avoid using "why" to solicit new information. For meaningful data collection, the interview processes can be divided into three sequential phases:

- **Engagement and exploring:** In this phase, the interviewer establishes a rapport with the interviewee. The relationship between interviewer and interviewee is essential for meaningful data collection. This relationship can also lead to effective collaboration during the entire engagement period. This phase is also focused on gathering diversified information about the topics of interest with multiple open-ended questions.

- **Probing and consolidation:** Probing means to respond to replies from the interviewee to get more specific and more exact information about the topic. The focus is on qualifying and quantifying the already collected information. Typical examples of these types of questions are, "please tell me in more detail" or "please provide one example of a bad experience you had with your earlier provider". The interviewer can sometimes lead the discussion and influence the interviewee's perspective.
- **Conclusion and exiting:** This phase is primarily for reflection and summarisation. The interviewers also discuss with the interviewee if further follow-up discussion is required.

Workshop

While interviews are conducted to get views from the individuals, the workshops allow us to access multiple perspectives simultaneously on specific complex topics. Besides, workshops are also used to get feedback and approval of interim work products like consolidated requirement documents or solution architecture documents. Deployment of any IT solution impacts multiple functional areas in any organisation. These functions frequently have contrasting expectations from the same solution. For example, for the marketing department, deployment of a campaign management solution indicates capability addition for new customer acquisition and getting more revenue from the existing customers. On the other hand, customer care would expect the new systems to enforce more control or safeguards (related to maximum number of campaigns/customers in a specific period and others), so that the customer's experience is not compromised. To bring multiple stakeholders to the same understanding, a workshop involving different functional areas becomes necessary.

The workshop involves getting a large number of the customer's senior managers at one location for a few hours. As many people are involved, the cost of not achieving the workshop objectives is very high. It is imperative to plan the workshop properly. The planning can focus on three main aspects:

- **Agreed purpose and outcome of the workshop:** The purpose of the workshop drives the rest of the planning. A workshop can be organised to assess the initial views of the multiple stakeholders from the customer's organisation. Another workshop can focus on deep diving (a detailed discussion) on a few identified vital issues. The purpose of the workshop impacts the expected outcome. The outcome can be an agreed document that details the high-priority issues impacting the customer's business performance. In many cases, the introduction of a new application or modification of the existing application leads to changes

IT PROJECT MANAGEMENT ESSENTIALS

in the current business process (such as customer onboarding or credit assessment of new customers). A document containing the impact of the new technology on the organisation's business process can also be considered a valid outcome of a workshop.

- **Identifying the right set of people for attendance:** A workshop would need participation from multiple departments such as marketing, finance, product management, and IT. Though organisations have documented most of their processes and application details, many senior employees still retain significant tacit knowledge. Besides, the involvement of senior managers or the departmental heads of the organisations is important to ensure their commitment. So, considerable effort should be made to identify and to ensure participation from the 1) impacted functional areas and 2) people with the right authority and knowledge in that area.
- **Process of conducting the workshop:** Here, the organisers need to work on multiple areas.

    - Deciding the workshop's venue: While a face-to-face (F2F) workshop is recommended, virtual workshops are also becoming popular due to travel and budget constraints. In virtual workshops, the facilitator needs to overcome additional challenges, such as keeping participants engaged over longer periods or any technology and access-related issue.
    - Organising the necessary logistics, keeping in mind the participants' profile.
    - The overall workshops and individual session's length and duration should be planned ahead of the actual workshop.
    - The facilitator should have experience in leading workshops. An experienced and trained facilitator would ensure that the discussions go through four distinct phases (as mentioned below) to ensure the emergence of diverse views and synthesise them into a usable outcome.

        - **Framing (goal and scope setting):** set expectations and goals and determine/communicate session objectives
        - **Investigating and probing:** explore new information, identify topics for expansion, and identify options
        - **Shaping:** in this phase, the discussion should be guided back to discuss a few agreed-upon and important topics to achieve objectives
        - **Harvesting (outcome):** translate new information into usable knowledge and conclude the workshop
    - **Follow-up actions:** Most of the workshop identifies a large number of activities to be followed up on

3.5 Risk management

PMI defines risk as "an uncertain event or condition that, if it occurs, has an effect on at least one project objective". This definition accommodates the possibility that the risk could have a positive impact on the project objectives. In IT project management, risk is considered a potential event or future situation that can have an adverse project impact. The underlying reasons for risks can be business, technical, regulatory, and others in nature, but all project risks share some common attributes:

- A risk can adversely or negatively impact the objectives of the planned IT initiative.
- Things that are certain to happen are not considered a risk. A risk is associated with the probability of how likely the event is to happen.
- Risks generally impact the project cost, schedule, quality, or customer satisfaction differentially; not all risks can cause similar damage.
- A manager should be able to manage the risk. Things that are not possible by the mangers to manage are not considered a risk. One example would be the remote possibility of a meteor striking the earth.
- Events that have already taken place should not be considered a risk. Rather, they should be treated as issues, and they need to be addressed based on the gravity of the situation. Table 3.1 provides examples to illustrate this.

3.5.1 Why risk management is essential in the proposal phase

Risk management advisors play a key role in assisting the proposal team by identifying and assessing the risks associated with a proposal and contract. Due to the very nature of the IT projects, a degree of risk is inevitable. As organisations need to get new businesses, risks cannot be avoided altogether. The risk management process allows these to be recognised and managed in a structured way and ensure that the IT supplier is suitably rewarded for the same.

For a complex and high-value proposal, an external risk advisor would do the risk identification and impact assignment, keeping in mind the technological as well as project management challenges. The outcome of this exercise would be a risk rating (on a scale of 1 to 10 or 1 to 5), where 1 means low or limited risk and 10 or 5 indicates the presence of significant and very high risk.

In addition to this, the risk advisors work with the proposal team for planning responses for each of the risks, or at least for the major risks, so that risks can be eliminated or contained. Without a solid containment plan, a proposal with high risk may result in a "no bid" decision by the senior

Table 3.1 Contrasting risk and non-risk events

	#*Can Be Considered a Risk*	# *Cannot Be Considered a Risk*
1	The project has many interdependencies and five near-critical path tasks, and a delay in any one will probably delay project completion.	The sea level in the major seas may rise until necessary steps are taken.
2	The technology proposed for digital transformation is new; we have only a prototype to show that it can work.	The State Bank of India has awarded an IT contract to Infosys at a fixed-price term.
3		The client project sponsor did not show up for the required discussion meeting and has not provided the important documents promised.

management. The bid rating is also used to define the contingency amount in the costing process; a proposal with a higher risk profile would demand setting aside a higher contingency amount. A higher contingency reserve might make the proposal unattractive, and the seller would be very unlikely to win the opportunity.

In the next section, we have explained the three steps of the risk management process: 1) risk identification and classification, 2) risk impact assessment, and 3) risk response planning.

3.5.2 Risk identification

During proposal development, risks are identified from all available project materials. The possible list of documents can be:

- RFP or RFI
- Proposed technical solution
- Documented discussions with key stakeholders of the customer
- A proposed commercial solution, including payment terms
- Schedule and cost estimates
- Resource plan
- List of identified dependencies, assumptions, and constraints
- Lessons learned from similar projects from the knowledge repository
- Team member's experience
- Discussion with an expert who has delivered similar solutions
- Any other secondary sources like published academic and business documents.

IT PROJECT MANAGEMENT ESSENTIALS

These categories are indicative and would also vary based on the project. To identify overall risks from a proposal, the proposal team should make use of any of the comprehensive checklists available in the literature. The following structured checklist can be used to identify the overall proposal and project-level risk (Pressman, 2005):

- **Key stakeholder commitment:**
  - Have the top management of the customers agreed on the importance of the project and committed to support the project?
  - Are end users enthusiastically committed to the project and the new application?

- **Requirement stability:**
  - Are requirements fully understood by the technical team?
  - Have customers been fully involved in the definition of requirements?
  - Are the requirements stable and the priority of the requirements agreed to by the customer?

- **Scope:**
  - Do end users have realistic expectations?
  - Is the project scope stable?

- **Delivery:**
  - Does the IT service provider have the right mix of skills available?
  - Does the project team have experience with the technology to be implemented?
  - Does the project team have prior experience of working with the sub-vendors?
  - Do the vendors (if any) have a local presence and adequate skill on the products to be implemented?

Risk classification

The risk drivers (or the underlying causes of the uncertainty) can impact different aspects of the proposal and project. These aspects impacted by the risk drivers are known as risk components. The risk components, in general, can be:

- Win risk: the degree of uncertainty related to winning the proposal, as well as managing the desired profit margin

IT PROJECT MANAGEMENT ESSENTIALS

- Customer satisfaction risk: the degree of uncertainty related to overall customer satisfaction during the proposal and delivery phases
- Performance risk: the degree of uncertainty that the resultant product will meet the requirement and create value for the customer
- Cost risk: the degree of uncertainty that the project budget will be adequate
- Schedule risk: the degree of uncertainty that the project would be delivered as per the agreed schedule
- Support risk: the degree of uncertainty that the application will be easy to manage, correct, and enhance.

Other than associating risk events with risk components, we can group them into five categories for efficient management. These categories are based on the sources of the risks and are listed here:

- Technical
- Client
- Project management
- Regulatory
- Resource

3.5.3 Risk impact assessment

In addition to identifying and classifying, the risk should be assigned a quantitative value known as risk exposure, based on the probability of its happening and its likely impact. The risk exposure of an individual risk can be summarised as the probability of the risk occurring multiplied by the risk's impact on the project. To get the overall risk exposure of a proposal or a project, we can plot each of the risks identified in a 3 × 3 grid, as shown in Figure 3.5, based on the probability as well as overall impact. The solution development and project management team can ignore the risks with a low impact as well as a low probability of happening. They need to focus more on risks that are high on both parameters or high on any of the two parameters.

Estimating total risk exposure on a proposal or project

The proposal team might want to understand the total monetary value of all the risks associated with a project. Let's assume that the risks are independent. So, the project's exposure to risk would be the sum of the individual risk exposures. We have already explained that individual risk exposure is equal to the probability of the risk occurring multiplied by the risk's impact on the project.

IT PROJECT MANAGEMENT ESSENTIALS

		Overall Impact of Individual Risk		
		Low	*Medium*	*High*
Probability	*High*	H-L	H-M	H-H
	Medium	M-L	M-M	M-H
	Low	L-L	L-M	L-H

Figure 3.5 Risk exposure matrix

Consolidated project risk exposure = risk 1 + risk 2 + risk 3 + ...

= (probability of risk 1 × impact of risk 1) + (probability of risk 2 × impact of risk 2) + ... + ((probability of risk n × impact of risk n)

3.5.4 Risk response planning

Once the risks are identified and prioritised, the planned action for each of the high exposure risks would need to be done.

Generally, there are four different options for planning the responses for each of the identified risks, as shown in Table 3.2.

3.6 Estimation

An estimate is an assessment of likely costs in quantitative terms for delivering the agreed-upon scope based on the available information. The available input could be very limited, noisy, and uncertain at the initial stage of a proposal, but could be based on more detailed information at the later stage.

Why do we need an estimate?

- The baseline estimate serves as a basis for generating the project price quoted to the customer.
- The baseline estimate can be used in opportunity qualification work. If the estimate is much higher than the client expectation or the client's approved budget, it may be better to avoid the opportunity.
- The estimate is used by the resourcing team to determine the skill level, number of resources, and location of the resources.
- The approved estimate can be used to establish a cost schedule against which to measure actual expenditures when the project starts.

IT PROJECT MANAGEMENT ESSENTIALS

Table 3.2 Risk response strategies

Options	Description	Example
Accept the risk	✓ The team might decide to accept the consequences of a risk without taking any further action. ✓ This is often the appropriate option for risks with low-risk exposure. These risks are accepted as not significant enough to justify expending any effort or money. No resources will be expended in planning for them. ✓ They will be handled as issues if they occur.	✓ Based on the assessment, it is found that the probability of delay in getting appropriate resources once the contract is signed is very low. The vendor team can accept the risk.
Set aside risk reserve	✓ Risk reserves are funds set aside for the project's use if a risk event occurs. ✓ There are two types of risk reserves: contingency and management reserves. ✓ Contingency reserve: A certain percentage of the project value is set aside as a risk reserve and included in the project budget. The amount of risk reserve depends on project value and complexity. ✓ The management reserve fund is kept outside the project; this reserve can be kept at the account, business unit, or program level. The advantage of keeping a management reserve is that the amount of money required would be less. It would be much lower than the sum of the risk reserve funds needed by each project individually. So, in many organisations, instead of keeping a project-level contingency fund, the risk reserve is kept at the management level.	✓ In case the implementation gets delayed, the risk reserve can be used to continue the work without raising additional change requests to the client.

Options	Description	Example
Transfer the risk	✓ Transferring risk means giving the responsibility for addressing all or part of a risk to someone else. ✓ The risks can be transferred to the client or sponsor, a supplier, or another organisation. ✓ Transferring a risk changes who is responsible, but it does not remove the risk from the project. ✓ Before you transfer a risk, consider the benefits and weigh them against the possible loss of visibility.	Transferring a part of work that involves new technology (Big Data analytics) to a subcontractor with appropriate expertise.
Contain the risk	✓ Taking steps to lower the probability of the risk. ✓ Reducing the impact of the risk if it does take place. The impact can also be reduced by defining an action plan proactively if a risk occurs.	✓ Remove high-risk elements from the solution/proposal. ✓ Add detailed assumptions to define the boundaries of a requirement. ✓ Add more skilled resources. ✓ Recommend a phased approach. ✓ Contingency plan of reverting back to old IT systems if the new system falters.

3.6.1 What are the important techniques used in estimation?

Parametric estimate: The parametric method uses an organisationally available productivity matrix and rate data to estimate the effort required to complete a sub-task or a particular work product. The two most important techniques used in this regard are function point (FP) and lines of codes (LOCs). The estimation team, based on a well-defined scope, attempts to decompose software that is to be developed into multiple problem functions that can be estimated individually. For each of the functions, LOC and FP can be estimated. Instead of problem function, requirement details or business processes can also be estimated. The baseline organizational metrics (LOC/per month or FP/per month) are then applied to estimate the cost of effort. For a particular scope, these estimates from multiple functions or other decomposed units are collated to get the overall cost or effort. These types of estimates tend to be more accurate than analogous or expert opinion–based estimation. But it is more expensive than the previous two methods. In addition, it assumes availability of organisational software metric data.

Analogous estimate or estimate based on experience: The analogy method, or comparison estimating method, uses the actual cost of a previous similar project as the basis for estimating. The following steps are used in this method:

1   Find comparable projects. If the attributes of the earlier project are not similar, the accuracy of the estimate will be significantly reduced.
2   Evaluate the cost of the previous project to identify factors that primarily contribute to the costs and underlying assumptions.
3   Apply the information from the previous project to estimate the current project. The cost of the previous project is modified to take into account the additional or lesser complexities and the number of components in the new initiatives.

Expert judgment: It is an estimating method that relies on information provided by one or more experts with specialised knowledge and training. The experts should have experience in developing solutions for a similar IT initiative. An expert judgment estimate is only as good as the expert. In addition to developing new estimates, this technique can be used to assess and adjust existing estimates to improve accuracy.

3.6.2 What are the types of estimation?

- *Top-down*

The top-down approach yields high-level estimates of the potential cost for delivering project scope. Top-down estimating is usually less costly and can be attempted when detailed information about the opportunity is not available. But it is also less accurate than other techniques. Top-down estimates are used most often early in the lifecycle for proposals or for estimating activities that would happen in the distant future. A common problem with top-down estimates is that they can be greatly affected by the subjective, personal biases of the estimators.

IT PROJECT MANAGEMENT ESSENTIALS

- *Bottom-up*

A bottom-up cost estimate involves receiving estimates for each work unit from the intended owners of the work units and then summarising them in a project cost estimate. A good bottom-up estimate demonstrates a detailed understanding of the work to be done on a project. Bottom-up estimates are considered to be the most accurate but are usually costly. A common problem with bottom-up estimates is that the overall project estimate might be artificially inflated because each contributing work unit might add its own estimate contingency. It is important to ask the estimators what contingency they used in their estimate so that you do not add another contingency. Bottom-up estimates are used later in the project lifecycle when more detailed data are available and the estimate must be more accurate. When large IT organisations act as the PSI, they need to work with a large number of suppliers. The estimation method may involve receiving independent estimates from all suppliers, adding them, as well as putting in additional effort for overall program management. This is akin to bottom-up estimating, which can be inflated, as every supplier would put their own contingency to their estimates.

3.6.3 What types of costs should be included?

In general, resource costs have the maximum impact on the overall cost structure of the IT project. As a result, IT vendors opt for offshoring (getting work done in a country with a lower resource cost). IT vendors also include more junior resources in the project team to optimise the cost, as senior resources are often much costlier. Offshoring (lack of adequate resources close to customer location) and inexperienced team composition often lead to customer dissatisfaction and troubled relationships. Table 3.3 depicts a typical resource cost estimation, where the project scope is delivered over two phases. The resource cost should also include planned resources from suppliers and partners.

Other than the resource cost, the following cost heads are included in IT cost estimation.

- Hardware cost
- Software license cost
- Annual maintenance contract (AMC) for software and hardware
- Expenses related to travel, training, and others

To optimise software cost, the solution team should explore open-source software and the possible implication of their usage in a commercial context. Similarly, instead of acquiring hardware, cloud-based Infrastructure as a Service (IaaS) can be used to provision the infrastructure.

IT PROJECT MANAGEMENT ESSENTIALS

Table 3.3 Resource estimation using the waterfall method

Project Phase 1

	Effort in Person Month	% of Total Effort
Requirement	49	4.3
Architecture and Design	44	3.8
Development and Unit Testing	68	5.9
SIT and Performance Testing	89	7.8
User Acceptance Testing	56	4.9
Go-live Support	9	0.8
Total Phase 1 Effort	315	27.5

Project Phase 2

	Effort in Person Month	% of Total Effort
Requirement	54	4.7
Architecture and Design	97	8.5
Development and Unit Testing	172	15.0
SIT and Performance Testing	185	16.2
User Acceptance Testing	136	11.9
Go-live Support and Service Migration	186	16.2
Total Phase 2 Effort	830	72.5
Total Project Effort	1145	100

3.6.4 Expected accuracy in different types of estimations

The average time required to close an IT opportunity successfully is long. So, the sales team would do multiple estimations for the same opportunity in its lifecycle. In the initial phase, the estimate for an opportunity is indicative and based on limited information. When the estimate is developed for the final proposal, the sales team has access to much more information; as a result, the estimate should be highly accurate. The accuracy of estimates, in general, is expected to increase later in the lifecycle as more information becomes available. A typical sales process would see the three different types of estimation with different levels of accuracy. They are explained in Table 3.4.

3.6.5 Best practices to be followed for estimation

- **Develop multiple independent estimates:** When the time and budget permit, it is better to build at least two independent estimates. They can

Table 3.4 Level of accuracies in estimation

Phase	Expected Accuracy	Methods
RFI /Indicative	−25%/+ 75%	Primarily top-down with limited data.
Initial Submission of Proposal/Budgetary	−10%/+30%	Mixing top-down and bottom-up methods with adequate data
Final Proposal/Definitive	−5%/+15%	Bottom-up estimate with detailed data about the customer environment, challenges, and expectations

be compared; in case of a wide variance between multiple estimations, further analysis would be required. When the variations between multiple estimates are within allowable limits, we can use their average for further calculation.

- **Include the appropriate contingency:** An appropriate contingency should be included in the budget based on the derived risk profile of the opportunity. Too high a contingency would make the proposal unattractive, while failure to include an adequate contingency might lead to a financial loss of the service provider.
- **Avoid force-fitting a presumed outcome:** Many times, due to competitive pressure and customer expectation, salespersons fall in the trap of justifying a presumed cost by working backward. This approach disregards the experiences, learnings of the service providers, and the uniqueness of the customer environment. Generally, in these types of scenarios, the delivery team often finds it difficult to meet customer expectations, leading to a troubled project and spoiled customer relations.
- **Document all assumptions:** It is very important for the sales team to document all assumptions, constraints, customer commitments, productivity and utilisation factors, and other supporting information. Documenting these would allow the team to defend their estimates in multiple review and approval meetings. These would provide sufficient background to the delivery team for the execution and control of promised benefits.

3.7 Schedule development

Other than the cost estimation, the duration of the project, as well as the sequence of the activities, are of great concern for the customer. To communicate that, the IT provider develops a project plan or project management schedule. A project plan or project management schedule defines the key activities with their durations, key milestone dates, the dependencies between internal activities, and dependencies with external activities. Once resources are integrated into the plan, we can also see who is responsible for the task. To integrate resources into the schedule, we must analyse and determine the effort and skills required for completing each of the tasks. The solution team can identify available resources with the required skills to assign them to those tasks.

If the solution proposed is very complex and the scope is large, it would be difficult to communicate the dependencies and implementation schedule in a single project plan. The complex program needs to split into a number of smaller projects, and project management schedules are built for each individual project. The program plan should summarise and integrate these interdependent smaller projects, capturing the interdependencies, as well as ensuring the consistency of the overall plan. A project management schedule of a typical IT project is shown in Figure 3.6.

A few of the important pieces of information related to scheduling terminology is explained here:

- An activity is an element of work performed over a period of time within the project. It has a measured beginning and end. In a project network diagram, each activity has an early start and early finish, as well as a late start and late finish.
- The amount of time an activity can be delayed without delaying the early start (ES) of any immediately following activities is called the free float associated with that activity.
- Similarly, the float of an activity can be described as the amount of time an activity can be delayed from its ES without delaying the overall project finish date.
- A task is a sub-division of an activity. Generally, to manage the activity, they are broken into shorter tasks.
- A milestone is an achievement in terms of completion of an important activity. Typical milestones are agreement on requirements document, completion of coding, completion of testing, and so on. A milestone activity has zero duration and zero resources.
- The critical path of a project is described as the longest of all paths in the project. A project can have more than one critical path. Critical paths do not have any float; any delay in executing the activities that fall in the critical path would delay the entire project.
- Two activities can have start-to-start, finish-to-finish, and finish-to-start relationships.

IT PROJECT MANAGEMENT ESSENTIALS

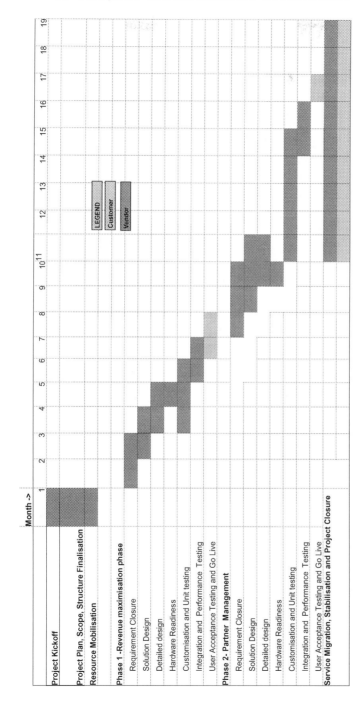

Figure 3.6 Typical IT project management schedule

3.8 Chapter highlights

- While selling IT is a complex activity, IT providers face challenges in delivering promised business benefits. Failure to deliver IT solutions and the associated feature would not only financially impact the service provider, but it would also lead to customer dissatisfaction and a poor reputation in the market.
- It is important for sellers to understand the IT solution development methodology, so the proposal includes a realistic timeline and price, which allows the service delivery team to deliver the promised solution.
- A project is a temporary endeavour undertaken to create a unique product or service. Specific to the IT service, we can think of the project as the effort required for the achievement of a specific objective, which involves a series of activities and tasks which consume resources.
- Project management often involves balancing time, cost, quality, scope, and customer satisfaction.
- A project management methodology is tightly coupled with the lifecycle it follows. A project lifecycle is a collection of project phases.
- Predictive software development methodology follows a sequential waterfall model with five project phases.
- The waterfall model is often found to be lacking in handling the dynamism and challenges of the turbulent business environment of the present day.
- The agile methodologies work better than the all-at-once model of software development, with their ability to handle changes and to provide visibility to the stakeholders. Agile fares poorly in handling complex, multi-vendor IT development.
- Identification, classification, and response planning of risks are important aspects of IT proposal development.
- Without a solid containment plan, a proposal with a high risk may result in a "no bid" decision by the senior management. The risk profile of the proposal is also used to define the contingency amount in the costing process; a proposal with a higher risk profile would demand setting aside a higher contingency amount.
- An estimate is an assessment of the likely cost in quantitative terms for delivering the scope based on the available information. The available input could be very limited, noisy, and uncertain at the initial stage of a proposal, but could be based on more detailed information at the later stage.
- The baseline estimate serves as a basis for generating the project price and the contract value.
- Top-down estimation involves less effort and can be done based on limited information, though it would have lower accuracy than the

bottom-up method. Bottom-up estimations are performed before the submission of the final proposal and have high accuracy.

3.9 Questions for discussion

1 Why is risk profiling a new opportunity so important in IT selling? Explain this with two possible scenarios.

   i)   A high-risk opportunity has been wrongly classified as having a lower risk
   ii) A low-risk opportunity has been improperly classified as having a higher risk

2 You are working for Wipro as a senior solution manager. Recently, one of your assignments is to develop an IT outsourcing proposal for Telenor's Asia business. Telenor's Asia business is spread over Bangladesh, Pakistan, Malaysia, Thailand, and Myanmar. The telecom operator is not the market leader in any of these markets. There is also no uniform IT stack across these countries, making economies of scale difficult to achieve. The parent company, Telenor of Norway, recently decided to review its investments outside Europe and exit from the unprofitable market. Please identify the risks that you would highlight as a proposal designer based on the scenario.

3 Do a comparative assessment of agile and plan-driven software development methodologies. Please comment when agile should not be recommended.

4 Why is it okay to accept an estimation with lower accuracy at the beginning of an opportunity?

3.10 References

Beck, K., Beedle, M., van Bennekum, A., Cockburn, A., Cunningham, W., Fowler, M., . . . Thomas, D. (2001). *Manifesto for agile software development*. Snowbird, UT. Retrieved from https://agilemanifesto.org/

Boehm, B., and Turner, R. (2003). *Balancing agility and discipline: A guide for the perplexed*. Addison-Wesley Professional.

Mukhopadhyay, S., and Gupta, R. (2019). *Reviewing commonalities between agile software development methodology and grounded theory methodology*. SSRN 3326376. Retrieved from https://www.researchgate.net/publication/328282326_Reviewing_Commonalities_between_Agile_Software_Development_Methodology_and_Grounded_Theory_Methodology_23_15102018

Munns, A. K., and Bjeirmi, B. F. (1996). The role of project management in achieving project success. *International Journal of Project Management*, 14(2), 81–87.

Pressman, R. S. (2005). *Software engineering: A practitioner's approach*. Palgrave Macmillan.

Sutherland, J. (2001). Agile can scale: Inventing and reinventing scrum in five companies. *Cutter IT Journal*, *14*(12), 5–11.

Turk, D., France, R., and Rumpe, B. (2014). Assumptions underlying agile software development processes. *Journal of Database Management*, *16*. arXiv preprint arXiv:1409.6610

4
SALES AND BID MANAGEMENT PROCESS

Learning Objectives

This chapter provides an overview of the different steps followed in the value-based selling process. By the end of this chapter, a reader will be able to:

* Understand the key activities in each of the four steps in the value-based selling process
* Appreciate different proactive and reactive methods of lead generation
* Understand how advanced analytic techniques can be used in qualifying leads
* Develop the different aspects of the technical and commercial solution
* Understand the types of contracts available and how to estimate the contract value in a specific opportunity.

4.1 Introduction to the value-based selling process

IT sales management is the process of opportunity identification and qualification, value articulation, technical and commercial solution development, and value delivery, as well as ongoing relationship management. The IT sales process is complex, time-consuming, and involves multiple stakeholders—often from different countries—with different technology and business backgrounds. So, following a consistent and rigorous sales process ensures that supplier firms increase their profitability and market share and at the same time create measurable value for their customers. Recent research has confirmed that the seller's success in assisting the customer derive greater value from the exchange also produces higher return for the seller (Töytäri and Rajala, 2015). In a competitive IT market, the ability to conduct value-based selling will differentiate winners from losers. But at the same time, we need to be aware of the challenges associated

DOI: 10.4324/9781003155270-5

SALES AND BID MANAGEMENT PROCESS

with the value-based selling approach. Töytäri and Rajala (2015) have listed multiple such challenges:

1. Different stakeholders involved in buying and using the new IT solution define value in a subjective way, which prevents the emergence of a shared perception of value.
2. Value creation and measurement depend on the context. Sub-optimal performance on areas outside the scope of new IT solution can impact value creation.
3. A significant part of value would only be realised in the future. As a result, value-based selling would need a long-term relationship between the buyer and the seller. This is in many cases considered risky and uncertain and would often involve a complex financial model.

Synthesising the literature on value-based selling (Töytäri and Rajala, 2015) and the managerial practices followed in large IT providers, we have broken the IT sales process into four steps, as defined in Figure 4.1. These steps are:

- Opportunity identification and qualification
- Value proposition articulation
- Solution definition
- Value delivery.

The mature IT organisations use reusable assets and knowledge artefacts from previous engagements in each step of the sales process. The large IT

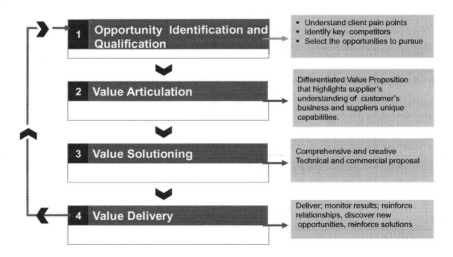

Figure 4.1 Value-based IT sales management process

80

companies have also developed a dedicated centralised pre-sales centre, known as the deal hub or bid management function. The deal hub is primarily involved in coordination between multiple stakeholders (technical, business, finance and pricing, project management, risk management, and other functions) associated with the opportunity. This arrangement allows the sellers and account managers to spend more time with the customers, while the deal hub coordinates the delivery of high-quality, more responsive solutions and proposals.

We have explained the input required for each of the steps of the value-based IT sales process, activities performed in those steps, and the expected output of the steps.

4.2 Opportunity identification and qualification

Two sub-activities are performed in this stage: identifying new opportunities and assessing them so that the sales team can focus effectively on more attractive opportunities.

4.2.1 Identification of the opportunities

Types of opportunities

In a broad sense, the new opportunities can come from new clients and the vendor's ongoing relationship with the existing customers. For an existing customer, the opportunities are primarily managed by the account management team. To fulfil these opportunities, the vendor would provide a range of services, and many times, an appropriate mix of those services. The services can range from high-end consulting to commoditised bug fixing and maintenance work (Figure 4.2).

Similarly, an opportunity can be classified based on its business and financial impact on the client's business. Transactional opportunities are short-term and, in many cases, related to cost-saving and solving immediate

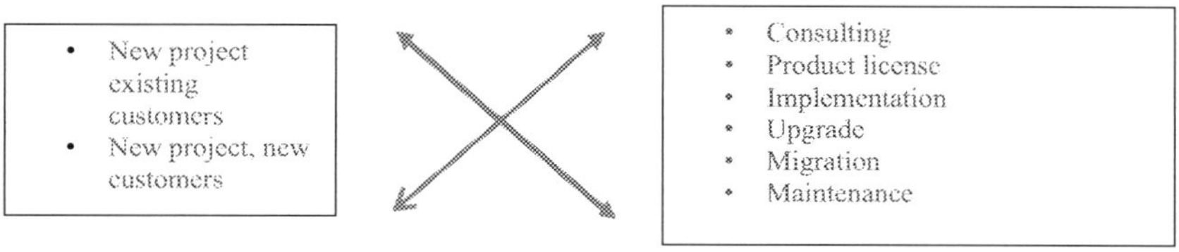

Figure 4.2 Mapping between customer and opportunity types

problems. While transformational projects are strategic in nature, buyers execute them to gain long-term, competitive benefits. While buyers of transactional opportunities demonstrate "value for money" buying behaviour, the buyers of transformational opportunities are associated with innovation and relationship-oriented buying behaviour.

Acquiring new opportunities

IT service providers become aware of these opportunities through multiple types of sales efforts. These sales efforts can be broadly classified into two categories: 1) proactive and 2) reactive (Table 4.1).

Within these two categories, IT vendors work with multiple methods to acquire new opportunities, which are examined next:

- **RFX process:** This is the most convenient way of getting involved in a new opportunity. The clients ask shortlisted partners or vendors (based on defined parameters) to participate in their procurement process. Clients generally share their expectations and requirements through the request for information (RFI) or request for proposal (RFP). We have explained the details about the RFI and RFP process in Chapter 5.
- **The outcome of consulting work:** Large IT companies provide business, technology, process, and methodology consulting to the user organisations. Though the consulting assignments are often of low value, they frequently act as door openers for significant IT implementation works. For example, while performing the IT capability assessment of a

Table 4.1 Proactive vs. reactive selling

#	Proactive Selling	Reactive Selling
1	In proactive selling, sales personnel create opportunities proactively.	In reactive selling, customers reach out to suppliers (vendors) seeking services or products.
2	Typical examples are a) a solution developed for a client based on analysis of its financial statements, priorities, and challenges and b) solutions developed based on some new regulations.	Typical example is shortlisting by customers for an RFP based on customer's prior knowledge.
3	This needs more effort from the seller, and the seller would have more control. The seller also has opportunities to differentiate it from its competitors.	In reactive selling, the customer controls the process to a much larger extent than in proactive selling. The amount of competition would be higher also.

retailer, the consulting team might recommend a major revamp of customer relationship management (CRM) systems. As the consultants are already aware of the customer's environment and the challenges they face, the buyer organisation would prefer them to implement the same. Even in a competitive RFP process, the consulting organisations would have an advantage due to their privileged access to the customer's IT environment.

- **Account mining:** Due to the ongoing relationships with large customers, the incumbent IT service providers are preferred for executing IT enhancement projects of low and medium value. Implementing these new IT features often involves integration and customisation in the existing IT systems. The buyers frequently assign these works to the incumbent IT vendors; as a result, the overall effort of coordination between multiple vendors is avoided. IT vendors on their own can also recommend new feature implementation, as they are aware of the limitations of the existing IT landscape.
- **Marketing activities:** Leads can also come from multiple marketing activities performed by the IT vendors. The leads can be generated from the trade fairs, exhibitions, conferences, other online channels, and field staff. The salespersons can also proactively do performance analysis of the target companies, the impact of new regulations, and suggest solutions based on those. Those are explained in detail in Chapter 7.
- **Partnership:** Though direct selling to customers remains the most preferred avenue for selling complex IT solutions to customers, smart collaboration with external players is becoming crucial. A joint go-to-market initiative with these players can create competitive advantages, achieve additional scale and reach, and access expertise outside one's organisation. A joint go-to-market strategy drives revenue in industries and regions where the IT provider cannot venture on its own due to multiple reasons. Broadly, there are two types of partnership options:

Partnership with other organisations: This is the most common form of partnering for go-to-market. The IT companies partner with other organisations primarily to address more customers and opportunities. Partnerships with other organisations need significant effort in partner selection, joint value proposition creation, partner enablement, and partner evaluation. So, partners should be selected carefully. From a sales perspective, partners should be onboarded for two specific purposes:

1 **Resource/capability acquisition:** The partner has capabilities (products, services, brand) valued by the customer and which the first organisation lacks. Many IT product companies (such as Oracle, Amdocs, and SAP) do not have service delivery resources and expertise required for product customisation and IT implementation work. They work with IT service

providers such as IBM, Infosys, and TCS to provide a customised solution (anchored on their product), keeping in mind the customer-specific pain points and context. Besides, large IT organisations such as IBM and Accenture work as prime systems integrators and act as a single point of interface to provide a host of varied computing capabilities to the buyer. The system integrator would not have in-house products that can fulfil the entire gamut of customer requirements. As a result, they select the products from other vendors to create a comprehensive IT solution that can address the customer's consolidated need.

2   **Increased customer reach:** A partnership is one of the quickest ways to address new customers or markets. There are four ways a partnership can help the IT provider achieve the same (Socransky, 2016):

   i   **Geographic expansion:** A partnership can allow an IT company to expand into a new geography without developing its own salesforce. The reasons for doing so can be many: 1) inability of the IT company to invest in the sales organisation, 2) the new market may be too small to justify a dedicated sales organisation, and 3) an uncertain regulatory framework for foreign companies in the target market.

   ii   **Market expansion:** A successful loyalty product vendor in the mobile services market might want to roll out the same product in the retail domain. Working with an established player with a retail industry background may allow the IT company to quickly roll out the product with the partner's salesforce, brand reputation, and domain knowledge. The partners would also have client contacts, which the first organisation would not have. Similarly, large IT companies can work with smaller partners with lower cost structures to push their products in the small and medium enterprises (SME) sector.

   iii   **Additional sales channel:** Partners are also selected to increase the impact of the sales channel. A partner with a large and successful salesforce can bring additional revenues. As these types of resellers work with multiple competitive products with similar functionalities, the product vendor needs to design incentives to motivate the salesforce of the partner to recommend its product.

   iv   **Selling to governments:** Governments (central, state, and municipalities) are increasingly using and procuring more IT solutions to provide better services to citizens and become more efficient. Selling to the government is different from selling to private enterprises. The underlying risks are also qualitatively different and have a much broader impact. Organisations often use experienced partners or tie-up with other government organisations to improve their chances of bagging these contracts.

A partnership between two or multiple organisations can be on a long-term basis or can be based on a particular opportunity. In a few cases, the partnership can lead to strategic alliances between two or more large organisations. Here, the participating entities invest significant complementary resource and management attention to develop a compelling value proposition. Examples of such collaborations are many, such as the IBM and Apple partnership, to serve the IT needs of enterprise customers (Satell, 2014). In this partnership, while IBM brings the strength of its analytical and productivity enhancement capability, Apple ensures superior employee and customer experience and higher satisfaction.

Collaboration with external organisations is generally beneficial, but one should be aware of the downsides of the inter-organisational collaboration (Gardner and Ibarra, 2017; Socransky, 2016).

The key limitations are:

- **Inefficiency:** Onboarding and managing partners involve significant search, evaluation, and management costs. The IT organisations should regularly review the partner's performance in comparison to the overhead and coordination cost. It should periodically get rid of dormant and ineffective partnerships, where cost outweighs the benefit.
- **Increased risk:** Trusting a partner to sell or deliver a part of the solution can create customer dissatisfaction and negatively impact the first organisation's brand reputation.
- **Competition among partners:** Popularly known as channel conflict, too many partners selling the same product to a customer creates confusion, customer dissatisfaction, and ultimately lowers the price. Besides, conflicting information received from multiple partners on an identical product reduces the credibility of the product.

Partnership to co-create with customers: Customers who have used a specific vendor's IT solutions for a longer duration often develop critical expertise with that product or solution. The customer generally also has deep domain expertise in their business. The IT vendor can collaborate with the client to extend its core solution's capabilities, leading to the industry-specific extension of the core product. There are multiple examples of the same. Philips NV has used Salesforce CRM for a long time. Going beyond the buyer–supplier relation, they decided to collaborate to develop a cloud-based healthcare solution (Philips, 2014). Similarly, in India, IBM and Airtel (India's second-largest telecom service provider) have collaborated for more than two decades. Taking advantage of this synergistic relationship, they work together to deliver services to other enterprises. IBM brings its IT product and services capabilities, and Airtel brings its telecom connectivity services.

For all opportunities, though they may come through different channels, their details are entered into the sales management or CRM systems.

An opportunity owner is assigned, and the opportunity's attractiveness is assessed to decide on the next steps.

4.2.2 *Qualification of the opportunities*

A better-performing sales process would qualify prospective sales opportunities accurately and earlier in the sales process. The sales team should focus their resources on the right and qualified prospects and would avoid investing unnecessary time and resource in other opportunities. A better opportunity management and qualification process would increase the win rate, reduce marketing expenses, and lead to a shorter sales cycle. In summary, opportunity qualification is becoming increasingly important due to:

1 Pre-sales activities involve a significant commitment to expenses incurred in mobilising resources, travel, and associated costs. For pre-sales and solution work, organisations need to deploy senior and more expensive resources. Opting out of an opportunity early that cannot be won means saving resources and management attention, which can be utilised in other more promising opportunities.
2 An IT service provider might decide to avoid certain types of work. For example, an IT service provider (vendor) focused on cloud-based service delivery might avoid traditional IT development work.
3 Customers might misuse the pre-sales activities of the service provider. Customers might get in touch with multiple providers, ask them to share information, and organise proofs-of-concept and trials. When the buying intention or need is not strong and the intention is not accompanied by budget allotment, customers can misuse the pre-sales discussions to accumulate information and develop internal capabilities at the vendor's expense.
4 The service provider also needs to assess its ability to provide the requested services. If the service provider does not have adequate competence and delivery capability for a specific work, winning the opportunity would lead to additional risk. Failure to deliver the agreed-upon scope can lead to loss of reputation and financial loss.

When assessing a new opportunity, large companies use a structured methodology with a few critical parameters. The lead resources from sales, architecture, and delivery associated with the opportunity provide their qualitative assessment on these parameters. In many cases, a rating scale of 1 to 5 is used. Here, 1 indicates a less favourable evaluation, and 5 indicates a highly favourable assessment. The opportunity can also be evaluated based on the agreed-upon parameters on a scale of low to high (low/medium/high). In the next section, we have described the four parameters used frequently for opportunity qualification.

SALES AND BID MANAGEMENT PROCESS

Client's perceived need

To understand this, the sellers (the vendors) should have insight into the client's actual business issues and the compelling reasons for acquiring the new IT capabilities. Though an RFP/RFI or other customer-provided documents might provide the explicit system requirement, it is critically important to go beyond those to understand underlying actual business issues.

To understand the client's perceived need, the pre-sales team should use secondary research and the insights coming out of their relationship with the client. As a part of a structured top-down secondary research, the macro-economic environment of the country, industry segment, the company, its competitors, and the customers are studied. Based on the data collected, the pre-sales team should focus on understanding the following specific questions:

1 What are the problems faced by the clients, and what is their impact on company performance?
2 What is the business goal that the client wants to achieve with the new solution?
3 Why has the customer not implemented this solution so far?
4 What would be the key barriers or challenges in implementing this?
5 If the project is delayed or not executed, how would it impact the client?
6 Does the client have adequate funds available for doing this now?

Executive relationship

As we have explained in Chapter 2, IT sales leaders need to understand their buyers well. Different stakeholders from multiple departments would come together to evaluate competing products and make buying decisions. It would be essential to understand their role and influence in the buying process and their attitude and level of support towards the seller. The key questions that need to be asked are:

- Who are the key stakeholders involved in the buying process?
- What are their roles in the buying process (e.g. gatekeeper, economic buyer, user, coach)?
- What is the seller's level of relationships with these key stakeholders?
- Does the relationship of the seller ensure that they can influence decision-makers?
- What is the level of trust and relationship that competitors have with these stakeholders? Can the seller have enough capabilities to counter those?

The seller should use the four types of role frameworks developed by Miller and Heiman (1985) for stakeholder mapping. In their book, *Strategic*

Selling, Miller and Heiman (1985) described four types of buyers involved in a business-to-business (B2B) purchasing relationship.

Economic buyer: The economic buyer owns the budget and provides the final approval to buy. There is generally one economic buyer in each sale. Due to his or her seniority in the organisational hierarchy, the economic buyer exerts maximum influence in the acquisition process. They are more interested in assessing the solution's benefits and business impact (cost reduction, competitive advantage, or new revenue). They also look into the business and financial risks associated with the solution, as well as the provider. These sets of people look for client references, return on investment, business case, and value modelling, showcasing the solution's financial and strategic impact.

User buyer: This set of stakeholders are the actual users of the proposed solution. There would be many users, and they would have personal views and interests. As they would use the solution daily, they want to understand its impact on their specific job outcomes. To make them comfortable, they should be provided a free trial, demonstration, and easy-to-use user documentation and online resources. Unlike economic buyers, the analysis of users would be detailed and cover most of the features. The decision-maker would not go ahead and buy any solution if they face opposition from users. On the other side, generating real interest among the user community can increase the potential solution's appeal. The sales team should provide these types of buyers with hands-on experience, free trials, demonstrations, and user documentation.

Technical buyer or gatekeeper: The technical buyer would do an objective evaluation and screen out various solutions from being considered. For an IT solution, the chief information officer (CIO)/IT manager would act as the most critical gatekeeper. The overall evaluation of IT solutions is generally done by the IT department. In addition to the functionalities, they evaluate the security and operational aspect of the solution. The finance manager and chief financial officer (CFO) can be another potential gatekeeper; the CFO would be more concerned about whether the solution can be developed in-house or if all possible alternatives have been considered. Based on their evaluation and feasibility analysis, they would make a recommendation. Generally, they can remove any solution from the consideration set by saying "no," but they cannot say "yes" by selecting a specific solution. The sales team needs to make them comfortable by incorporating their points of view on contractual terms and conditions, sharing compliance with the different standards, and making them part of the trial and demonstration. In terms of communication and messaging, they should be provided with trials, demos, and compliance matrixes, including security and non-functional requirements.

Coach: The coach is the champion of the seller's solution within the buyer organisation. This individual has a positive attitude towards the seller's solution and wants it to succeed. This person is also confident of the value

SALES AND BID MANAGEMENT PROCESS

creation potential of the proposed solution. The seller needs to find at least one coach in every deal and develop that relationship. The person should be supported by the seller with relevant sales and marketing material so that he or she can work on promoting the seller's offer internally. The coach also acts as an internal guide to the outside business entity on the inner intricacies of making a specific sale. The coach should be provided with sales and marketing material for internal promotion.

We should not label people in the buyer's organisation based on their organisational title, but based on their role on a specific opportunity. An excellent way to understand the key stakeholders would be to ask the following questions:

- Who will pay for this sale?
- Who will be using the proposed solution?
- Who is making judgments about the technical merits?
- Who can provide guidance?

Once the right stakeholders for an opportunity are identified, the sales team should assess the relationship with these identified individuals. A relationship matrix (Table 4.2) would help visualise the present level of relationships with the key stakeholders and the corrective action plans.

Impact

It is crucial to understand the economic impact of the solution on the client's business. The sales team needs to understand the fundamental economic

Table 4.2 Stakeholder management plan

#	Stakeholders	Nature of Relationships	Perception About Seller	Perception of Key Competitors	Planned Actions
1	Economic buyer (head of customer service)	Well established	Positive	Positive	• Organise reference client site visit
2	Technical buyer 1 (IT head)	Coach	Highly Positive	Neutral	
3	Technical buyer 2 (CFO)	Weak	Neutral	Positive	
4	User buyer 1	Developing	Positive	Negative	• Provide a demo of the system's functionalities

drivers impacted by this program and the quantum of the impact. The economic drivers could be revenue, cost, working capital requirement, and capital expenditure. The sales team should be able to quantify these benefits and convince the customers that these are achievable.

Though a robust economic rationale is desirable, IT solutions are also implemented to acquire strategic advantages or comply with the local regulations. A few strategic interests would be access to additional information about customers or competitors, which allows for better product and service design. Many organisations also work with emerging technologies, though they might not get any immediate economic benefits from this project. Based on these two criteria (economic and non-economic), the sales team should be able to do impact analysis of any opportunity.

Delivery capability

The sellers also need to internally analyse whether they possess the right capabilities to execute the jobs. In case the skills are not available internally, they also need to ensure whether they can acquire it from the market as per the solution timeline. If the capabilities are very specialised and the resources could not be utilised in other projects, the sellers might avoid onboarding those resources.

The large IT companies have partnerships with many product and services vendors; the analysis should also consider these partners' capabilities. As customers are increasingly looking for resources close to their location, the sellers need to see the cost and other feasibility of having onsite (client location) resources. Implementing any IT solutions would require business or domain, technical, and project management capabilities. The resource analysis should take into account all three types of capabilities. The sellers can also differentiate their solution by showcasing assets developed by their innovation and research team. The sellers can also highlight their achievements in implementing similar solutions elsewhere and the high business impact generated. The buyer compares the solution proposed by a specific IT vendor with similar solutions provided by the competitors. So, the sales team should find out their relative positioning considering other competitors.

Once the analysis for a particular opportunity is done based on these four parameters, we can allot a qualitative score for each of them. We might decide to use the high, medium, and low categories to indicate attractiveness. Table 4.3 provides a framework for using these parameters to qualify an opportunity.

For an opportunity to have a high chance of winning, it should have a high or medium score in all four quadrants. The seller organisation can take corrective actions to improve its positioning in these four quadrants, where it has scored low. In case the capability for delivering the opportunity is absent in-house, the organisation can consider partnering with someone

SALES AND BID MANAGEMENT PROCESS

Table 4.3 Structured opportunity assessment

	Score Low if	Score High if
Need	• The current business environment and application environment are stable • Unclear or marginal business benefits • No significant competitive advantage available from the opportunity • The purpose behind the project is not clearly understood	• The requirements are regulatory in nature and must be complied with • It addresses the significant competitive threat of the buyer or opens up a new opportunity • Clear business benefit
Impact	• The opportunity scores low both on strategic value and financial value • Net present value (NPV) is low or negative • Project return on investment (ROI) is less than the expected return	• The opportunity scores high on both strategic and economic value • NPV is positive and significant • Project ROI is significantly higher than the expected return
Relationship	• Senior management is not easily accessible • The senior executive from the sellers have not met or rarely met the chief executive officer (CEO) and other top managers.	• Has easy access to senior management and project sponsor; can set up a meeting on short notice • Ongoing regular meeting/contact between senior management of the buyer organisations and the sellers
Capabilities	• Uncertain whether the seller can deliver the business benefit with the agreed timeframe • Never delivered the solution—first of a kind • It would be difficult to guarantee the promised business benefits	• Have implemented similar work multiple times • Confident that the seller can deliver the business benefits to the client in the agreed-upon timeframe • The seller is in a position to commit to the promised business benefits

who brings relevant experience. But if the relationship with senior management of the buyer is lacking, it might be better not to aggressively pursue the opportunity. The relationship-building takes a longer time, and it would be difficult once the buying process kicks off. If the impact is low and the client is not important and strategic, it would make sense to opt out of the bidding process. But if the customer is important, the seller should participate but without investing too much.

SALES AND BID MANAGEMENT PROCESS

Analytics-driven opportunity assessment

In today's markets, the big story is Big Data. Technological advances are enabling the organisation to capture rich and diverse data throughout the lifecycles of customer interaction. Though big or traditional data alike, on their own, do not reveal significant insights, using machine learning and other analytics techniques can provide critical input for decision-making. The dependence on data for decision-making allows corporations to move beyond qualitative or past experience-based decision-making on new opportunities. IT vendors or service providers already possess significant analytical capabilities. They can also incorporate a structured opportunity assessment methodology to predict the sales conversion probability of new opportunities. Due to better classification of opportunities, sales and profitability objectives are achieved, even after a significant reduction of marketing (pre-sales) spend.

Though there are multiple types of machine learning algorithms, the classification family of algorithms would be appropriate for this scenario. Classification is a technique where we categorise data into a given number of classes. The classification algorithm differs from linear regression; the dependent variable in classification is categorical, wherein the dependent variable in the linear regression is continuous. If the number of classes is two, we call the classification a binary classification. The main goal of a classification problem is to identify the category/class to which new data will fall under. A number of explanatory variables (also known as predictors, independent variables, and features) are used for the same.

The opportunity assessment problems can be modelled as a classification problem, where the dependent or target variable would be binary (likely to win/not likely to win). For predicting the target variable, several independent variables such as industry segment, geography, profit margin, customer's financial status, deal value, and the relative strength of the service provider (and many others) can be used. A classification technique predicts the opportunity's outcome and highlights each of the independent variable's relative contribution to the outcome. The modelling exercise can help the sellers in two distinct ways: 1) to avoid the challenging opportunities and focus on winnable opportunities and 2) identify and work on the factors that positively or negatively impact the probability of winning. Though a detailed analysis of different classification techniques is not part of this book, the classification techniques are of two varieties:

Parametric method: Here, the probability of winning the opportunity (outcome/target/dependent variable) is expressed in the form of an equation consisting of functions and coefficients. The widely used parametric methods are logistic regression and linear discriminant analysis.

Non-parametric method: Here, the algorithm does not worry about choosing the right functional form and does not provide an equation to predict

SALES AND BID MANAGEMENT PROCESS

the outcome variable. It works better with a large amount of data and offers easy-to-interpret business rules and tree diagrams. The decision tree is a widely used non-parametric method. Decision tree output is straightforward to understand even for people with a non-analytical background. It does not require any statistical knowledge to read and interpret them. Its graphical representation is very intuitive. It is also advantageous to identify the independent variables (which the seller can control) having maximum impact on the outcome. For example, an organisation can have access to hundreds of variables related to the opportunities they have won or lost in the past; the decision tree will help to identify the most impactful variables.

Outcome of opportunity assessment process

The opportunity assessment process would lead to a go/no-go decision related to pursuing the opportunity. In case of a go decision, the seller would invest in responding to the client's RFP or RFI as per the bidding process. In case of no-go, the buyer might decide to withdraw from the opportunity. In some cases, the buyer might try to discover the significant gaps that have led to the opportunity of being classified as unfavourable. They can identify actions to close the gaps.

The seller with a deep relationship with the buyer's organisation and significant experience in that domain sometimes can decide to influence the opportunity's scope to make it more winnable. They might propose a different solution compared to what has been asked for. The new solution might create more value for the buyer while addressing the actual problem. Due to the differentiated nature of the solution, the seller would have a higher chance of success. Doing this is not an easy task; it requires a strong relationship with the client's key decision-makers, a convincing business case that is superior to the business case of the original scope, and obviously, identifying the challenges associated with the new approach. In case of a decision to not pursue the opportunity, the buyer might decide to increase the cost of the competitors. One way to do that is to increase the customer expectation. The purpose of the process and the multiple outcomes associated with it are mentioned in Figure 4.3.

Bid team formation for validated opportunities

Once the seller decides to pursue the opportunity, it would form a cross-functional team (Figure 4.4) to develop a value proposition and a detailed solution and responses to the customer's requirement. The team formed to address the preparation of the relevant bid documents is known as the bid team. The response to customer's requirements and the associated financials is known as the proposal. In the next section, we have discussed the different team members of the bid team and the roles they play.

SALES AND BID MANAGEMENT PROCESS

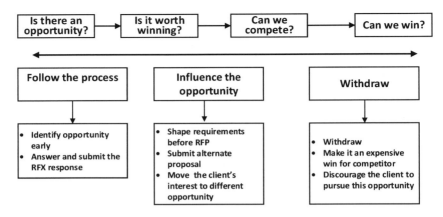

Figure 4.3 Possible outcomes of the opportunity assessment process

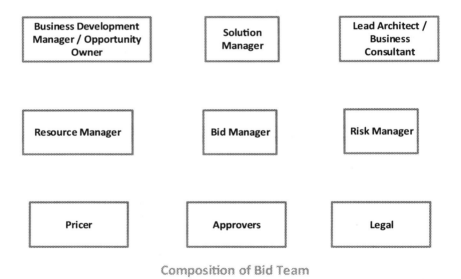

Figure 4.4 Bid management team composition

Business development (BD) manager: The BD manager (associated with a particular customer) owns the opportunity. The BD manager manages the customer relationship, articulates customers' views and challenges, and decides on the overall sales strategy.

Solution manager: The solution manager works in conjunction with the opportunity owner and is responsible for the overall solution strategy, quality, and effectiveness.

Lead architect/business consultant: They are the domain experts, architects, and technical resources. They develop the business and technical architecture, the interfaces with other applications, and the overall impact on the business processes.

Bid manager: The bid manager acts as the project manager and central point of coordination. The person develops and manages the bid response development plan, assigns work to multiple participants, and is responsible for maintaining the bid response's approval process.

Other than those four principal roles, the risk manager, pricer, legal, and resource manager are responsible for specific activities in the different phases of the bid response development. The resource manager, in conjunction with the solution manager, develops the resourcing strategy, such as whether internal resources are available to be deployed in this opportunity or if resources need to be acquired from the market. In case the capabilities required are in tune with the long-term organisational plan, they would look for the recruitment of the critical resources. Otherwise, they might try to access resources available with their partners or other smaller vendors, which might be immediately available. The risk manager reviews the risk profile of the opportunity and identifies gaps (a few of them can be addressed by the solution team). The risk manager also provides an overall risk rating of the proposal. Competitive pricing is critical in ensuring the success of a proposal. The pricer works with the solution team to develop multiple innovative pricing options, where concerns for both buyer and sellers merge.

4.3 Articulating value propositions

In Chapter 2, we have seen that buyers often compare the (value/price) differences between multiple solutions offered by different providers and often select the vendor's solution which provides the highest difference. Three distinct strategies as explained in Chapter 2 (all benefits, favourable point of differences, resonant focus) can be used to develop a favourable value proposition. The core of these three value propositions lies in identifying the point of parity (POP) and point of differentiation (POD) for a particular need of the customer. Customers often assume the presence of several relevant points of parities in any solution, so that the vendor's solution can be considered for evaluation. Sometimes, the sellers would be able to convince the buyer to consider a POP as a POD; as a result, the customer would consider the supplier's solution superior to its next-best competitor. In reality, its offer is comparable with competitors' offerings (Anderson, Narus, and Van Rossum, 2006).

Specific to IT solutions, the POPs would be the development and deployment method and tools, global delivery and global reach, industry knowledge and industry-specific research and point of view, and compliance with the buyer's technical and commercial requirements. All large IT companies would have these capabilities. The PODs would be different in different situations. However, they would be derived from the unique insights 1) from its relationship with the seller's senior management, 2) secondary research, and 3) prior experience with similar types of business problems. We have explained these multiple sources of input used in developing a compelling value proposition in Figure 4.5.

In this section, we have mentioned a few of the guidelines for developing compelling value propositions. It is better to follow a resonating focus strategy by highlighting a few important themes of benefits (ideally five or fewer). The benefit themes are developed by combining several similar types of benefits. Cost reduction as a significant theme in a CRM implementation would combine multiple benefits related to cost reduction. The cost reductions can be achieved due to automated customer onboarding or service fulfilment processes or due to the introduction of chatbots for customer care. A major value theme (popularly known as a winning theme) should satisfy two conditions:

- The benefits associated with the theme are important for the client's business and an important part of the client's ask.
- The vendor's solution should have a clear advantage in providing these benefits compared to the next-best alternative solution from the competitors. The vendor can use this opportunity to change the client's focus on the areas where it has its own strength.

A well-articulated value theme allows the vendor to demonstrate its understanding of the client's real business and technical problems. While creating

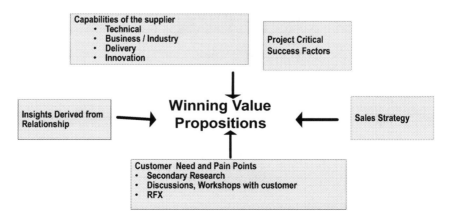

Figure 4.5 Developing winning value propositions

SALES AND BID MANAGEMENT PROCESS

the value proposition, the sellers should keep in mind the important stakeholders in the buying unit and their needs. It is also recommended not to exaggerate benefits that cannot be delivered.

It is often challenging for the sellers to convince the customers about the value proposition. Expecting the customer would trust the verbal or written explanation of the seller may not work. The sellers need to show how exactly their firm would achieve these benefits. The evidence can be a proof of concept or a trial with a limited scale. In some cases, if it is not possible, the sellers should highlight case studies based on past achievements in terms of delivery of similar business outcomes or reports of the analysts like Gartner, IDC, or other independent research providers. It can also highlight the skill and experience level of the key resources to instil confidence in the customer's mind. The value proposition is used as a reference in developing the detailed solution and is useful in computing the actual value delivered later. It is recommended that the sellers associate several key performance indicators (KPIs) with each of the benefits. They can highlight the improvement by comparing the pre- and post- (solution deployment) values of the KPIs.

To provide an example, suppose a telecom (Mphone) operator is facing stagnant revenue, and it got in touch with a large IT provider after their internal analysis. The IT provider, after discussion with Mphone, found that:

1 The market is saturated; hence new customer acquisition would be slow
2 To increase overall revenue, the operator needs to increase average revenue per user (ARPU)
3 As customers are already using the voice calling service to the fullest extent, Mphone needs to launch new applications and content to increase usage
4 To do so, Mphone needs to tie up with multiple partners and content owners.

Considering this scenario, one of the important value propositions (themes) would be **to increase overall non-voice revenue by 45% in three years**. The message can be further fine-tuned by identifying the KPIs (Table 4.4) associated and the changes in them (post–IT solution deployment).

4.4 Solution development

The solution design process is one of the crucial formal activities within the pre-sales process, and it consumes significant effort—between one-third and one-half of the total pre-sales effort. The output of this activity would be a formal and internally approved proposal that can be submitted by the seller to the buying team. While developing a solution, the pre-sales (bid management) team should integrate their knowledge of the client's business and the

Table 4.4 Value proposition with KPI

Value drivers	Present Status of Key Performance Indicators (KPIs)	Post IT Transformation (expected KPI Value)
Time to onboard a new partner for developing services	3–4 months	1.5 weeks max
Time to market—new plans/ promotions	2–3 months	One week max.
Non-voice services contribution in ARPU	13%	20–25%
Contribution of subscription services (recurring services) in non-voice services	10%	25%

environment with a deep understanding of their own organisation's capabilities and offerings. In doing so, the solution manager might need to combine multiple solutions offered by the company and its ecosystem partners. The focus should be on achieving outcomes expected by the client instead of a standard vanilla solution. To address a complex customer issue, specialists need to work together across the boundaries of their expertise. The solution team should reach out to the multiple appropriate experts within its own company and the partner's company for information and knowledge. The solution thus designed would earn a higher margin, customer confidence, and a competitive edge. While it is imperative that the solution provides tangible value to the client and addresses their concern, it should also be of value to other parties involved. It should be valuable for the IT service provider (by providing revenue, profitability, and successful client references) and sellers involved in the bid process (incentive, experience, and career progression). So, the sales leader should make a conscious effort to acknowledge the contribution of all individuals involved in the successful proposal development.

At a high level, a proposal would have three components: 1) technical solution, 2) commercial solution, and 3) legal terms and conditions.

4.4.1 Technical solution

The key components of the technical solution are:

- Solution approach and scope
- Value proposition themes
- Overall technical architecture, including modules and the integration framework

SALES AND BID MANAGEMENT PROCESS

- The timeline, including phases and associated deliverables
- Details of the partners and vendors working with the seller
- Responsibility matrix between buyer and sellers
- Program governance and risk management
- Reusable assets, best practices, and innovation coming out of the seller's knowledge management and research
- Evidence related to the capability of the solution and seller (in the form of a planned demo, client references, and other testimonials).
- Compliance matrix for functional and non-functional requirements

4.4.2 Commercial section

The commercial section contains important information such as the type of contract, contract value, and payment terms. The primary purpose of selecting a specific type of contract is to ensure a reasonable distribution of risk between the buyer and seller. The contract should also provide incentives for the seller's efficient and economic performance. Several factors play an important role in selecting the appropriate type of contract. They are:

- Scope: How well-defined the scope of work is.
- Scope change expected: The amount or frequency of changes of scope expected after the contract is finalised.
- Buyer's expertise: The level of expertise and time the buyer has in managing the seller. A fixed-price contract allows the buyer to move out of the active management of vendors.
- Industry-standard: In many cases, a particular type of contract is preferred for certain types of work.

Selecting the right type of contract

The buyer and sellers have the choice of broadly five different types of contracts. They are explained in detail:

- Cost reimbursable (CR)
- Time and material (T&M)
- Fixed price (FP)
- Pay per use/transaction
- Shared risk/reward

Cost reimbursable: In this type of contract, the buyer reimburses the seller's cost incurred for completing the contractual job. Besides, the seller is provided an agreed amount of fee representing seller profit. This type of contract is preferred if the scope of the work could not be described in detail by the buyer and is also expected to change during the contract period.

SALES AND BID MANAGEMENT PROCESS

Table 4.5 Multiple types of cost-reimbursable contracts

Cost Reimbursable	
Cost Plus Fixed Fee (CPFF)	CPFF is the most widely used cost-reimbursable contract. In addition to reimbursing the cost incurred, the buyer pays a pre-defined fixed fee. This type of contract does not provide any incentive for the seller to inflate the cost (cost overrun). Fees can only be changed with an approved change order. A typical contract of this type would be: Contract value = Cost plus a fixed fee of $200,000.
Cost Plus Incentive Fee (CPIF)	This type of contract pays all costs incurred on performing the work agreed in the contract and an agreed-upon fee. Besides, the buyer can receive a bonus or incentive for performing better than the assigned target. A typical contract of this type would be: Contract value = Cost plus a fixed fee of $200,000. For every month the project is completed sooner than agreed upon, the seller receives an additional $20,000.

Here, the buyer carries the financial risk, as the total costs are unknown to the buyer in the initial period. There are a variety of CR types of contracts (Table 4.5).

Cost-plus percentage of cost (CPPC) (another variety of CR contract) is not a legal type of contract and can be highly risky for buyers. As the sellers get their fee as a percentage of costs incurred, they would not have any motivation to control the costs.

Organisations can also innovate and limit the impact of budget overrun by deploying a cost-plus model. Here the other things remain the same as a standard CR contract, but there would be an upper limit or ceiling that can be charged by the vendor.

Fixed price: In this category, the contract involves a fixed price for a well-defined scope to be delivered by the seller. These types of contracts need less supervision from the buyer's side. The sellers also bear the financial risk in case 1) the project entails more requirements than anticipated originally or 2) the actual cost is more than budgeted due to project delay or some other reasons. As the cost risk is primarily with the sellers, the buyers generally prefer these types of contracts, and it is the most widely used form of contract in the IT industry. To keep better control over the delivery promised by the seller, the buyers also link the payments (as a percentage of total contract value) on achieving the different milestones in the project delivery.

SALES AND BID MANAGEMENT PROCESS

Although fixed-price contracts provide the buyer with a defined cost without chance of overruns, the initial cost charged by the seller may be higher to account for risks and unknown factors. In this type of contract, if the scope is not well defined, both parties are at risk—the buyer may not receive the desired product, or the seller may incur additional costs to provide it.

The buyer's contracting organisation can include the additional penalty for not achieving the timely and quality delivery. Similarly, the contract can have some provision for incentive in case the seller's performance is better than the agreed-upon target.

Time and material: T&M is a hybrid type of contract combining the features of FP and CR contracts. This type of contract is especially useful for projects where the scope is difficult to define, the contract value is less, and the duration is shorter. This contract protects the seller from cost overruns while passing the burden to the buyer. With this type of contract, vendor management is easier, and often the chances of conflict between buyer and seller are low.

In this type of contract, a resource's time spent is priced on a per hour basis. In addition, the expenses or cost of any material used is reimbursed by the seller. A typical example of this type of contract would be an agreed-upon per hour rate of $100 per hour for a Big Data developer with five years of experience. To limit the cost out-go, this type of contract can specify the maximum allowable working hours in a week. In addition, buyers (customers) can decide to pay the expenses incurred for delivering the work, such as travel and lodging.

It is also possible to go for a T&M model with a cap to restrict the maximum amount, allowing the buyer to have some level of control over the cost risk.

Transaction (per unit)/consumption-based pricing: The client pays an agreed rate for a specified transaction or event (i.e. each resource unit) used by the client. This type of pricing is popular for on-demand or cloud-based offerings. This approach works well when the price can be aligned with a well-defined commodity transaction. Many services would be difficult to model on a per-unit price. Besides, as prices are volume-driven, the vendor or seller would have no incentive to add value.

Sellers need to invest in setting up the infrastructure for providing the service. If overall volume or demand is less than anticipated, the seller is exposed to financial risk. The seller's investment/fixed cost exposure can be minimised by ensuring a minimum revenue commitment. It can be done either by charging a monthly fixed charge independent of the volume or imposing a minimum baseline consumption. Minimum revenue commitment is often used in outsourcing contracts, where a seller makes specific investments for a large buyer. It allows the buyer to recover its investment and fixed cost. A reasonable revenue commitment also ensures that the services provided remain financially viable,

Risk and reward sharing: Though there are many variants of this contract, we have discussed two important types of risk and reward sharing contracts. Increasingly, the types of contracts are becoming popular in large IT projects.

Business metric based: The client pays agreed charges based on the client achieving agreed business metrics (e.g. revenue increase, customer churn reduction, etc.). Clients are increasingly demanding these types of transactions, as the cost is aligned to overall business results. This type of contract shows that vendors share the client's gains and "pains" instead of selling some IT capabilities. But the IT vendor may be subjected to unacceptable financial loss or delivery risk, as the delivery cost and price are not linked in this type of contract. Besides, the cost recovery may not be in the IT vendor's control. IT capabilities alone cannot ensure the attainment of business objectives. Instead, those capabilities need to work with other organisational capabilities and processes (which would be difficult to influence by the IT vendor) to achieve the desired business objectives.

Gain share: Like the earlier methodologies, this contract price here is not dependent on the investment required for the project. Rather, the vendor's return is determined by an agreement on sharing cost savings related to operational efficiencies, supply chain optimisation, or other arrangements. In case the vendor is not able to achieve the promised objectives, there would also be pain-sharing elements. The seller should have a deep understanding of the client's business so that it can reach an agreement with the buyer about the original cost and resulting cost savings. The advantage of this method is that if structured properly, it can drive client business to lower cost while creating a significant return for the seller. It also addresses the buyer's concern about the IT vendor's tendency to make excessive profits.

There are several challenges associated with this type of contract. A few of them are:

- This contract looks good conceptually and in theory, but it is complicated to structure and monitor
- The seller has to bear all the delivery risks, but it would have a limited upside in most cases.

Contract value (price)

One of the most important pieces of information in the signed contract is the overall contract value. For T&M and cost-plus types of contracts, the contract value is indicative in nature. For the FP type of contract, the seller cannot charge more than the agreed contract value, even if the project is

SALES AND BID MANAGEMENT PROCESS

delayed or there is a cost overrun. The overvalue of the project is derived from three components:

- **Total estimated cost:** It would include resource cost, travel and living expenses, and software and hardware costs for the vendor and its partners and sub-contractors. As mentioned in Chapter 3, there are multiple methods to do cost estimation. A complex opportunity would be evaluated using different methodologies and by multiple sets of experts.
- **Risk contingency:** Based on the risk profile (rating) of the opportunity, a certain percentage of the total estimated cost (risk contingency) would be added. For the projects that carry higher risk ratings (risky projects), a higher amount of contingency would be required. The total of estimate and the risk contingency is known as the "budgeted cost".
- **Profit margin:** The vendor would also include a certain amount of profit (generally a percentage of the budgeted cost). The profit margin depends on the client profile, industry segment attractiveness, and the type of services delivered.

We have provided one of the more straightforward examples of deriving the total contract value in Table 4.6.

Payment milestones

For many of the IT opportunities (particularly for FP deals), the payment milestones are important negotiation items. In a large FP IT deal, the payments are staggered. It becomes due on achieving pre-defined milestones. The most common milestones used in the industry are:

- Business requirements are agreed and approved by the client
- Software development and customisation are completed successfully, and the same has been installed on the client's machines

Table 4.6 Estimating contract value

Cost Description	Amount (in US$)
Hardware	99,000
Software licenses	250,000
Implementation services	300,000
Total Baseline Cost	**649,000**
Risk contingency added (10% of baseline cost)	64,900
Total Budgeted Cost	**713,900**
Gross profit (20% of the total budgeted cost)	142,780
Total Contract Value	**856,680**

- Testing of the implemented solution is successfully completed with or without known minor issues
- Service is live.

The other vital components of the commercial solution are the financing plan. This section is optional and would be required when the seller finances directly or collaborates with other finance companies the full or partial IT investment of the client.

4.4.3 Legal section

The legal section would be negotiated by the buyer's and seller's procurement teams with help from their legal specialists. The essential sections included in this section are:

- Contract terms and conditions
- Penalty clauses
- Arbitration
- Exit criteria
- Legal binding.

4.4.4 Proposal audit

Once the solution is prepared, the seller's internal quality and risk management team would audit the proposal from multiple perspectives. They review the proposal from commercial, delivery, technology, and regulatory perspectives to identify and manage the critical risks.

At the end of the proposal lifecycle, it is essential to do a retrospective analysis to improve the process. The retrospective analysis should be done for both types of opportunities, those that are won and those that are lost. IT companies make extensive use of knowledge management solutions to consolidate the learnings from multiple opportunities and store the artefacts to reuse them in the future.

4.4.5 Major reasons for unsuccessful proposals

To reduce overall marketing spend without compromising the revenue, IT companies need to increase their success rate in the conversion of opportunities. Multiple analyses have identified several major reasons for the failures of the proposals. They are:

- Inability to appreciate the customer's requirements, pain points, and context.
- The value proposition is generic and not linked to the customer's pain point and the business environment.

SALES AND BID MANAGEMENT PROCESS

- There is no tangible evidence to support the claim related to the proposed value creation.
- The solution proposed is not in sync with customer requirements and outcome expected. It might happen due to the seller's propensity to focus on solutions, where the seller has a strong capability or which provide high margins.
- Inadequate use of the past experiences, knowledge, and artefacts available within the organisations
- The buyer perceives the solution proposed as having high risk.
- Poor compliance with the RFP/RFI shared by the buyer.
- Failure to gather marketing intelligence related to the competitors. The proposal is pricier than the similar solutions offered by competitors. The vendor has not provided convincing justification for premium pricing.
- Less experience of the seller in technology, business, and areas related to the solution.
- Risk aversion nature of the seller. Many times the seller does not want to participate in deals that are gain sharing or business metrics based.
- Pricing constructs are not innovative and not tuned with customer's expectation.
- Many of the mid-sized IT companies do not have strong brand equities, particularly outside their home market. They would find it difficult to compete and win against the globally known large brands. Besides, they would frequently not be considered for opportunities related to higher-end consulting and emerging technologies.

4.5 Value delivery

The primary activities in this phase are:

- Delivery of the solution as per the agreed contract
- Demonstrating the business benefits and quantifying the value
- Ongoing relationship management (account management).

IT companies use structured project management methodologies to deliver a complex project, and the relevant topics are covered in Chapter 3. The ongoing account and relationship management processes are described in Chapter 6. In addition, a mature sales organisation should create a client-reference case repository. The steps for doing so are 1) asset harvesting or documenting customer cases in standardised format. It might also need removal of client names or direct references. 2) Indexing to allow a structured search based on industry, technology, geography, and opportunity size. 3) Making client reference stories available for relevant sellers (Töytäri and Rajala, 2015). This repository can be very effectively utilised for convincing customers about the promised value propositions.

105

4.6 Chapter highlights

- The large IT companies follow a four-stage structured sales process. One of the objectives of using a structured approach is to make the best use of reusable assets and knowledge artefacts from previous engagements.
- The IT organisations also make use of a dedicated centralized pre-sales centre, known as the deal hub or bid management function. The deal hub is primarily involved in coordination between multiple stakeholders (technical, sales, finance and pricing, project management, risk management, and other functional areas) associated with the opportunity.
- The IT providers are increasingly focusing on the better opportunity qualification process. A better opportunity process would increase the win rate, reduce marketing expenses, and lead to a shorter sales cycle.
- The availability of historical data and adoption of analytics has allowed IT providers to move to the data-driven opportunity qualification process.
- The solution or proposal design process is one of the crucial formal activities in this process. Developing an effective proposal consumes significant effort—between one-third and one-half of the total pre-sales effort. The output of this activity would be a formal and internally approved proposal.
- A proposal would have three components at a high level: 1) technical solution, 2) commercial solution, and c) legal terms and conditions.
- The technical solution contains a solution approach, value proposition, solution architecture, schedule of solution delivery, and major risks.
- The commercial solution plays a vital role in the vendor selection process. The buyer and seller should identify the appropriate contract to share the risk and reward fairly.

4.7 Questions for discussion

1. Discuss the different steps in value-based selling and the activities performed in each of these steps.
2. Researchers have commented that effective value-based selling can take the sales out of selling; please provide your comments and views on this.
3. Consider this scenario: From TCS, you recently have been appointed as the key account manager of Ronald's Bakery (RB). RB has 234 outlets in NCR, Jaipur, Indore, Hyderabad, and Bengaluru. So far, all these outlets have operated on a commonly used point-of-sale (POS) and billing solution provided by a small vendor in Gurgaon. The existing software used by RB has performance issues affecting peak-time transactions. Recently, Mr Jacob has joined as CIO of RB. You have earlier worked with Jacob at Accenture, and both of you appreciate each other's capability. Jacob is also known for his passion for the increased adoption of

technology for business impact. Jacob thinks that the current vendor is not able to provide the necessary support, and the legacy POS and billing systems need urgent replacement. He wants to upgrade to a modern, scalable, cloud-based POS, inventory, and financial management solution. He has got the in-principal go-ahead from RB's CEO and secured the necessary funding for this program.

a   On behalf of TCS, please do a structured opportunity assessment for this opportunity.

b   Suppose, post-opportunity assessment, TCS has decided to submit the proposal. Describe a high-level proposal structure, keeping the scenario in mind. Make suitable assumptions wherever necessary and state the same.

4   In both fixed-price and business metrics–based pricing, the risk is primarily with the IT vendor. So, why do the IT vendors prefer fixed-price contracts over business benefit-based contracts?

4.8 References

Anderson, J. C., Narus, J. A., and Van Rossum, W. (2006). Customer value propositions in business markets. *Harvard Business Review*, 84(3), 90.

Gardner, H. K., and Ibarra, H. (2017). How to capture value from collaboration: Especially if you're skeptical about it. *Harvard Business Review*. Retrieved from https://hbr.org/2017/05/how-to-capture-value-from-collaboration-especially-if-youre-skeptical-about-it

Miller, R., and Heiman, S. (1985). *Strategic selling* (pp. 97–98). New York: Miller Heiman Associates Inc., Time Warner Books.

Philips. (2014). *Philips and Salesforce announce a strategic alliance to deliver cloud based healthcare information technology*. Retrieved from www.philips.com/a-w/about/news/archive/standard/news/press/2014/20140626-Philips-and-Salesforce-announce-a-strategic-alliance-to-deliver-cloud-based-healthcare-information-technology.html

Satell, G. (2014, December 10). *What's behind the new Apple-IBM partnership?* Retrieved from www.forbes.com/sites/gregsatell/2014/12/10/whats-behind-the-new-apple-ibm-partnership/#5302d8c02ec6

Socransky, B. (2016). *Partner go to market strategy for enterprise software/SaaS*. Retrieved from www.linkedin.com/pulse/partner-go-market-strategy-enterprise-software-saas-socransky-mba/

Töytäri, P., and Rajala, R. (2015). Value-based selling: An organizational capability perspective. *Industrial Marketing Management*, 45, 101–112.

5

BUYING IT

Learning objectives

This chapter provides an overview of the different steps followed in the vendor management process. By the end of this chapter, a reader will be able to:

- Understand the key activities in each of the four steps in the IT acquisition and vendor management process
- Appreciate the implication of strategic options such as in-house vs. outsourced IT development, multi-vendor vs. single vendor, and transaction vs. relationship orientation
- Understand how to develop different bid solicitation documents such as RFP and RFI
- Understand the structured vendor evaluation process to select a vendor from multiple options.

5.1 Introduction

In the earlier chapters, several examples have highlighted that enterprises use IT capabilities in multiple ways to achieve various business objectives, including gaining a competitive advantage. Large enterprises have several options to acquire IT capabilities. They might decide to develop those solutions in-house. Alternatively, the enterprises can work with external vendors to source those capabilities. As a result, there is a high level of competition among IT vendors for acquiring new clients and retaining existing customers.

The sellers and account managers of IT organisations should have a good understanding of vendor selection and vendor management processes. While developing the proposals for their customers, the sellers should focus on the attributes impacting the customers' decision-making process. The sellers should also have a fair idea of how the buyers' senior managers receive information for vendor evaluation (such as information on new technologies and their business impact and analysis of competing

108   DOI: 10.4324/9781003155270-6

IT vendors). Knowing the sources would allow the vendors (sellers) to improve their coverage on those information channels.

As there are a limited number of enterprise buyers for IT solutions, it is essential to make the necessary efforts to retain the existing accounts. Historical data shows that despite high switching costs and the steep learning curve associated with vendor migration, large enterprise buyers frequently switch vendors. The most important reasons for this phenomenon are 1) poor relationship management with the senior stakeholders of the buyer's organisation; 2) dissatisfaction with the technical performance of the vendor's human resources and the solution provided by it; 3) technological superiority of a new vendor, particularly in an emerging area; and 4) better commercial terms from a new IT provider, which reduces the total cost of ownership (TCO) of the buyer. Retaining existing customers is less expensive than acquiring new customers. A well-managed relationship not only ensures the guaranteed revenue but the chances of additional revenue through proactive selling.

5.1.1 The importance of vendor management in IT

Based on their internal analysis, enterprises can decide to delegate all or identified aspects of IT service delivery to an external vendor. The external sourcing can be achieved through a contractual arrangement. In this scenario, effective vendor management becomes a very critical management responsibility.

IT vendor management enables organisations to gain higher value and mitigate risks from their vendors throughout the relationship lifecycle. The higher value from the relationship can be obtained by 1) lowering the cost of IT service delivery, 2) improving the service quality, and 3) innovating collaboratively. Vendor management achieves the dual objectives of risk reduction and value enhancements by making effective strategic choices. The choices are related to decisions about the number of vendors (single vs. multi-sourcing), vendor selection approach and criteria, selecting an appropriate type of contracts, and the right type of metrics for vendor performance evaluation.

In many cases, large buyers of IT services enter into a prime system integrator (PSI) agreement with one of the large IT providers. As no vendor can provide solutions for all aspects of a business, the vendor nominated for the PSI role, in turn, collaborates with a number of other IT product or service vendors. As a result, the vendor selection and management capability is not only relevant for the IT managers of the user organisations but also for the IT sellers working for large IT vendors.

This chapter will go through the overall vendor management process and describe each sub-activity in detail. The terms vendor, seller, and provider have been used interchangeably in this chapter. Similarly, the terms buyer, customer, and user have been used interchangeably.

5.2 The IT vendor management process

Vendor management or supplier management refers to all the business processes and activities that deal with a vendor's entire lifecycle for an organisation. The vendor management process scope includes strategy formulation, vendor selection, and relevant analysis of the vendors' performance to maximise value from IT investments. In the context of IT products and services, we have divided the vendor management process into six sub-processes, as shown in Figure 5.1.

They are:

- Sourcing strategy formulation
- Managing bid process
- Vendor selection
- Contract negotiation
- Contract execution
- Contract closure and sourcing analysis.

In the next section, we have described the key activities of each of these six sub-processes.

Figure 5.1 IT vendor management process

BUYING IT

5.3 Sourcing strategy formulation

The components of sourcing decisions related to 1) internal vs. external sourcing and 2) single vs. multiple providers have implications for the overall corporate strategy of the firms. The managers in the firm need to analyse several strategic and tactical factors. However, in many cases, firms adopt short-term perspectives with a primary focus on cost reduction. This type of decision-making does not consider the impact of the decisions on other areas of concern, like loss of knowledge or competitiveness due to outsourcing. The possible impact on business due to vendor insolvency also should be factored in. We suggest that managers perform their cost–benefit analysis of three fundamental decision problems to formulate an effective sourcing strategy. The sourcing strategy, like other components of corporate strategy, should be periodically evaluated and updated.

As mentioned before, the sourcing strategy looks into three decision alternatives in onboarding new IT capabilities or functionalities. They are the decisions related to 1) make or buy, 2) single or multi-vendor, and 3) buying behaviour.

5.3.1 Make or buy decision

Though most large organisations have their own IT departments, more and more organisations depend on vendors for their IT service fulfilment needs. A study conducted in 2016 by the CIO Executive Council found that 71% of IT leaders spend up to half of their budget on external IT service providers. In the context of IT services, make or buy decisions focus on the cost and benefit comparison of delivering IT functionality internally with the costs and benefits involved in hiring an outside supplier for the functionality in question. We have provided a short case study to elaborate the different options available for buyers.

Caselet 5.1

A large multi-country automobile component manufacturer, MSP, wants to revamp its supply chain management systems and intends to introduce an online portal for buyers. Implementing the Internet portal would allow manufacturers and dealers to purchase parts from MSP and update their expected demand. MSP's mission statement is to ensure the availability of the right spare part to the right dealer or manufacturer at the right time. MSP also deals with more than 100,000 types of spare parts, and this is a daunting task. MSP management can evaluate multiple options available

111

to implement the advanced supply chain functionality. The various options available to MSP are:

- Purchase standard supply chain and enterprise resource planning (ERP) product license from an established product vendor and consulting and implementation services from established service providers
- Purchase standard supply chain and ERP product license from established product vendor and involve in-house IT team for implementation activities
- Hire IT service provider and develop customised IT solution, keeping in mind the unique requirement of MSP
- In-house and customised implementation of all IT needs.

To resolve this decision-making issue, MSP can develop in-house IT capabilities (option 4) if the following three criteria are met (Table 5.1).

Table 5.1 Framework suggesting a make decision

#Criteria	Decision	Justification
Strategic Objective	Make	• Technology is an integral part of competitive strength, and there is a need to remain ahead of the technology curve.
		• The business process involved is unique, and standard products would not address their proprietary process's needs.
		• The supplier market is controlled by competitors or having a close relationship with competitors.
Risk Mitigation		• Only a few providers of the requested services.
		• The rapid change required in IT applications and the lower lead time would justify the involvement of internal IT departments.
		• The IT application involves sensitive intellectual property and associated business processes; hence the organisation cannot depend on external providers.
		• Better control required over the process of IT development, instead of only focusing on a developed product or services.
Cost and Resource Factors		• Internal cost advantage or cost parity, so there is no economic justification of external sourcing.
		• Enough unutilised resources available who can deliver the requirement.
		• The work is not unattractive, and resources can be acquired with some effort. New investment by the company meets the internal return on investment (ROI) target.

In many scenarios, there can also be a strong case for using external vendors for managing IT services. The key benefits of IT outsourcing would be cost reduction, complexity reduction, and access to vendor's premium skills. It also allows the customer to focus on the core business processes while allowing the IT partners to focus on technology infrastructure development and management.

Transaction cost economics and the make or buy decision

Transaction cost economics (TCE) (Williamson, 1979) is often used to justify the way the economic activities are organised. It tries to find an answer to the typical decision problems faced by the organisations, whether to perform an activity within the boundary of a firm or to buy the same from an external company. The concept of transaction cost was introduced by Williamson to explain the multiple types of costs involved in purchasing products or services from an external organisation in comparison to producing them in-house. In the context of IT services acquisition, these sets of costs would be the effort involved in the search and selection of appropriate vendors or service providers, negotiation, and drafting appropriate contracts and cost for vendor management and contract enforcement. Similarly, the cost of developing IT services in-house would be the effort involved in 1) identifying and sustaining an appropriate sub-organisation with the desired skillsets and 2) controlling and coordinating its activity. As per transaction cost theory, if the internal coordination and control cost is higher than the transaction costs, firms would decide to buy the services and products from an external provider. The theory also states that transaction cost, or the cost the firm incurred for getting any work done by any external providers, would depend on two crucial parameters. They are:

- **Frequency of the transactions:** If the transactions are conducted more frequently, the transaction costs increase. So, the firm would be better off doing it internally. The spread of technology and newer ways of contracting, like outsourcing, has reduced the cost of executing and managing transactions between firms.
- **Asset specificity:** If the task needs specific assets (computing resources and human resources with specific skills) that are not re-deployable outside and hence have limited value outside that work, the firm would be better off doing that task internally. If any IT service provider needs to invest in these types of locked-in assets, it will face a financial loss if the relationship ceases. This type of lock-in situation could be opportunistically exploited by one party or the other to the detriment of the overall relationship (Williamson, 1979, 1985), leading to conflict and reduced satisfaction.

Path dependence, or impact of accrued experience in the sourcing decision

The buyer's external sourcing decision reflects the firm's vision on the make or buy problem. But the same is also moderated by the buyer's experience or learning related to external sourcing. The learning depends on 1) the firm's overall experience with external sourcing and 2) the kind of IT capabilities previously acquired from external sources (Lewin, Massini, and Peeters, 2009). Generally, for external sourcing of IT, most of the organisations primarily learn by doing. As a result, progressively complex capabilities are acquired from external sources.

While the decision to insource or outsource IT functionality is an essential part of the IT sourcing strategy, other two aspects of sourcing strategy also need close consideration. We would discuss some of the important aspects of the sourcing strategy.

5.3.2 Decisions related to single/multi-sourcing

Once the external sourcing decision is committed, the organisations need to decide on the number of IT vendors for collaboration. To minimise the technical or managerial complexities of multi-vendor scenarios, a few organisations have consolidated their IT supplier base by moving to a single-vendor scenario or reducing the number of vendors to a manageable level. On the other hand, the multi-vendor scenario minimises the dependency on any single IT provider and reduces the enterprise risk. To minimise undue risk, many organisations with single-vendor scenarios have inducted additional vendors. We compare single- and multi-vendor strategies, keeping in mind the benefits and the challenges associated with them (Table 5.2).

5.3.3 Buying behaviour matrix

While selecting a vendor or several vendors, a transaction-focused buying behaviour indicates that the buyer is looking for well-understood IT functionalities at the best possible price. There are multiple suppliers of the same services, the customisation requirement is limited, and the existing market is well established. Alternatively, the buyers can be focused on identifying a collaborative partner with a longer time horizon. The transaction-focused buyer is interested in a specific delivery (of agreed functionalities); the relationship or innovation-focused buyers look for collaborative value creation in a long-term relationship. In a collaborative scenario, the IT provider works as an extended arm of the buyer and has a deep understanding of the buyer's technology and business environment. They are also respected for the expertise they bring. The buyer intends to reward the seller based on objectives or outcomes achieved instead of monitoring its performance

BUYING IT

Table 5.2 Factors affecting single/multi-sourcing decisions

#*Criteria*	*Justification*
Best of Breed	• No single vendor can offer the best product covering multiple IT functionalities; the single-vendor strategy often leads to an integrated product composed of modules that are not best in their category. In the earlier example of MSP, if MSP decides to select any single product vendor having ERP, supply chain functionalities, portal, and analytical modules, the individual modules may not be the best in the industry.
Cost	• Single-vendor scenarios would lead to favourable cost scenarios due to the improved bargaining power of the buyer. • The implementation cost would also be lower due to less effort in integration and lower skill diversity.
Implementation Complexity	• The implementation complexity would be much higher in the multi-vendor scenario. The complexity arises due to the technical complexity of integrating diverse products, and project management complexity arises due to interdependency. • The buyer may hire another consulting organisation to act as a system integrator to manage the dependencies between multiple vendors.
Procurement Efforts	• A multi-vendor solution involves a large amount of vendor selection and contract negotiation. The procurement effort would increase proportionately with the number of providers. • In a multi-vendor scenario, contract renewal needs to be synchronised, keeping in mind the dependency among solution components.
New Feature Development	• As IT functionalities are not static, organisations need to introduce new features continuously. An integrated solution makes it easy to introduce new features. The relative ease stems both from a vendor management perspective and limiting changes to a few modules. • In a multi-vendor scenario, new feature development often needs significant impact analysis and customisation and change in multiple products supplied by different vendors.
Supplier Management	• A single-vendor scenario calls for less effort to track supplier performance and manage the relationship. • Information exchange is easier in a single-vendor scenario. • A single-vendor scenario might lead to closer collaboration and co-innovation. India-based Reliance Industries and its associates are the largest users of SAP products in Asia. To provide special focus to this large customer, SAP has developed a dedicated practice for Reliance, keeping its unique requirements in mind.

(*Continued*)

BUYING IT

Table 5.2 (Continued)

#*Criteria*	*Justification*
	• The customers generally avoid the single-vendor scenario to avoid vendor complacency. Competition among providers leads to better service quality and problem resolution.
	In the Razorpay case (provided at the end of the book), we have come across Rivigo, an India-based logistics company, that uses technology extensively. The ability to accept payment from its customers and ensure timely payment to its partners (fleet owners) is a critical business requirement. To incorporate high availability, speed, and robustness into the payment systems, Rivigo uses multiple payment gateways for accepting payments from the clients and reimbursing the fleet owners. Rivigo uses a dynamic switching algorithm that evaluated the payment gateways' performances based on 1) success rate (how many transactions went through successfully in one go), 2) turnaround time (TAT, time for the payment gateway to respond with a confirmation of success or failure of the transaction so that further disbursements or auto-refunds could be processed), and 3) bluff rate (a transaction which was earlier termed as a success but later termed as a failure or vice versa is called a bluff). The dynamic switching algorithm estimates these parameters in real time and diverts exponentially more traffic to the better-performing gateway, creating enough competition among the payment providers.
Vendor Risk	• Generally, large vendors with significant revenue and a more stable financial outlook are selected as single vendors. In a multi-vendor scenario, small vendors with specialised products are also chosen for a specific component of an overall solution. In a dynamic market, smaller vendors have a higher chance of going out of business or being acquired by a larger party.
	• So, the probability of vendor insolvency and other financial risks are much higher in a multi-vendor scenario.
	• On the other hand, the impact of vendor insolvency would be much higher in a single-vendor scenario.
Training	• A new IT solution deployment calls for training of different departments within an organisation (business, customer care, technical). Training and knowledge dissemination of a single integrated system is easier than systems with multiple components from different vendors.
	• A single IT solution makes deployment of operation and support staff easier, reducing skill diversity.

BUYING IT

continuously. A significant part of this long-term relationship might focus on how the buyer and seller would co-create value and reduce the TCO. The vendor is ready to invest in value co-creation. Between the two extremes of the transaction and relationship-focused behaviour, the buyer can also opt for a trusted supplier. The trusted supplier has a strong reputation and is highly regarded for a particular offering and associated implementation services. The buyer keeps the overall control over the project but delegates a significant project management role to the seller (vendor).

For an effective negotiation, the expectation of buyers and sellers (short-term transactions versus long-term collaborative relationship) should be in sync (Jackson, 1985). The inability to understand the customer's buying behaviour can lead to disappointment. Table 5.3 explains the key aspects of three types of buying behaviour.

5.4 Managing the bid process

Once the decision to procure IT services from the market is established along with sourcing guidelines, the buyers need to identify the relevant vendors for the services. The prospective vendors are identified and provided with the business requirement, technical requirements, and high-level commercial expectations. The vendor's proposal is developed based on 1) the

Table 5.3 Transaction vs. relationship-oriented buying behaviour

TRANSACTION FOCUSED ⟵⟶ *RELATIONSHIP FOCUSED*		
Value for Money	*Trusted Supplier*	*Collaborative Partner*
• Low price • Delivered quickly and on time • The scope is well defined and simple • Seller's brands are known • Project management is primarily done by the buyer	• Best in class/ innovative offers • Seller's brand is trusted and respected • The seller has good project management expertise and strong industry and domain knowledge • Overall project control lies with the buyer	• The vendor is embedded within the buyer's environment or understands the buyer's business environment well. • The vendor is entrusted to provide a solution to complex strategic problems or opportunities. • Solutions and offerings are customised to the buyer organisation. • Relationship balances value and risk. The relationship takes a longer-term view.

117

client's business context and asks about 2) the vendor's ability to deliver similar solutions. The buyer uses this proposal to evaluate and identify the best possible provider(s) of the services. The successful management of the bid process is vital for buyers and sellers. Many sellers might decide not to participate in a bid process if the opportunity's attractiveness falls short in their bid qualification process. The vendor working on preparing a bid response document deploys its resources and capital to fund the activity and often shortlists the most attractive opportunities. The seller's bid qualification process has been detailed in Chapter 4.

From the buyer perspective, the bid management process can be split into two components:

- Bid document preparation
- Bid response management.

Bid document preparation

Here the buyers put together the details of the requirements and other related information in a RFI or RFP document.

Request for information (RFI): It is a preliminary document used by buyers when they do not understand the range of providers available for specific IT functionalities and features. Suppose SBI (the largest bank of India) wants to explore the blockchain technology for providing cross-border trade-related services. SBI has no prior experience working with blockchain vendors. It can use the RFI route to understand the range of options available. The objective of RFI is to gather information, which the buyer uses to shortlist the prospective vendors and draft a more cohesive request for proposal (RFP). In RFI, the buyers want to ask open-ended questions; these questions allow the vendor to talk about its full range of capabilities and offerings. The RFI states the broad business challenges the buyer is facing. The seller develops its response with case studies, industry expertise, and skill matrix within the context of those challenges. To argue its case, the vendor also highlights its relative positioning in the marketplace compared to other providers. In a typical RFI response, the vendors generally need to provide the following information:

- High-level architecture with details of software and hardware components
- Technical information related to the solution
- Case studies of successful completion of similar projects in a similar context
- A budgetary estimation of the efforts and costs for the project work
- A budgetary estimate of the costs for the maintenance activities
- Training availability and costs
- Brief company information.

BUYING IT

Request for proposal

Generally, the RFP follows the RFI. The RFI process is not mandatory. Organisations with prior knowledge about the intended products and services and the vendor landscape in that domain generally avoid the RFI process and save time and effort. During the RFP process, vendors are invited to propose a solution to meet the customer's objectives. RFP brings more clarity and specificity; it provides the background and the objectives of the initiative and the requirements that need to be addressed. It provides the vendors with sufficient detail to develop a valid solution and the price, timeline, and other terms and conditions associated with it. Broadly, a well-drafted RFP would have the following sections:

- General information
  - Background information
  - Procedures for applying
  - Guidelines for the preparation of the proposal
  - Evaluation criteria
  - Pricing details
- Scope of the work
- Terms and conditions of the contract.

Most of the buyers also put evaluation criteria in the procurement documents to give the seller an understanding of the buyer's evaluation process, which helps them to decide if they should spend their effort on the bid. During vendor selection, the evaluation criteria become the basis by which the buyers evaluate the proposals. Though commercial aspect of the proposal plays an important role, it is not the only factor in selecting a seller. The following criteria, along with the financial attractiveness of the proposal, are often used in vendor evaluation:

- The vendor's understanding of the customer's industry and region
- Project management capability
- Customer reference
- Local presence
- The financial strength of the seller.

A detailed and well-designed RFP is beneficial for both buyers and sellers. The key benefits of putting forth effort in designing an RFP would be:

- The seller would be able to understand all the work that requires completion; this would allow the seller to adequately understand the scope of the work and price the project appropriately. This clarity would result in a better and more complete proposal.

119

- A good RFP reduces the ambiguity and, in the process, also reduces the seller's risk. This would lead to more accurate pricing.
- As interpretation of a well-defined scope would be easier, there would be less conflict during the implementation period.
- Well-captured requirements ensure fewer changes to the project scope once the contract is awarded.
- Easier comparison of proposals from multiple sellers (by the buyers).

Bid response management

Once the bid documents are created, they are shared with identified vendors. The buyers also provide information to address the seller's questions and queries that might come while preparing responses for the RFP. Based on the initial information and clarification, the seller prepares the response. Sometimes the buyers organise the bidders' conference with selected sellers to make sure that they all have a clear and common understanding of the RFP and the procurement process.

A detailed bid management process is followed in procuring IT products and services, keeping in mind the customer's context and aspiration.

For the procurement of standardised IT and IT-enabled business process outsourcing (BPO) services in a competitive framework, government organisations and large enterprises are increasingly using the reverse auction method. In a reverse auction, the buyers put up a request for the defined services. Multiple sellers or vendors submit their bid, indicating the prices they are willing to provide for their services. The customer selects the seller with the lowest price at the end of the auction period. The reverse auction method is effective for the acquisition of non-differentiated commodity services with limited vendor evaluation overhead.

5.5 Vendor selection

Vendor selection is a decision-making process to select the best supplier from a pre-qualified pool based on pre-defined objectives and decision criteria (Wetzstein, Hartmann, Benton, and Hohenstein, 2016). It consists of receiving and reviewing the proposals and selecting a vendor. Several evaluation parameters are used to assess the potential seller's ability and willingness to provide the requested services. Because the vendors are compared on available data, they provide a basis for quantitatively evaluating proposals to minimise the influence of personal biases and motives. IT vendor selection is one of the most critical management responsibilities performed jointly by the IT, finance, and purchase and supply chain functions of the enterprise.

Response solicitation, vendor selection, and contract closure are time-consuming and need significant financial resources. While the cost and time spent on selecting the right vendor are increasing with time, an inappropriate or inaccurate decision related to vendor selection can:

- Lead to project failure, either increasing the cost of IT acquisition or reducing or delaying the potential value creation opportunity
- Lead to loss of reputation for both providers and buyers, many times leading to litigation.

That is why there is an increasing focus on organisations on a well-structured and data-driven process for vendor evaluation. Frequently external consultants like Gartner are also included in the process. Though the importance of a structured vendor selection is well understood, organisations face the following challenges in executing these activities. For many of the buyers, vendor evaluation and selection is not a core competence. An ad hoc team comprising resources from procurement and the IT team is assigned this task.

- The team involved in vendor selection and evaluation is expected to complete the activity in a short time, which makes detailed assessments difficult. Many times, the team may not have an adequate budget for travel and other activities. Travel becomes essential to get a first-hand experience of the vendor's office, lab, and other infrastructure or to meet the vendors' key customers.
- Sometimes, particularly for emerging technologies, the requirements and scope of the functionality are not well understood by the business and IT team of the buyers.
- Political agendas of different divisions of the buyer's organisation can also negatively impact the objectivity of the process. For a telecom operator, the IT team is more comfortable and well-connected with multiple IT vendors (i.e. IBM, Accenture, Oracle), whereas the network vendors (i.e. Nokia, Ericsson) are well connected and have good access to the network planning and operation team of the same firm. Any new technology functionality onboarding often creates conflict between these two sets of decision-makers, as their vendor preferences are very distinct.
- Many organisations do not make efforts to develop an overall vendor management strategy; instead, they acquire new capabilities in a tactical manner. They might onboard a vendor who offers the best prices for a particular bid. Over time, they might end up managing a large number of vendors with the additional complexity of integration and governance.
- The vendor selection team often finds it difficult to explain/justify their approach and methodologies to different stakeholders in the

organisation. This can happen if the vendor evaluation team focuses more on qualitative or subjective parameters while ignoring empirical methods.

To complete the vendor evaluation process, the buyers gather information from multiple additional sources (other than the information available in the vendor's proposals) to evaluate the relative merits of various vendors. So, it is also important for the sellers to understand the sources of the information that influence the buyer's decision-makers. It might also be important to find out the relative importance of different sources of information. The primary sources of information which impact the IT buying process are listed here:

- Proposal and requirement compliance matrix supplied by the vendor
- Case studies and information on the past implementation provided by the vendors
- Input from satisfied and dissatisfied customers of the vendors
- Product demo and workshop conducted by the vendors
- Hired consultants or experts
- Reports from reputed rating and advisory companies like Gartner and Frost & Sullivan.

In a study conducted in India, Mukhopadhyay and Nath (2001) found out the relative importance of six different information channels in the chief information officer's (CIO's) buying decision-making. They used a 5-point Likert scale, where 0 indicates that the information channel is not at all important, but 4 indicates it is very important. Their findings are presented in Table 5.4.

Once the information from multiple sources is acquired, the buyers focus on the vendor evaluation process. A systematic vendor evaluation process would deal with the following questions to decide on the vendor evaluation structure:

- What criteria should we use to measure the quality of the proposals submitted by the vendors?
- What is the relative importance of each of those criteria?
- How do I measure vendor performance data related to each of those criteria?

A structured framework (Table 5.5) for vendor selection would have the price and non-price criteria for vendor selection. In general, the cost or acquisition price mentioned in the IT proposal carries maximum weight in vendor selection. The importance of the price factor might vary in different scenarios based on the complexity of the solution and the type of

BUYING IT

Table 5.4 Information that impacts the vendor selection process

#	Information Channel	Score
1	Direct interface (Interaction with sales and pre-sales team, presentation, proposal quality, demo, proof of concept [POC])	3.3
2	Consultant/expert/industry report (This can be hired consultants, experts to help in the evaluation, and recommendations from an external agency like Gartner. Many CIO s use Gartner's magic quadrant to understand the relative positioning of a vendor and its offerings.)	2.95
3	Prior experience (incumbent IT providers would have a higher chance than a new provider)	2.9
4	Seminar/tradeshow/publications/case study	2.65
5	Word of mouth (satisfied/dissatisfied customer)	2.4
6	Media/advertisement/digital presence	2.4

Table 5.5 An empirical approach for vendor selection

CRITERIA	WEIGHT	SCORE SCALE (min-max)	How Will It Be Assessed?
Price Criteria			
TCO	60%	min. 1 to max. 5	Based on TCO calculated over the useful life of the IT solution
Non-Price Criteria			
Requirement Compliance	20%	min. 1 to max. 5	Based on requirement compliance matrix
Project Management Capability	10%	min. 1 to max. 5	Methodology suggested and reference implementation
Knowledge of the Industry Segment and Geography	5%	min. 1 to max. 5	Based on references/ description of projects on the geography and industry
Ability to Support Value Realisation	5%	min. 1 to max. 5	1) Based on their past experience with in-service migration/business benefits realisation 2) Their willingness to link percentage of the payment to post go-live milestones (like achieving 50% of the planned TPS in their network)

relationships the buyer wants to develop with the vendor. A buyer looking for a long-term relationship with one or more selected vendors might accept higher prices and negotiate contract terms that specify how they would co-create value and reduce the TCO. In turn, the supplier would re-invest part of its profits into research and development (R&D) with a long-term view. As mentioned in Chapter 2, the buyer generally compares the TCO to include all explicit and implicit costs in their vendor comparison.

For the non-price criteria for vendor selection, the quality of the technical solution and compliance to the buyer's requirement would play the most important role. If the proposed solution does not address the requirements mentioned in the RFP of the buyer, it is unlikely to be selected. The RFP generally would have three types of requirements: 1) business requirement or functional requirements, 2) non-functional requirements, and 3) requirements related to support and maintenance. The non-functional requirements deal with redundancy and high availability of the solution and security aspects and support for reporting and analytics. The buyer generally specifies a few of the critical requirements as mandatory. Failure to fulfil those might disqualify the proposal of a vendor.

Based on the resource-based view (RBV), described briefly in Chapter 2, project management can be an important capability for IT vendors, particularly in the context of complex programs and where the buyer is planning to entrust the complete project delivery responsibility or a part of it to the selected IT service provider.

Vendors should also possess and demonstrate a good understanding of the industry and geography in which the client is operating. For example, some Indian customers may be uncomfortable with a western vendor who is successful in its home country but has no exposure to the Indian or any other emerging market. The IT systems in emerging markets like India face additional challenges of scalability due to their large population size. Understanding the established processes in an industry and the challenges associated with a particular geography is critical for the success of enterprise sales efforts. The IT vendors frequently highlight their industry competence through the whitepaper, point of view (POV), or industry-specific product customisation. In many cases, failure in IT investment can be traced to poor linking between technology capability and the business environment. Hence, selecting a vendor with demonstrated industry and geographical knowledge reduces this risk.

The ability to support value realisation primarily evaluates the capability and intention of the vendor to go beyond the traditional IT functionality delivery. The vendors should work with the buyers to increase the adoption of the new technology by the intended users. In many cases, existing users continue to use the old IT application instead of migrating to a new application. The main issues are generally related to their need for additional training, the comfort with the existing systems, and their inability to convert the new features offered by the new application into tangible business benefits.

These non-price criteria explained here are indicative. The vendor selection team develops these criteria and decides on their relative importance in the vendor selection process.

5.6 Contract negotiation

Backed by legal authority, formal contracts are designed to detail the rights and obligations of buyers and sellers. The contract also explicitly mentions the assumptions that underline the transactions and highlights the roles and responsibilities of the buyer and seller. For IT services, multiple different types of contracts based on linear and non-linear pricing models are used. We have discussed the different types of contracts and the associated pricing model in Chapter 4 (sales and pre-sales process).

The primary purpose of contract negotiation should be the equitable distribution of value and risk between buyers and sellers. The negotiation phase may also be used to tie up the loose ends of the proposals, which may have been missed in the earlier round of activities. For example, while buying a product license for a software product, buyers can decide to influence the product road map by requesting to include their preferred features in the next release of the product. For a service provider, the buyer may ask for the local presence of the services team in case the services are planned to be delivered remotely. In the contract negotiation process, the finance and procurement team takes the lead, and the legal team aids them in the journey.

5.7 Contract execution

Once the contract is signed and awarded to the deserving vendor, the IT project management office and the procurement team of the buyer would ensure the vendor delivers the solution as per the agreed statement of work in the contract.

5.7.1 Contract execution activities

The primary activities during this phase are discussed in the following sections.

- *Vendor enablement and ongoing coordination*

The buyer's project team needs to provide the necessary logistics support to the onboarded vendor. The buyer should fulfil the dependencies as per the agreed project plan. The buyer's organisation ensures physical space for the vendor's engineers and analysts within their premises and provides the existing as-is documentation of processes and IT systems. Besides, the vendor should provide other required information and access to the client's IT network. The buyer's business team needs to approve the requirement documents for the new IT solution and agree with the process impact, if any, due to the introduction of a new application.

In many cases, the new IT solution implementation might lead to minor or major changes in a few existing IT applications, which are not covered in the vendor's statement of work (SOW). In this case, the buyer needs to plan and manage these changes. For example, the introduction of a new customer relationship management (CRM) application might impact the existing integration with a payment system. As the payment system is not included in the scope of the seller's solution, the buyer needs to analyse the impact on the payment solution. The buyer should also ensure that payment system-related work is executed as per the CRM vendor's timeline.

- *Managing conflict*

It is not unusual to have a conflict between the vendor and the buyer's project implementation team. For the benefit of the project and the ongoing relationship, it is crucial to manage the conflict fairly and transparently. The conflict primarily happens due to the different interpretations of the contract. The primary questions needed to be answered are "What does the contract really say?" and "Who is responsible for what part of the work?" The project managers from the buyer's and seller's organisations may resolve many of the conflicting issues. Few of the unresolved issues are generally earmarked for the steering committee, consisting of both sides' senior executives.

If the issues remain unresolved even after the involvement of the senior management of the buyer and seller, the contract provides an option to the aggrieved party of going to court. By doing so, the contract promises protection against the opportunistic behaviour of one of the partners. Nevertheless, we also need to be aware of the limitations of depending too much on contracts for vendor governance.

As mentioned in the discussion related to transaction cost theory, drafting and enforcing a contract is time-consuming and expensive. The contracts are supposed to formally document all assumptions, roles, and responsibilities, as well as the scope. But the contracts are always considered incomplete (Grossman and Hart, 1986; Williamson, 1979) due to the following two reasons. The companies want to limit the costs associated with contract development and enforcement, as it is challenging to document all contingencies. Many times by design, companies want to keep strategic flexibility in the contract so that newer needs and interests can be accommodated. As a result, the buyers should strive to complement the governance based on the contract with mutual trust and cooperation.

- *Managing the change control process*

A complex and long-duration project always involves some unexpected changes in the scope or timeline. The contract should specify the process for modifying some expect of the contract (scope, time, price, and others). Whenever a change is raised, it is analysed based on the agreed scope mentioned in the contract to determine whether it can be considered a change. The impact of the changes on the overall architecture, other components inside and outside the project, and timeline are analysed. For a change to be implemented, the change management processes mentioned in the contract should be followed, including the final approval from the change control board. A large number of changes can create additional complexity and uncertainty.

- *Ongoing performance and risk analysis*

The vendor's project team regularly reviews the IT program's performance in terms of scope delivered, planned vs. actual time and cost, and the projection for the remaining work. The project team should also review the risk profile of the project and take appropriate corrective action. The risk management concept is explained in Chapter 3. The vendor's project team should appropriately report the project performance and highlight issues and risks to the concerned person (SPOC) of the buyer's side. The additional discussion on change management is provided in Chapter 6.

5.7.2 Control mechanisms to align the vendor with the buyer's objectives

Management researchers view control mechanisms as a process that aligns the action of the vendor with the action of the employing firm. The buyer organisation can use control mechanisms to direct the attention and motivation of the vendor's team to act in desired ways to meet the organisation's objectives (Cardinal, 2001; Eisenhardt, 1985) and, in this process, reduces the risks and uncertainties for the buyer's organisation. From the organisational literature, the buyers can use two types of formal control: behavioural and outcome.

Behavioural control: When a desirable behaviour necessary for a task is identified and can be observed, behavioural controls are recommended (Choudhury and Sabherwal, 2003). Behavioural control is mostly implemented by explicitly specifying the appropriate behaviour (e.g. development methodology, internal testing guideline) that the buyers can observe and evaluate. Behavioural controls need more supervision, effort, and time and a better understanding of the underlying processes. Sometimes, behaviour controls are assumed to have a negative impact on creativity and innovation (Adler and Borys, 1996).

Outcome control: In an outcome control scenario, the focus is limited exclusively to understanding, evaluating, and monitoring the results. The results are related to the closure of requirement document, delivery of code in the servers, and successful closure of the acceptance testing. Vendors are free to decide how they will achieve the desired outcome. Although outcome control focuses mostly on outcome-based incentives, there may be elements of punishment for failure to achieve the goals (Merchant, 1985). One of the drawbacks of this control mechanism is that, often, the controller focuses on outcomes that are easy to measure instead of on more complex outcomes that are harder to measure but that are more in line with the desired goals (Merchant, 1985).

The supplier management process does not just end once the buyers choose the suppliers. After their selection and onboarding, the buyers need to periodically evaluate their performance to see how well they fulfil the set objectives and requirements. To ensure proper evaluation, the buyer and seller together should have agreed and established key performance indicators (KPIs) to measure performance. Identifying and measuring appropriate KPIs over a more extended period provides insights for improvement in supplier performance. It also provides information about the supplier management process's effectiveness and areas where it can be further improved or optimised.

5.8 Contract closure and sourcing analysis

Contract closure can happen either when the deliverables specified in the contract are delivered and accepted by the buyer or when an agreement is terminated before the work is completed. The process primarily includes the verification and acceptance of deliverables and financial closure (payment reconciliation between the customer, vendor, and the vendor's partners) and activating the IT operation and maintenance process. Contract closure indicates that all resources like human resources, computing resources, and office spaces are returned to the originator. We have listed a few other activities done as part of contract closure:

- Review of the lessons learnt as well as documenting key findings.
- Identify the follow-on opportunities where both sides can work together.
- Identify any intellectual capital that should be retained by any of the organisations or multiple organisations together.
- Review the performance of the team members and provide feedback based on their work, both to their managers and to the employees. The respective project managers of the vendor and the customer should complete their team members' performance evaluation and feedback

sharing process. Making these extra efforts ensures that people involved receive due credit for their work and get the chance to improve their level of functioning.

- Sourcing analysis: Though sourcing performance analysis is a continuous process, it is essential to capture the lessons learnt at contract closure. It should focus on:

  - Delivery performance
  - Quality of delivery
  - Innovations co-developed
  - Price performance: Is there any additional cost incurred which was not budgeted into the proposal?
  - Actual usage of the feature by business
  - Long-term relationship with the vendor.

5.9 Chapter highlights

- Vendor management and vendor selection are becoming increasingly critical management responsibilities, as companies prefer to acquire IT services from outside instead of developing them internally.
- For a complex IT service delivery, large IT vendors also collaborate with other vendors (partners) for specific products and services.
- We have envisioned vendor management as a six-step process; initially, it starts with developing an appropriate vendor management strategy, considering long- and short-term objectives.
- While formulating a sourcing strategy, the buyers need to review the trade-off on three key decision points: make or buy, single or multi-sourcing, and transactional vs. relational buying approach.
- A well-crafted RFP or RFI makes it easier for vendors to submit a high-quality response, with a lesser scope of conflict during implementation.
- Vendor selection is a decision-making process to select the best supplier from a pre-qualified pool based on pre-defined objectives and decision criteria. It consists of receiving and reviewing the proposals and selecting a seller.
- While vendor-provided RFP/RFI response documents are used for vendor evaluation, the sellers need to understand that the buyers have access to multiple other sources of information, like the external consultant, recommendations from advisory service providers such as Gartner, the testimony of existing customers of the vendors, and past experience of the managers of working with the same vendor.
- While the commercial part of the proposal plays a vital role in vendor selection, several non-price criteria like quality of the technical solution, requirement compliance, and domain expertise play a critical role. The sellers should highlight these types of capabilities instead of focusing only on the proposal's price aspect.

BUYING IT

- Backed by legal authority, formal contracts are designed to detail the rights and obligations of the buyer and seller. Contracts also explicitly mention the assumptions that underline the transactions and also highlight the roles and responsibility of the buyer and seller.
- The buyers usually implement contract-based vendor governance. Buyers should try to develop trust and collaborative relationships with the vendors to reduce vendor management overhead and the scope of conflict.

5.10 Questions for discussion

1. A large retail organisation wants to acquire state-of-the-art CRM software to provide better services to its customers. Please advise the CIO by listing the benefits and challenges associated with the three options: developing in-house, the entire scope of the proposed solution outsourced to a large IT provider, and different components outsourced to different IT providers.

2. How do you differentiate between RFI and RFP?

3. Consider this scenario: You have been appointed as the CIO of Tea-lite—one of the large online and offline stores serving tea and snacks in a modern format that has 123 outlets in the country. So far, all these outlets have operated on a commonly used billing ("point-of-sale solution") and inventory software provided by a vendor in Gurgaon. This billing solution, however, has performance issues affecting peak-time transactions. You also realize that the current vendor is not able to provide the necessary support. Based on your experience, you have assessed the need to upgrade to a modern, scalable, cloud-based POS and inventory solution. You have an in-principle go-ahead from the CEO. The venture has got adequate financial backing and is keen on focusing on technology to differentiate. You are preparing to release an RFP and are working on it.

   a. Write your thoughts about the business background, including the strategic context, of this requirement. It should bring out your pain points and the objective you are trying to achieve through the new technology and the additional capabilities you desire to acquire. The section helps the vendors understand your business intent behind this RFP.

   b. Based on the earlier descriptions, what type of buying behaviour is expected from you? Please also write expected key deliverables from the prospective vendors and the timelines to achieve those.

   c. Develop a framework for a transparent and data-driven vendor evaluation process. The framework should show the criteria and their relative importance in selecting the right vendor.

5.11 References

Adler, P. S., and Borys, B. (1996). Two types of bureaucracy: Enabling and coercive. *Administrative Science Quarterly*, *41*(1), 61–89.

Cardinal, L. B. (2001). Technological innovation in the pharmaceutical industry: The use of organizational control in managing research and development. *Organization Science*, *12*(1), 19–36.

Choudhury, V., and Sabherwal, R. (2003). Portfolios of control in outsourced software development projects. *Information Systems Research*, *14*(3), 291–314.

Eisenhardt, K. M. (1985). Control: Organizational and economic approaches. *Management Science*, *31*(2), 134–149.

Grossman, S. J., and Hart, O. D. (1986). The costs and benefits of ownership: A theory of vertical and lateral integration. *Journal of Political Economy*, *94*(4), 691–719.

Jackson, B. B. (1985). Build customer relationships that last. *Harvard Business Review*, *11*, 120–128.

Lewin, A. Y., Massini, S., and Peeters, C. (2009). Why are companies offshoring innovation? The emerging global race for talent. *Journal of International Business Studies*, *40*(6), 901–925.

Merchant, K. A. (1985). *Control in business organizations*. Boston, MA: Pitman.

Mukhopadhyay, S., and Nath, P. (2001). Decision metrics for CRM solutions. *Customer Relationship Management: Emerging Tools, Concepts and Applications*, 185–192.

Wetzstein, A., Hartmann, E., Benton, W. C., and Hohenstein, N. O. (2016). A systematic assessment of supplier selection literature—state-of-the-art and future scope. *International Journal of Production Economics*, *182*, 304–323.

Williamson, O. E. (1979). Transaction-cost economics: The governance of contractual relations. *The Journal of Law and Economics*, *22*(2), 233–261.

Williamson, O. E (1985). *The Economic Institutions of Capitalism: Films, Markets, Relational Contracting*. New York, NY: Free Press.

6

CLIENT AND ACCOUNT MANAGEMENT

6.1 Learning objectives

This chapter provides an overview of client management. By the end of this chapter, the reader will be able to:

- Develop a client account management strategy
- Classify clients and identify key accounts
- Understand the process and complexities of managing clients
- Develop a client services strategy
- Identify risk and risk mitigation strategies.

6.2 Introduction

Studies have shown that acquiring a new client is five times more expensive than retaining and growing an existing client. Client relationships have been recognised as a key intangible asset for a company. As IT vendors are focused on selling to large enterprise clients, retaining these large accounts is vital. In such an environment, the responsibility for client relationships is not confined to the client management team. It is the equal responsibility of all touchpoints that a client has with a vendor. This includes pre-sales, sales, transition, operations, client relationship management, and leadership. Given the diversity of touchpoints and the constant hand-offs, it is essential to have robust guidelines, processes, metrics, and feedback capture mechanisms for client management. What makes client management more critical is that a dissatisfied client can switch to competitors. As a result, the supplier not only experiences a loss in the revenue from this client, but there is a possibility of this lost client becoming a negative reference in the future sales efforts.

The process of client relationship management has been studied extensively in academic literature since the mid-1990s when the focus moved from product marketing to services marketing and relationship management.

132   DOI: 10.4324/9781003155270-7

CLIENT AND ACCOUNT MANAGEMENT

During this period, many definitions of client relationship management were proposed. One of the more comprehensive definitions was provided by marketing guru Jagdish Sheth and Parvatiyar:

> Customer Relationship Management is a **comprehensive strategy** and process of acquiring, retaining, and partnering with **selective customers** to create superior value for the company and the customer.
>
> (Parvatiyar & Sheth, 2001, p. 6)

It involves **the integration** of marketing, sales, customer service, and the supply-chain functions of the organisation to achieve **greater efficiencies and effectiveness** in delivering higher customer value.

This chapter focuses on the key elements identified in this definition, which are:

1 Developing a key account management strategy
2 Integrated relationship management and metrics
3 Governance and risk mitigation.

6.3 Developing a key account management strategy

The relationship with a client begins when the client is first contacted during the pre-sales process and then carries through the sales, onboarding, and delivery phases. It is therefore critical that a firm has seamless processes to manage these phases.

CRM technologies and client database

The first step in building a client relationship process is having a comprehensive database of clients. A large part of this task has been automated with the use of customer relationship management (CRM) technologies that support pre-sales, sales, and ongoing delivery processes.

While this book does not focus on selection of a CRM tool, some of the key elements of information in a CRM tool that are required for building a client strategy are outlined in Table 6.1.

Though these processes appear simple, in many companies the required information is in disparate databases across sales, operations, and finance functions. These issues get further aggravated in large IT vendor companies, where different divisions are dealing with the same client, managing varied services. A critical first step in developing a client strategy is to consolidate all data into one database.

CLIENT AND ACCOUNT MANAGEMENT

Table 6.1 Information elements in a CRM platform

Category	Information Requirements (by client)
Client contact information	Organisation structure of the client
	Key contacts in a client organisation by function
	Roles and responsibilities
Buyer information	Current buyers in the organisation
	Current "non-buyers"
	History of interaction with "non-buyers"
Product/service mapping	Mapping of products/services by various functions in the client organisation
	Current sales by product/service mapped to the client organisation
Qualitative data	Historical qualitative feedback received from both buyers and non-buyers within a client

Client portfolio management

Vendors have limited resources and therefore need to allocate resources across clients judiciously. Most vendors have an "80–20 rule". That is, 80% of its revenues come from 20% of its clients. Segmentation through portfolio management is critical to ensure that this 20% of clients—popularly known as key accounts—receive the required focus as they drive the vendor's growth and profitability. Though revenue earned is the most important parameter for identifying key accounts, in the IT industry key accounts can be identified using other measures as well.

Client portfolio management (CPM) is defined as "an activity by which a company analyses the current and future value of its customers for developing a balanced customer structure through effective resource allocation to different customers or customer groups" (Terho and Halinen, 2007).

In business-to-consumer (B2C) marketing, various statistical techniques like cluster analyses are used to segment clients. However, in a business-to-business (B2B) scenario, this is still mostly a manual process and based on the intuition and experience of the sales and account management teams.

Some of the conventional methods used to segment clients are described next.

Demographics: This is segmenting accounts by some characteristics of the firm that could be linked to their propensity to purchase services. Typical characteristics include total revenue, revenue growth, number of employees, geographic spread, and industry segment (based on standard industry codes (SICs) in the United States).

The use of demographic data in segmentation varies. In IT product sales, demographics data can help estimate the total revenue potential of a client. For example, a company that sells payroll software (that is charged "per employee") can use client headcount data to determine the total account potential. In the case of IT services, demographic data will need to be used in conjunction with other metrics to assess account potential. Demographic data are the easiest to collect and verify and are therefore used extensively in client segmentation.

Client needs: This form of segmentation is based on the type of products and services required by individual clients. By segmenting needs, a vendor can evaluate the skills and capabilities required to support their clients and build capabilities where gaps exist. For example, a vendor may find that a higher proportion of its clients require digital support in the future as against legacy maintenance services. This will be a trigger for the vendor to build digital skills.

Products and services offered: This is the converse of the previous form of segmentation and helps in mapping clients against the strategic priorities of the vendor. For example, a vendor may want to focus on certain types of service offerings, as they are more profitable or are a differentiated offering. Clients who require these specific offerings will get prioritised in this form of segmentation.

Perceived prestige value: Working with iconic brands such as Apple, Tesla provides higher visibility for the IT providers. In most cases, it also leads to a higher margin and better employee satisfaction. So, these types of customers would get special attention, irrespective of the revenue contribution.

Customer buying behaviour: Relationship-focused customers treat IT as strategic, spend more on IT than the industry average, are more interested in innovative solutions, and look for longer term relationships and collaboration with IT providers. The transaction-focused customers are more concerned about getting the features and functions at the best possible price (Waaser, Dahneke, Pekkarinen, and Weissel, 2004). While the first set of customers (key accounts) deserves a consultative approach, deploying the same for the second type of customers would unnecessarily increase sales expenses.

R-F-M model: Recency-Frequency-Monetary (R-F-M) is a widely used client segmentation model. This is a quantitative behavioural model that examines how recently a client made a purchase, the frequency of purchases, and the value of purchases to predict future purchases. The model is used primarily in B2C scenarios and not used very often in B2B client management. However, the three elements of the R-F-M model can be used individually to segment clients. For example, clients can be segmented based on the value of recent orders. Most IT companies use this as a basis to determine and manage their top clients. These vendors classify their clients into categories such as platinum, gold, and silver purely based on criteria such as the value of an account and the cost to service the account (see Figure 6.1).

Client segmentation is critical for all vendors. It helps in determining the key accounts to focus on and the capabilities required to service these

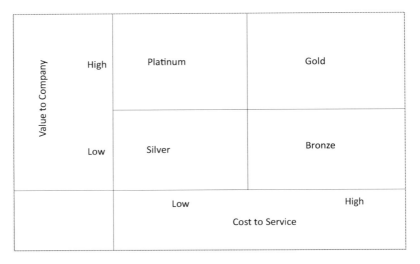

Figure 6.1 Customer portfolio management matrix
Source: Thakur and Workman, 2016

accounts. Depending on the size of the vendor and the number of clients it has, a combination of segmentation techniques is generally used. Also, the basis for segmentation is dynamic, with vendors continually adapting based on experience.

A sample key account segment is provided in Figure 6.2.

Segmentation is used to allocate account management resources to manage individual accounts. Most large IT companies are organised vertically by industry groups and horizontally by service delivery capabilities. In most vendor organisations, clients are first segmented by industry segments and assigned to the corresponding industry vertical group. Each industry vertical group then segments its clients using a matrix of geography, services required, and billing potential.

Accounts are assigned to account managers, who are responsible for preparing account plans at a client level. The key accounts enjoy several benefits above other accounts, as explained below:

- Higher mindshare of senior managers of IT vendors
- Better service level agreement (SLA)
- Key account's suggestions influence vendor's product roadmap or service strategy
- Important customers and vendors often collaborate for joint go-to-market or joint product development work.

CLIENT AND ACCOUNT MANAGEMENT

Sample Key Account

Industry : Consumer Banking, Retail (Brick and mortar and ecommerce)

Revenues : USB 10 Billion

Geographies : North America (US and Canada)

Technology:
- Digital savvy – started their digital transformation process
- Implementing omni-channel

Budget
- IT outsourcing budget of USD 50 million plus

Figure 6.2 Sample key account

Key account planning

The next step after segmenting a client portfolio is to develop account plans. Key accounts require detailed account plans, while other accounts can be managed with high-level plans. Every vendor has their own definition of key accounts but typically this definition constitutes an account that generates a significant proportion of a vendor's revenue.

Account managers are responsible for developing account plans. For key accounts, the plans go through multiple levels of reviews and in some cases all the way to the chief executive officer (CEO)/board. The format for account planning is relatively standard across most vendors. The information required to build out an account plan is given in Table 6.2.

After analysing this information, account managers build a detailed action plan by account. In addition to summarising each of the earlier areas, the account plan typically has the items discussed in the following sections.

Evaluating the relationship

Account managers need to evaluate the status of the current relationship. Some of the commonly used models are described next.

Contractual performance vs relationship

Plotting clients on the grid shown in Figure 6.3 helps in determining the state of a relationship. Clients who fall into the "At-Risk" or "Looking"

137

CLIENT AND ACCOUNT MANAGEMENT

Table 6.2 Information for creating an account plan

Category	Description
Company overview	Revenues
	Profitability
	Growth rate
	Recent events and corporate actions—M&A; product launches
	Other relevant information from previous financial statements
	Risks and challenges as identified in financial statements
Industry (of company) overview	Industry overview
	Competitors
	Growth of the industry
	Technology/other trends
	Disruptions in the industry
Company products and services	Current products
	New product launches
	Product road map
Organisation structure	Organisation chart
	Key decision-makers
	Key influencers
	Key gatekeepers
Current relationship	The existing suite of products/services purchased
	Products/services purchased from competitors
	Share of wallet
	Account size—trends
Potential for growth	New services in each stage of the pipeline
	Competitors and SWOT analysis against competitors
	The revenue potential for the next three years
Client feedback	Feedback (both positive and negative)
	Areas of strength
	Areas for improvement—action plan, including resource requirements

categories need additional focus, as they are the most likely to attrite. Specific retention strategies are included in the account plan.

Vendor vs. trusted advisor

These terms are the two ends of a relationship spectrum. While "vendor" is a generic term, it is often used to describe order takers whose relationship with the client is purely transactional. Vendors are usually signed on through competitive requests for proposals (RFPs), and incremental business from the client must be gained through the same route. Typically,

138

CLIENT AND ACCOUNT MANAGEMENT

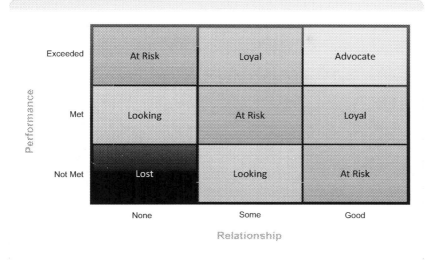

Figure 6.3 Mapping the state of client relationships

sellers of commodity products and services are referred to as vendors. At the other end of the spectrum are trusted advisors. Such vendors have excellent relationships with their clients, and clients consult with them on their strategies. To become a trusted advisor takes time and consistent delivery of value along with a good relationship. Most vendors are somewhere along this continuum. The academic and business literature uses various terms to define the intermediate stages along the continuum. Some of the terms used are preferred vendor, credible vendor, partner, etc. While the definitions of these intermediate stages are ambiguous, vendors need to understand where they are on this journey.

Loyalty ladder

A loyalty ladder is also used to describe the state of a client relationship (Figure 6.4).

A client moves from a prospect (pre-sales) stage to becoming a customer and then a supporter and finally an advocate, where they recommend a vendor proactively to others.

Same account revenue growth (SARG): The next step of an account plan is to analyse the data and identify the business potential for the next financial year. A modified version of the popular Ansoff matrix (Ansoff, 1957) is used to determine the strategy for existing accounts.

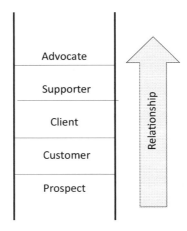

Figure 6.4 Loyalty ladder

		Offerings	Benefits	Risks/Challenges
Quadrant 1	Existing services Existing geos/divisions	(1) (2)		
Quadrant 2	New services Existing geos/divisions	(1) (2)		
Quadrant 3	Existing services New geos/divisions	(1) (2)		
Quadrant 4	New services New geos/divisions	(1) (2)		

Figure 6.5 Mapping future services using an Ansoff matrix

The classical Ansoff matrix helps develop a product/service strategy using a product vs. market grid. A modified version (as shown in Figure 6.5) is used to determine the products/services an IT vendor offers its existing clients. Quadrant 1 is a list of existing products/services being provided to existing internal clients within an organisation. Quadrant 2 consists of new offerings that can be made to this same internal client (for example, if a vendor offers SAP maintenance services to the credit card division of a bank, it can consider offering digital services to the same division). Quadrant 3 offerings are current services to other divisions or geographies within the same client (for example, if a vendor currently offers digital services to the

CLIENT AND ACCOUNT MANAGEMENT

credit card division of a bank, it can plan to provide the same service to the mortgage division of the same bank). Quadrant 4 consists of new offerings to new divisions/geographies within the same client and is the lowest priority, as it involves extensive selling.

Another useful way to classify revenue potential is described next:

- Continuing contracts: Current services that will continue into the next year (Quadrant 1 of Ansoff).
- Contracted but not delivered: Services for which contracts have been signed but delivery will begin in the next year (any quadrant).
- Pipeline: Services for which discussions have commenced but no formal agreement has been signed (any quadrant).
- New services: Additional services that the client may need but where discussions have not commenced. These could also be services currently being outsourced to a competitor (Quadrant 2 or 4).

Action plans are drawn up for each of these initiatives to ensure that the account revenue target is met.

For continuing contracts, the focus is on ensuring smooth delivery. Account managers work closely with the delivery teams and help in overcoming any challenges. These challenges typically relate to an inability to meet service levels or lack of resources to complete the project on time. In some cases, the challenges also relate to the relationship between the process owner within the client organisation and the delivery team.

For services contracted but not delivered, the focus is on ensuring that the project setup is smooth, and that delivery commences on time. Some of the typical challenges faced for these services are lack of resources, hiring delays, and delays on receiving specifications from a client. The account manager must work with both internal teams and the client organisation to overcome any obstacles.

For pipeline and new services, the account plan needs to outline what it will take to close the deal. This could be a combination of relationship selling, pricing, marketing, product demos, etc. The account plan will need to outline the support required from the vendor organisation for each of these areas. Probabilities of closure can be assigned to each of the new contracts depending on the stage at which they are, the urgency on the client side for the service, and competition dynamics. The probability adjusted revenue is an input to the revenue plan.

Revenue plan: The final part of the account plan is to develop a monthly revenue plan. The revenue plan must take into consideration the anticipated date for closure of new contracts, the set-up time required, and time for revenue generation to commence.

Actions: The final section of an account plan consists of an action checklist. The plan outlines the actions required to execute the account plan, the resources required for each of the actions, responsibilities, dependencies, and timelines.

Building an account plan is an iterative process. For large accounts, the plans go through two to three rounds of reviews with senior management. Once a final plan is given the go ahead, the account manager is responsible for its execution. Plans are updated once a quarter to reflect any new developments.

Incentives and compensation of account managers are tied to the revenue plan and achieving of goals in the account plans. Progress on the plan is reviewed periodically by senior management to ensure that the plan is being executed and to help overcome any obstacles. Plans for large accounts are reviewed as frequently as once a week. Any deviation from the plan has a significant impact on the revenues and profitability of the vendor.

Most account managers validate key elements of the account plan with their counterparts on the client side (e.g. vendor manager). This is to ensure that the plan is not too widely divergent from reality. Summaries of key account plans are also used by senior management in investor meetings and conferences.

In summary, the account plan document is one of the key elements of client management. It forms the basis for managing a client relationship and sets up clear goals and action plans to achieve the same.

6.4 Integrated relationship management

Client expectations

An account plan provides the structure for the account management process. On the other side of the relationship, clients have certain expectations from account management that go beyond meeting SLAs and contractual terms. The following section outlines these expectations.

Partnership: Clients expect their vendors to be business partners and not just vendors of services or products. They expect their vendors to fully understand their business and business issues and work towards helping them succeed. In this rapidly changing world with constant disruptions, the expectations in a partnership have gone up even further. A vendor providing support services to one part of a client organisation is expected to understand the end-to-end process of the client and the business implications of the service being provided. Clients expect vendors to proactively propose solutions that will help them be ahead of their competitors and the innovation curve in their industries. It is therefore a common practice for account managers to bring in industry experts into meetings to help clients think through their strategic direction for their business.

The expectation of being a business partner has its challenges. In many relationships, clients are unwilling to share information beyond what is required to provide contracted services, citing confidentiality reasons. Clients also use multiple vendors across the same process to de-risk their dependence on a single vendor. Another challenge that vendors face at this stage is that clients listen to their ideas and then share them with competing vendors. These issues can make it very challenging for vendors to suggest transformational changes. However, the role of the account manager is to ensure that clients receive the added value they expect while overcoming these challenges.

Accessibility: Clients have an expectation that account managers and operation leaders are accessible. This becomes a challenge in global organisations with operations in multiple countries and time zones. In such situations, clients expect vendors to have account teams under their account manager. Most large clients also provide office space to their account manager and expect the individual to be co-located with their vendor management or operations teams. This benefits vendors as they have the ability to attend some of the client's internal meetings and be involved in their IT planning process. Co-locating also helps account managers to build deeper relationships with clients, as "water cooler" discussions are as important as formal reviews.

Responsiveness: While accessibility is about a client's ability to reach a vendor, responsiveness is about the speed at which issues are resolved. As part of their contract, clients specify responsiveness for operational issues. This is covered in greater detail in further sections. Outside of operational issues, clients expect vendors to respond to any issue, including those relating to ramp-ups or ramp-downs, additional resources, pricing, invoicing, etc., within reasonable timelines. As many of these issues are non-operational, it is important for account managers to understand the expected timelines in terms of response.

Communication: Timeliness and quality of communications are big challenges when working across time zones and cultures. Clients expect that their account managers are well informed about all aspects of service delivery and that they facilitate smooth communication between the two organisations. They expect that the process for the flow of routine information is clearly established by account managers. For ad hoc and urgent communication, clients expect that account managers judge the severity of the issue and escalate the information appropriately.

The client service process

As outlined earlier in this chapter, meeting client expectations is a shared responsibility across the company and is not restricted only to the account management team. However, this team is responsible for setting up and managing the client services processes. Figure 6.6 provides a high-level overview of a client service process.

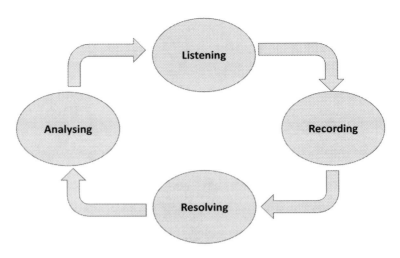

Figure 6.6 Customer service loop

Table 6.3 Touchpoints for capturing feedback

Capture Opportunity Stage	Employee Group	Type
Sales and pre-sales	Sales team, channel partners	Internal—Informal/formal
Contracting	Finance, legal	Internal—Informal
Implementation	Internal implementation team, external partners, external partner like integrators	Internal—Informal/formal
Ongoing delivery	Operations, client service, account management, leadership, quality	Internal—Informal/formal
Account management	Account management, leadership	Internal—Informal/formal
Service management/call centre	Service team, account team	Internal—Informal/formal
Social media (e.g. Google and Amazon reviews, Twitter, etc.)	Customer care, account management	External—Informal

Listening: Client feedback is both formal and informal and can be captured at multiple touchpoints.

As a vendor, it is important to list all the potential touchpoints with a client to ensure that nothing is missed. Table 6.3 outlines the various

CLIENT AND ACCOUNT MANAGEMENT

opportunities to capture feedback, the employees who interact with clients at each of these opportunities, and the type of feedback.

Client feedback can be formal or informal. Formal feedback is gathered from a combination of surveys and client review meetings. A process is set by vendors to capture formal feedback. At a minimum this includes:

- One-time feedback after the sales and contracting process
- Multiple times during implementation
- Half-yearly feedback post-sale
- Feedback after every service call or complaint

Complaint and service interactions are another good source for formal feedback. These interactions can be through voice calls, chats, emails, or apps. The availability of omni-channel client services has become basic.

Feedback needs to be sought from multiple stakeholders in a client organisation including the CEO, operations or business heads, and operations managers. A good practice for formal feedback is to send surveys to all these stakeholders.

While most companies have some form of formal feedback mechanism, capturing informal feedback is equally important. These could be in the form of comments during meetings or reviews, feedback given to third parties, etc.

In the digital world, the number of external sources for informal client feedback is increasing. Given the "viral" nature of this feedback, it is very important for vendors to identify all the potential external sources and monitor them. While this is more applicable in B2C scenarios, it is becoming as critical in B2B delivery when the end user of the service is a consumer. For example, a vendor who develops a banking app for a client should directly monitor feedback on the app from the client's end customer.

Recording: The next stage in the client service loop is capturing all formal and informal feedback from identified sources. A client could provide feedback through any of the channels, and one interaction can straddle across multiple channels simultaneously or linearly. For example, a client's operations team may call the vendor's operations team to log a complaint, and then the vendor manager sends an email to the account manager. This makes client service more challenging, as the client experience must be seamless irrespective of the channel and source of complaint. The more avenues for interaction, the greater the need for an omni-channel client services platform.

Resolution: When client feedback is received, the first action is to classify the feedback:

- Is it a query or a complaint?
- If a complaint—what is the level of severity?

145

CLIENT AND ACCOUNT MANAGEMENT

Table 6.4 Client service metrics

Type of Measure	Measure	Description
Operational	Volume	Number of complaints received
Operational	Response time	Time taken to respond to an interaction
Operational	Average handle time	Time taken to resolve
Operational	Accuracy	Accuracy of resolution as measured by lack of repeat interactions on the same issue
Experience	Client satisfaction	Satisfaction scores measured as part of periodic client satisfaction surveys
Experience	Net promoter score	Willingness to recommend as captured in client satisfaction surveys

A good practice followed by vendors is to acknowledge the interaction and provide some timelines for a response immediately. This reduces the chance of repeat interactions through other channels.

Some of the key metrics used to measure the effectiveness of complaints are provided in Table 6.4.

In B2B client services, these measures are difficult to implement, as clients may not be willing to log all complaints via the CRM tool. It then becomes the responsibility of the account manager to ensure that all complaints are logged into the CRM irrespective of the channel through which they are received.

Analysis

The final step of this loop is to conduct periodic analysis of all the data collected through the client service process.

Broadly the analysis should be conducted at two levels.

1 Efficiency analysis. This is an analysis of how efficient the client service process runs. It is an analysis of all operational metrics, and the aim is to make the listening, recording, and resolving processes more efficient.
2 Effectiveness analysis: This part of the analysis focuses on the effectiveness of the products/services that are on offer rather than the client service process. Client satisfaction, net promoter score, number of complaints, etc., are indicators of how good or bad client perceptions of the services are. The end goal of the analysis of effectiveness parameters is to improve services by providing feedback to the delivery teams.

Account managers include the analysis of effectiveness and efficiency parameters as part of the quarterly reviews. These metrics are also a critical component in the evaluation of the account management team.

6.5 Managing global clients

Managing global clients brings additional complexity to a relationship. Some of the typical challenges that need to be taken into consideration while building account plans are described in this section.

Engaging with global teams: With client teams dispersed globally, they, in many cases, lack the processes for internal coordination. For example, the vendor management team may be in the United States, while the operating teams are dispersed across multiple geographies. In such a scenario, vendors need to understand the global structure and ensure that the vendor team is responsible for all internal coordination. In most master service agreements (MSAs) and statements of work (SoWs), vendors include what are referred to as "reverse SLAs". These SLAs specify the dependencies on the client for delivering services. Vendor teams are responsible for ensuring that clients meet these reverse SLA.

Cultural differences: Another challenge in global contracts is dealing with the cultural, national, and social differences. For example, within the same contract, certain countries are more relational, whereas other countries may be more contractual. Language barriers accentuate these differences. Even if the language of the business is English in an organisation, local languages are more suitable for relationship building. This is a difficult challenge to overcome, as the deal economics may not allow for local account management in every country. Some of the methods for mitigating these challenges include phased roll-out (to limit risk at any point of time) and creating global project teams within client organisations to handle localised issues. In the latter, individuals from the client organisation act as virtual account managers for the vendor.

Varying degrees of importance: The significance of one project may vary across geographies. For example, an omni-channel technology implementation may be more relevant to one country and less in another where retail is still largely brick and mortar. This results in varying levels of engagement from local client teams in the overall project. Reverse SLAs are used to overcome these kinds of issues.

Account teams need to identify these challenges up-front and ensure that solutions like reverse SLAs and global governance structures are identified and included in the contracts.

6.6 Governance structure

An outsourcing engagement is a complex multi-year transaction. It involves a shift of responsibilities from an internal IT team to one or multiple vendors located globally. The vendors do not have the legacy knowledge and the relationships with the operations teams in the client organisation. A well-recognised way to mitigate the risks arising from such a shift of responsibilities from client to vendor is the constitution of a joint governance structure.

A good governance structure has been identified as the key to success in any outsourcing arrangement and protects the interests of both vendors and clients.

Governance structure in outsourcing is broadly divided into two categories—contractual governance (also referred to as the promissory contract) and relational governance (also referred to as the psychological contract). Contractual governance, as the name suggests, is based on the terms of the contract and what has been agreed in it. Relational governance, on the other hand, is based on unwritten and peer-to-peer relationships. In academic literature, these two forms of relationships have been positioned as two counterviews to governance structures.

In the paper *Evolution of Governance: Achieving Ambidexterity in IT Outsourcing* (Cao, Mohan, Ramesh, and Sarkar, 2013), the authors introduce the concept of ambidextrous governance and show that the governance pendulum swings from relational to contractual and back and eventually finds a mid-way equilibrium. In the initial stages of an engagement, account managers and sales teams rely on relational governance, as no formal structures exist at this stage. As a contract gets firmed up, the pendulum swings back towards a contractual relationship. In the early stages of a new engagement, many issues tend to crop up that are not written into contracts. To resolve these issues, account and vendor managers push the pendulum back towards the relationship side. Eventually, as the two parties get to know each other, a mid-way equilibrium is established.

In practice, an effective governance structure needs to have a balance of contracts and relationships. Account managers need to ensure adherence to the governance agreed in the MSA and SoW and, at the same time, establish an informal governance mechanism with their clients. The risk of adhering strictly to a formal governance mechanism is that these tend to not allow for the flexibility that is required in managing a complex relationship.

Typical objectives of a good governance structure include:

- Monitor the health of the outsourcing arrangement and direct reporting requirements to support this monitoring adequately
- Perform long-term strategic and operational planning and execution
- Provide support to strengthen the relationship and coordinate activities between business organisations
- Periodically review and support change management procedures
- Review and resolve issues that have been escalated to the different levels of the governance framework
- Discuss and promote continuous process improvement ideas and initiatives.

CLIENT AND ACCOUNT MANAGEMENT

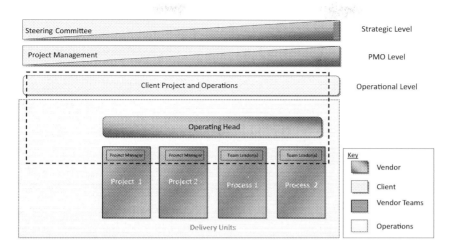

Figure 6.7 Sample governance matrix

A comprehensive governance structure will have multiple levels, each addressing one part of the relationship (Figure 6.7).

Level 1: Steering Committee—Responsible for the overall success of the relationship, strategic alignment between the two organisations, tracking of the return on investment (ROI), and review of the relationship goals. The steering committee consists of senior executives from the client and vendor.

Level 2: Project Management Office (PMO)—Responsible for the overall delivery of services. The PMO is tasked with handling key issues such as project prioritisation, contract, SLA monitoring, change management, volume forecasting, etc. Most IT relationships are governed by a single MSA with multiple SoWs. The PMO is responsible for the governance of all the SoWs that exist with the vendor. The PMO typically consists of the account management team on the vendor side and the vendor management team on the client side.

Level 3: Project Management and Operation Teams—Responsible for managing the day-to-day execution of projects and systems management activities, executing/enhancing management processes, establishing effective communication mechanisms, promoting shared learning and re-use, and feeding the PMO with relevant information and updates. Most large relationships have multiple such teams, with each responsible only for the governance of their respective project. The project management and operation teams consist of the operating leads in both organisations.

Communication plan

A formal communication mechanism must be put in place to support the governance structure. These interactions occur at multiple levels at varying

CLIENT AND ACCOUNT MANAGEMENT

Table 6.5 Sample communication plan

Category	*Mechanism*
Quarterly steering committee meetings	Monthly and quarterly review meetings involving the leadership from both organisations. These meetings are used as toll gates for reviewing the engagement and taking decisions on major initiatives and escalations.
Monthly/weekly PMO calls	PMO calls are typically held weekly to monitor the health of a relationship and plan for the subsequent periods. All escalations from the various operations calls are also reviewed as part of these interactions. The outcomes of these meetings are summarised as an input for the steering committee meetings.
Weekly operations calls	Weekly team meetings are conducted with operation and project teams from both sides to monitor service delivery progress. The account manager attends most critical operation calls in addition to the functional teams.
Issues and metrics tracking reports	Vendors are expected to report all metrics and issues in pre-defined formats. These reports are reviewed in the operations and PMO calls.
Ad hoc calls	In addition to the previous interactions, there are several ad hoc calls that get set up to discuss topics and issues that were not covered as part of the structured calls.

frequencies and facilitate the smooth flow of information between client and vendor. Table 6.5 shows the typical communication channels adopted in a project.

6.7 Role of service management standards

Most IT services providers have undergone certifications such as Capability Maturity Model Integration (CMMI) and International Organization for Standardization (ISO). These certifications require vendors to define processes for service management, including client services.

ISO/IEC 20000–1:2018: The standard provides a specification document that requires an organisation to establish, implement, maintain, and continually improve a service management system (SMS). The requirements specified in this document include the planning, design, transition,

CLIENT AND ACCOUNT MANAGEMENT

delivery, and improvement of services to meet the service requirements and deliver value.

Among other uses, the document can be used by:

1 A client seeking services and requiring assurance regarding the quality of those services
2 A client requiring a consistent approach to the service lifecycle by all its service providers, including those in a supply chain
3 An organisation to demonstrate its capability for the planning, design, transition, delivery, and improvement of services
4 An organisation to monitor, measure, and review its service management system (SMS) and the services
5 An organisation to improve the planning, design, transition, delivery, and improvement of services through effective implementation and operation of an SMS
6 An organisation or other party performing conformity assessments against the requirements specified in this document
7 A provider of training or advice in service management.

CMMI

CMMI is specific guidance derived from the Capability Maturity Model (CMM) methodology that has been developed by the Software Engineering Institute (SEI) of Carnegie Mellon University in the late 1990s. The methodology was initially developed for military contractors and then was adapted for commercial organisations' certification. CMMI provides certifications at five levels:

Level 1 — Ad Hoc: The processes are undefined and unstructured. There is chaos in each organisation's process area.

Level 2—Managed: The processes are defined at the project level. The solutions are very reactive.

Level 3 — Defined: The processes are defined at the organisational level. It is one of the most important levels, since it suggests that the company has learnt how to put the processes to the project level and how to make them work in each case.

Level 4 — Quantitatively Managed: All the key processes are properly managed and controlled. The project metrics are gathered and analysed.

Level 5 — Optimising: The processes are improved based on the gathered metrics.

151

Most large vendors have undergone one or both certifications, and therefore these are no longer differentiators. However, implementing these guidelines assures clients that service processes are in place and are being adhered to.

Account managers are the owners of all processes relating to capture and analysis of client services issues as described earlier.

6.8 Risks and risk mitigation

As discussed earlier in this chapter, client management has two distinct drivers: contractual and relational. It is important for account managers to identify risks that impact client satisfaction and document risk management strategies. We have described a few of the common risks and issues that client and account managers need to be aware of:

Client dissatisfaction: This is the most common risk in any relationship and is captured through both formal and informal mechanisms. The severity and reasons for client dissatisfaction determine the course of action. Most contracts outline the action plan and escalation mechanism for client issues, especially those relating to service delivery (see Figure 6.8). In addition to escalation, it is essential to have a plan for resolution. As part of the service agreement, a high-level process for resolution of complaints is also outlined (Figure 6.8).

Lack of coordination between vendor and client teams: Failure in coordination between teams happens due to multiple reasons ranging from lack of a formal communication plan, cultural differences, and intercompany dynamics. While communication issues can be fixed using processes and procedures, the relational issues are more complex to deal with. These issues get further aggravated in global outsourcing contracts. In many cases, client teams have colleagues who have been retrenched due to the outsourcing deal, and this leads to resentment of vendor personnel and eventually a breakdown in relationships. There are no easy fixes for these issues, but some of the common steps taken by vendor organisations include the hiring

	Expected Resolution Time	Operations Team responds within	Heads of Operations + PMO	Steering Committee
			Escalate if not resolved by	
Level 1 (Not severe)	12 hours	2 hours	3 days	NA
Level 2	8 hours	2 hours	2 days	NA
Level 3	6 hours	2 hours	1 day	NA
Level 4 (Extremely severe)	2 hours	0.5 hours	1 day	3 days

Figure 6.8 Sample escalation matrix

CLIENT AND ACCOUNT MANAGEMENT

Table 6.6 Client–vendor relationship mapping

Client Organisation	Vendor Organisation
Vendor Manager	Account Manager
Operations Head	Delivery Head
CFO	Account Manager
COO	COO/CEO
CEO	COO/CEO

of some of the retrenched vendor personnel in account management and other roles. One of the critical roles of an account manager, especially in the early stages of an outsourcing engagement, is to identify key personnel within the client organisation and build one-on-one relationships with them.

Breakdown in the relationship: A breakdown in the relationship can happen due to an inability to meet service levels, a change in vendor management or operations teams within the client organisations, disagreements on contractual terms, the introduction of new vendors, change in client strategy, etc. Multi-level relationships are key to ensure that relationships remain strong irrespective of changes (see Table 6.6). Vendors identify key client personnel at each level and make active efforts in maintaining relationships.

Inviting key client personnel to visit vendor facilities, invitations to conferences and speaking engagements, and invitations to sports and other events are some other methods used to ensure organisational connect. Account managers are responsible for ensuring that these periodic "informal" interactions are held at each of the levels.

Terminating the relationship: In very rare scenarios, the vendor and buyer can amicably decide to move out of the relationship. This can happen due to several reasons: 1) the vendor's inability to deliver or manage the relationship; 2) evolution in technology, regulation, or customer's preference has made the project unviable; and 3) the financial problem of the buyer or its changed priority.

Scope creep: One of the biggest challenges of account management is the continuous change in the specifications or boundaries of a project. The causes of scope creep can be classified into controllable and uncontrollable. The uncontrollable reasons are beyond the control of the vendor team, such as acquisition of the client's business by its competitor, change in regulations, or emergence of newer technologies. Some of the reasons for controllable changes in scope include:

- Not having an SoW in place. Clients sometimes push vendors to begin work without a detailed SoW due to time pressures or not wanting to go through paperwork.

- The scope of the project is not defined in detail.
- Poor expectation management. Other than the SOW, the sellers should set and manage the expectation of the client from the beginning.
- Client's IT team does not understand the scope.
- Informal commitment. The supplier's sales, account, and delivery leadership team might have informal conversations, off-the-record-chats, or side deals with the client's team, which might have impacted the client's expectation.
- Poor estimation by supplier's pre-sales team of the effort required to complete a project, as well as improper estimation about the risks.
- Lack or low involvement of business users from the beginning. In multiple occasions, business leadership gets involved at a later stage, and any change in developed systems impact the budget and timeline.
- Lack of reverse SLAs where responsibilities of client personnel are clearly defined. The buyer should ensure that the key stakeholders are engaged.
- The scope change management process is slow or not properly used by the supplier's resources.

A project may require additional work, even after managing the controllable reasons. This could be because of changes related to the needs or preferences of a client's end customer, competition-driven changes, or unanticipated regulatory changes. To handle scope creep in such scenarios, vendors should use the change management process, which is part of the MSA. The scope creep problem may also arise if the budget of the clients gets exhausted, but the project needs important changes to be incorporated. The negative impacts of the scope creep are many:

- Client loses confidence in IT provider's delivery and technological capability
- Conflict between teams buyer and seller teams
- The project milestones are missed
- The delivery team of the seller is overstretched
- The seller or IT provider realises a much lower gross profit, compared to what was planned.

Agile methodologies are better suited to handle changes in project definitions. By design, these processes incorporate end users in the design and allow for short development cycles followed by the feedback process.

Account managers play an important role in handling scope creep. They need to implement a process where all scope changes are flagged to them by the project operations teams. It is then their responsibility to work with the client's team to negotiate the changes and incorporate them into a revised SoW. If handled well, it results in a better outcome for both the client and

CLIENT AND ACCOUNT MANAGEMENT

the vendor. Many times, saying no to a customer-requested change can be beneficial in the long term.

6.9 Chapter highlights

- CRM is a complex but critical process.
- Existing clients are the fastest route to growth and profitability for most vendors, and therefore managing and growing existing clients have received the attention of both academics and practitioners in the last few decades.
- The process of building and managing client relationships consists broadly of three activities:

  - Developing the client relationship strategy
  - Integrated relationship management and metrics
  - Governance and risk mitigation

- Developing a client relationship strategy starts with fully understanding a vendor's portfolio of existing clients, the market in which they operate, their product strategy, revenues, and revenue growth. Vendors then map these profiles with their own aspiration for growth, profitability, and product strategy and arrive at a portfolio mapping of clients.
- Clients are classified into various categories depending on their importance. Various terms are used to describe the accounts to focus on, including "top clients", "key accounts", and "platinum/gold customers".
- The next step in developing a client strategy is to create detailed account plans for each of the key accounts and then build revenue plans. Key account plans form an important part of investor presentations.
- This is followed by implementing the account plan through effective relationship management.
- Client management consists of four individual elements: 1) listening, 2) recording, 3) resolving, and 4) analysing. The role of account management is to ensure that robust processes exist for each one of these elements.
- Account management can be broadly divided into two parts: 1) contractual and 2) relational. While contractual management is driven by written-down processes and procedures, relational is "fuzzier" and depends on interpersonal relationships.
- The chapter describes the processes for the former and provides guidelines on how processes can also be implemented to support relationship building.
- The challenges of client management get enhanced in global contracts where effectively vendors are dealing with multiple clients under one contract, each with their own needs and priorities. It is important for

155

CLIENT AND ACCOUNT MANAGEMENT

vendors to specify their expectations from the vendor management team, including through "reverse SLAs".

- Governance structures must encompass various levels of interactions, including strategic, project management, and operational, to be effective. Standards such as ISO provide vendor guidelines for implementation of effective governance structures and communication plans.
- Despite all the planning, client management is fraught with risks. It is important for vendors to identify these risks and build-in mitigation strategies.

6.10 Questions for discussion

1 What are the three steps of a typical client management process? Briefly explain each of the steps.
2 What is client portfolio management? What are some of the frameworks used to assess a portfolio of clients?
3 What are the attributes for segmenting clients? Discuss which of these are easier to implement.
4 What are the four key steps of customer service? Why is this a loop?
5 What are the risks in client management? Provide mitigation strategies for each of the risks outlined.

6.11 References

Ansoff, H. I. (1957). Strategies for diversification. *Harvard Business Review*, *35*(5), 113–124.
Cao, L., Mohan, K., Ramesh, B., and Sarkar, S. (2013). Evolution of governance: Achieving ambidexterity in IT outsourcing. *Journal of Management Information Systems*, *30*(3), 115–140.
Sheth, Jagdish N. *Customer relationship management: emerging concepts, tools, and applications*. Tata McGraw-Hill Education, 2001.
Terho, H., and Halinen, A. (2007). Customer portfolio analysis practices in different exchange contexts. *Journal of Business Research*, *60*(7), 720–730.
Thakur, R., and Workman, L. (2016). Customer portfolio management (CPM) for improved customer relationship management (CRM): Are your customers platinum, gold, silver, or bronze? *Journal of Business Research*, *69*(10), 4095–4102.
Waaser, E., Dahneke, M., Pekkarinen, M., and Weissel, M. (2004). How you slice it: Smarter segmentation for your sales force. *Harvard Business Review*, *82*(3), 105–111.

7

MARKETING AND SALES ENABLEMENT

7.1 Learning objectives

This chapter provides an overview of the role of marketing and sales in a technology organisation. By studying the chapter, the reader will be able to:

- Understand the role of marketing in an IT organisation
- Develop a marketing plan
- Understand the role of marketing in supporting the sales team
- Appreciate the sales process in an IT organisation
- Develop a sales toolkit.

7.2 Introduction

Marketing activities are vital to the business development process in IT companies, and they go hand-in-hand with the sales process. Marketing activities also span the entire client lifecycle from pre-sales to sales, solutioning and proposal development, deal closure, and ongoing relationship management.

This chapter starts with explaining the role played by the marketing function in product-centric and service-centric IT organisations.

The first part of the chapter focusses on the role of marketing across product management, demand generation, branding, and communications.

The chapter then focusses on the importance of developing a sales toolkit and also developing appropriate communication for each phase of a sales process. The chapter finally discusses some technologies that have become integral to the marketing process.

7.3 Role of the marketing function

The five critical tasks performed by an IT company's marketing function are product management, demand generation, branding, communications, and

DOI: 10.4324/9781003155270-8

157

industry research and analysis. The magnitude of these tasks varies across IT products and IT services companies. In an IT products company, product management is a critical role, with product managers owning the "4Ps" of a technology product in partnership with the product development team. In an IT services company, product management is less relevant, with the marketing function focusing on driving corporate branding, supporting the sales team in demand generation, and working closely with the account management teams in building and managing client relationships. This is best illustrated in the difference in the chief marketing officer (CMO) role of product companies like Intuit or Oracle versus the CMO of a traditional services company like TCS or Tech Mahindra. As IT companies move up the value chain, from pure services to intellectual property (IP)–based products, the marketing function's role is getting recast in most organisations. From being a support function, they are now becoming a part of the executive decision-making process. More and more CMOs in IT companies are being hired from consumer product companies to reflect this shift. Marketing department is responsible for developing a comprehensive marketing plan. The marketing plan forms the backbone for the functioning of a marketing department. With increased competition from global players, clients have multiple vendors to choose from. Also, there is general fatigue among clients to meet sales personnel from newer or untested vendors. Marketing plays a critical role in building bridges, beyond transactional sales and account management, and keeping a company relevant in a client's mind. The focus of marketing given by IT products and services companies is reflected in the growing number of such companies that appear in Forbes' The World's Most Valuable Brands list.

In the next section, the role of marketing in each of these areas has been detailed.

7.4 Product management

Product management in an IT company is best defined by an annual marketing plan, which is the first step of an effective marketing strategy. While smaller companies develop a single marketing plan, most large companies develop marketing plans by industry segments and geographies. These are finally consolidated into a corporate marketing plan.

A typical marketing plan consists of the following:

Product Mix: A mix of products/services that are going to be offered by the company. In software product companies, products are well-defined. In services companies, the term product usually refers to a broad set of services. Special focus is given to newer services like digital that the company plans to focus on.

MARKETING AND SALES ENABLEMENT

Target Segment Identification: The next step of a marketing plan is to identify the target segments for products and services.

The segmentation could be:

- By industry
- By buyers or buyer groups within the industry
- By size and operations range
- By geography/region
- List of potential targets by target segment/region.

7.5 Demand generation, branding, and communications

Demand generation is the most crucial role played by the marketing function in an IT company. The marketing function supports the sales team in generating demand. Branding and communication go hand-in-hand with demand generation activities. For branding, a comprehensive set of objectives are set at a corporate level. This includes:

- The overall image the company would like to project
- Branding objectives
- The vision and mission (and changes, if any)
- Focus for the next few years.

The demand generation has several sub-activities, which we have explained next.

7.5.1 Target industry and segment identification

Industry profiling is used to map target industries and segments within the industries using demographic information. Some of the variables used to profile industries are as follows:

- Standard industry codes (SICs) and the newer North American Industry Classification System (NAICS) are used for broad classification in the United States.
- Number of players by company size—based on revenues and sales.
- Players by number of employees.
- Geographic location: A vendor must decide which geographies they plan to target. For example, will they target a client for its global operations or a few geographies? If the target is the global operations, will they follow a phased approach by region or country?

Some other information that is used in arriving at a list of potential industries and segments include:

- The current needs of the segments that can be fulfilled by a vendor
- Industry or segment-specific differentiated services that can be offered by a vendor
- Growth rate of the industry: Is the industry in a high-growth mode and therefore needs support from an IT services vendor to expand?
- Cyclicality of the industry: Is the industry cyclical and therefore needs to outsource IT services to keep fixed costs low?
- What are some of the recent trends in the industry that make it attractive to IT vendors? For example, is there a disruptor in the client industry, forcing traditional players to rethink their strategy?
- What are the potential changes in regulations and the impact of these changes on business processes and technologies in an industry?
- Which industries and segments are the vendor's competitors currently targeting?

The Ansoff matrix (Ansoff, 1957) is a useful tool to look at target industries (Figure 7.1)

A company can choose to be in any of the four quadrants or an optimum mix of these. For example, a vendor can decide to remain in Quadrant 1 to expand their client base within the existing industry segments. A vendor may also choose to expand their service offerings to the current industry segments (Quadrant 2). A vendor may choose to enter new markets or geographies that need their existing products or services (Quadrant 3) or develop new services for a new market (Quadrant 4). Most vendors try to minimize their exposure to Quadrant 4, as it is high risk and adopt around a 40%-30%-25%-05% mix of their expansion across the four quadrants. This implies that a large proportion of their business (~70%) comes from existing segments.

There is no scientific way of finalising the list of industries a vendor should target. It depends on several factors such as risk appetite, availability of resources, investments into new products and services, shareholder pressures, and competition. However, structuring all the data discussed in this section by the marketing team helps senior management take an informed decision. The final decision on target industries cannot be too broad, or sometimes referred to as macro segmentation (for example: "We will target Fortune 500 companies"). Similarly, it cannot be too narrow, leading to micro-segmentation (for example: "We will target banks with assets between USD 500 million and 1 billion in the northeast United States"). Having too broad a classification will dilute the vendor's market positioning, while having a very narrow definition will reduce the available market size. Most vendors have a target segment definition that consists of at least three variables. A sample target profile is provided in Figure 7.2.

MARKETING AND SALES ENABLEMENT

	Existing Products	New Products
Existing Markets/Segments	Status Quo (Q1)	New Product (Q2) Development
New Markets/Segments	Market Development (Q3)	Diversification (Q4)

Figure 7.1 Ansoff matrix

Sample Target Segments

Industries : Consumer Banking, Retail (Brick and mortar and ecommerce)

Revenues : USB 10 Billion to 100 billion

Geographies : North America (US and Canada)

Other characteristics:

- Have some experience with IT outsourcing
- Have a stated intention of providing omni-channel services (from annual reports and other sources)
- High growth companies (growth rate of 15% in the 2 years)

Figure 7.2 Sample target profile

7.5.2 Database generation

Once a list of industries and company characteristics is drawn up, the next step is developing a database of clients who fit the profile. Several sources are available to help build the database.

Internal sources: As discussed in the earlier section, most companies target 60% to 70% of their next year's business from existing clients. As a result, the best starting point to build a database is internal sources. The internal sources include:

- Accounting software which has data from past billings
- Account management software (customer relationship management [CRM]) or data with the account management team

161

- Past sales management data, including pipeline data
- Lists subscribed to by the marketing team in earlier years
- Sales and account management teams

Integrated CRM software is discussed later in the chapter. However, it is common to find client data and lists in multiple databases across different departments. The marketing function plays an important role in consolidating these data into one usable database.

While generating a list of companies is a key task, the more critical and complicated task is to consolidate, clean, and update the database. The marketing departments of many large corporations outsource this process of master data management. The master data list contains companies, key contacts, offices, demographic data, and previous interaction history. An entity on the list could be a current client who can be offered a new service, a new client, or a past client who is no longer buying services. It is important to record why the client is no longer using a service in the latter case. As an illustration, the following clarifications can be asked:

- Was it a one-time requirement?
- Were there service issues?
- Did the client move to a competitor, and if so, what were the reasons for this movement?

The master data management (MDM) process also involves de-duplicating the lists. (For example, one database may have Microsoft listed as MS while another as Microsoft Inc and a third as Microsoft Corporation). The cleaner the database, the easier and more efficient its usage.

External sources: In the last decade, many good sources for databases have become available.

Database companies: Companies such as Dun and Bradstreet, InfoUSA, Zoom Info, and Experian provide extensive databases of companies. A vendor can specify their criteria and receive a sample list from these companies to conduct a pilot campaign. In the recent past, social platforms such as LinkedIn Marketing Services have also gained a significant market share in database marketing.

Industry associations: Most industry associations make available their member lists. While these lists may not be comprehensive in terms of the data available, they are a good starting point.

Primary data gathering: This remains the best source for building a database and can be combined with any of the internal and external sources discussed in the chapter. Most large IT providers use primary data gathering to refine the data they receive from the databases. This exercise needs to be repeated periodically, as data on companies and contact information are dynamic.

MARKETING AND SALES ENABLEMENT

	Role
Initiators	These are the individuals who first recognize the problem.
Gatekeepers	These individuals control the flow of knowledge, either by being proactive in collecting information, or by filtering it. (e.g. assistants to the CEO)
Buyers	The individuals given the task of sourcing suppliers and negotiating the final deal. (e.g. Commercial/Sourcing department)
Deciders	These are the people who make the final decision (e.g. CEO/BU Head)
Users	These are the people who will be using the products which are supplied (e.g. Business Operations)
Influencers	These people "have the ear of" the deciders (e.g. Consultants)

Figure 7.3 Roles in buyer organisations

Source: Wind and Webster, 1972

7.5.3 Tailored messaging

Before starting a campaign from a database, it is important to understand various individuals' roles in the decision-making process followed by a client. In Chapter 4, we have explained the four types of roles conceptualised by Miller and Heiman (1985). Figure 7.3 provides an alternative but similar conceptualisation (Wind and Webster, 1972). The figure explains the five types of roles.

The decision-making team usually consists of multiple individuals. The same individual may also play multiple roles. It is important to understand the role individuals play so that messages can be tailored. For example, at a transactional level, "Buyers" may be more interested in pricing and industry references, while "Users" may be more impressed by quality methodologies and implementation speed. The "Deciders", on the other hand, may be interested in strategic fit and shareholder value. The choice of media for this targeted messaging will also vary across the roles conceptualised in any of the two above models.

7.5.4 Marketing support

The marketing function works closely with the sales in lead generation. Figure 7.4 illustrates a typical sales funnel created by a sales team to determine the number of leads/prospects required to meet their annual target.

Figure 7.5 outlines the various sources of demand. The sales and marketing teams work together to distribute the number of prospects across various lead sources. Lead sources can be multiple and non-exclusive. Figure 7.4 provides

MARKETING AND SALES ENABLEMENT

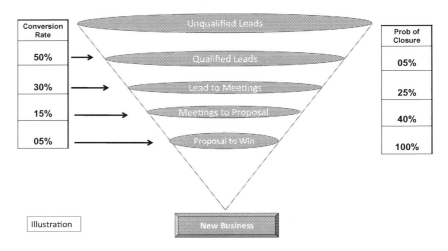

Figure 7.4 Illustrative pipeline

Figure 7.5 Sources of demand

an illustrative view of how leads/prospects get distributed across multiple sources. While the categories listed under the marketing pillar are the marketing team's direct responsibility, the team also enables the other pillars.

Digital Campaigns: These are campaigns focused on the chain of decision-makers (described in Figure 7.3). Digital marketing can be used in several ways in a business-to-business (B2B) context.

MARKETING AND SALES ENABLEMENT

1 Search Engine Optimisation (SEO): This type of activity is typical for newer services or vendors targeting small businesses.
2 Search Engine Marketing (SEM): Like SEO, SEM is used mostly for specialised services or targeting smaller clients.
3 Social Media: This includes targeted campaigns on platforms such as LinkedIn or Instagram. Videos on platforms such as YouTube are also used to disseminate information about a vendor's services. Video platforms are also used to publicise client case studies and testimonials.

Each social media platform attracts different users and is effective for certain types of messages (Figure 7.6). To execute an effective digital campaign, vendors need to select a variety of these platforms.

Webinars: Webinars on specialised topics are another effective form of client communication. Most vendors create live webinars to disseminate information and benefits of their offerings to clients. Webinars are

Medium	Benefits
LinkedIn	• Best for business-to-business marketing • Real people • Lead generation tools • Thought leadership through groups and posts
Google AdWords	• Instant traffic to your website unlike all other media • Set-up a campaign in less that 5 minutes • Highly targeted to exactly what people are searching for • Pay by use (PPC) • More focused than Facebook AdWords (intent is not searching)
YouTube	• 2nd biggest search engine • Largest for "How To" (70%) • Educational videos ; brand telling videos; entertainment videos • Redirect back to product
Facebook	• 2.5 billion active users • Broad-based user profile • Average Fb users has 200 friends (viral) • Mostly real profiles (businesses can see who their viewers are; good for analytics) • FB ads Integrated with WhatsApp and Instagram • Powerful ad platform
Twitter	• Interacting vs broadcasting • Sharing information/driving engagement/building brand • Search for clients directly • Social listening
Instagram	• Over a billion users - millennials • Visual content • Good for brand building – humanizing your brand • Growth tools for businesses • Influencer marketing

Figure 7.6 Benefits and uses of social media platforms

effective, as they are interactive and allow potential clients to interact with the host. Vendors use the expertise of both internal and industry experts to host these webinars. The audience for a webinar is usually gathered using some of the other activities outlined earlier in this section, and direct mailers. One of the primary advantages of a webinar is that participation is a sign of interest in discussing the topic. It provides for an easier route to seek an appointment. Webinars also demonstrate industry authority on a subject for a vendor.

Email/Mailer Campaigns: Email and mailer campaigns are the more traditional form of lead generation activities. There are broadly two objectives of such campaigns. The first is to provide information that helps in brand building. The information could range from announcing a new suite of services, informing a client about an industry award, client cases, etc. The second and more important use of email campaigns is to have a definite "call to action" like asking for a meeting appointment or requesting the receiver to join a webinar. The challenge with email campaigns is multi-fold. There is a clutter of such emails, and most corporate email filters block out such emails. Vendors are experimenting with going back to physical mailers, as there is less clutter in such mailers now and they cannot be deleted by the press of a button.

Industry Conferences and Events: These events are held across the globe and focus on specific industries or products. Vendors use these conferences to showcase their products and services and build their brand. For example, vendors targeting banks typically attend all major banking conferences in the target geography. The attendance can be in multiple forms—sponsorship of the event, setting up a booth to display products, sponsoring workshops, speaking events or lunches within the events, etc. Marketing teams work closely with the sales team to select the right conferences and develop the conference's branding and messaging. Most modern conferences allow participants to view a list of attendees and pre-set meetings with the attendees. Marketing teams use the apps provided by conference organisers to schedule appointments for senior management and sales personnel with potential clients. These events have some advantages over digital marketing. They provide face-to-face connections and can generate a high volume of leads over a short period.

There are multiple categories of conferences. We have explained a few of them.

Tradeshows: Conferences focused on specific trades and industries. They are usually organized by industry associations and managed by event management companies. Tradeshows have a large number of attendees and are typically held annually. The Consumer Electronics Show[1] in Las Vegas and the various regional tradeshows on banking and fintech organised by Money 2020[2] are some examples.

MARKETING AND SALES ENABLEMENT

Specialized tradeshows: These are also tradeshows but organised across industry horizontals. Gartner IT Symposium and Forbes CIO Summit are examples of such conferences. The conferences revolve around the challenges and opportunities for chief information officers (CIOs) and are not industry-specific.

User Conferences: IT product companies with large user bases organise conferences for their users. IT companies use these conferences to showcase their products and services and client success stories. User conferences usually have a mix of existing clients, existing partners, and prospective clients. Google Cloud Next and Salesforce Dreamforce are examples of large user conferences. Smaller IT services companies also organise user conferences that are usually held annually. Prospective clients are invited as guests and speakers to these conferences. In addition to meeting the vendor, prospective clients get the opportunity to interact with senior managers of existing clients.

Roadshows: Roadshows are used by vendors to showcase new products and services. Marketing teams work with sales to develop a travel schedule and host smaller events in locations with higher client concentrations. Roadshows are useful in conveying focused messages but require significant marketing and logistics support. One of the challenges of roadshows is ensuring the right number and quality of attendees.

Most leads from a conference and events are directly at Stage 2 (see Figure 7.2) of the sales pipeline (qualified leads), unlike digital leads that are typically at Stage 1 (unqualified). There has been some dilution of the attendance at conferences due to budget and travel restrictions in many client organisations in recent times.

The marketing teams of IT companies are responsible for measuring the effectiveness and return on investment (RoI) of various conferences and selecting the right conferences to attend. Their role also extends to ensure best practices are adopted while attending the conferences. These include pre-scheduling of meetings, ensuring that the CRM is updated, post-conference report generation, and managing follow-ups.

Websites/Apps: A corporate website is the anchor for all marketing activities and is therefore critical for any B2B marketing activity. Most prospects visit a vendor's corporate website early in the sales process. While in this chapter we will not cover how to design a good website, marketing teams need to ensure that the following items are checked off on a corporate website:

- Content: The website should, at a minimum, contain information about the company, its purpose, service offerings, target industries, leadership, and investors
- Value proposition: What differentiates the company, and what is its value proposition to its clients? This could include the vision and mission of the vendor.

MARKETING AND SALES ENABLEMENT

- Contact information: A way for potential clients to contact the sales teams. Clear expectations need to be set on the timelines within which potential clients will be contacted.
- Ease of navigation: The corporate website should be clear and easy to navigate and search for specific content.
- Multi-cultural: Clients access most websites from across the globe. The sites should therefore reflect the multi-cultural nature of the vendor.
- Language and scripts: Many IT companies, especially those based in Asian countries, have not invested in good editing capabilities for the content on their website. The lack of quality, incorrect grammar and spelling, verbose statements, and clichés reflect poorly on the company.
- SEO optimisation: The corporate website needs to be optimised for most search engines to include keywords.
- Security and social media integration: IT services companies offer these as services to their clients. Clients therefore expect that vendors should have implemented these basics on their own websites.
- Mobile ready: Clients access websites through mobile and tablets. The site needs to be optimised for multiple devices.
- CRM integration: Most modern corporate websites are integrated into the corporate CRM software.
- Currency: The website needs to be current and relevant.
- IP tracking and Google analytics to capture and analyse website traffic.

Websites form a vital part of the demand generation process. While the attributes described earlier are the basic requirements, vendors use several techniques to generate leads by capturing visitor information from their websites. For a visitor to access any of the following, they are required to input their contact details. This information flows directly to the sales CRM.

- Inclusion of white papers and technical documents
- Calculators: Return of Investment (RoI) calculators, pricing calculators, calculators to determine efficiency gains, etc.
- Videos from industry experts
- Offers for consulting.

IT product companies integrate their entire sales process to their corporate websites. Clients, especially small and medium enterprises, can complete a product purchase through the website.

In addition to corporate websites, vendors have to establish a presence on social media platforms such as LinkedIn, Twitter, Instagram, and Facebook.

MARKETING AND SALES ENABLEMENT

Telemarketing: Telemarketing has traditionally been used by IT companies to generate leads. Most companies have set up inside sales teams mainly in offshore locations, both insourced and outsourced, to assist in lead generation. However, the effectiveness of telemarketing as a lead generation source is reducing. Clients are getting inundated with such calls and blocking or ignoring them. Some best practices used by telemarketing teams include:

- Start a campaign with an email or social media message (e.g. LinkedIn), providing an introduction to the company and its offerings.
- Follow up with a call and refer to the email/message.
- Have well-defined templates for the first email and each of the follow-up calls.
- Have a clear "call to action" for each of the contact points. For example, the call-to-action on the first call could include offering to send some additional information and setting up a follow-up call with a local salesperson. The second call's call to action could consist of introducing the onshore sales personnel, going through the information, and scheduling a face-to-face meeting.
- Clients tend to avoid reading messages or receiving calls close to weekends and holidays. Most telemarketing activities are therefore best scheduled Tuesday to Thursday of a week.
- If there is no response from a prospect, add their contacts to the drip-marketing list.

A sample telemarketing plan is provided in Figure 7.7.

Drip Marketing and Newsletters: Drip marketing is a less intrusive form of marketing and is used in addition to email campaigns. Relevant emails to the target audience are sent at pre-scheduled intervals. The intervals can

Steps	Action Items
1	– Business proposal email sent (Via Mail merge Process by the pre-sales Team) – Emails which get reverts are dealt accordingly.
2	– Three Call attempts made to reach out to the Right Party Contact (RPC) – Calls where discussions are started are converted into appointments and handed over to Sales lead
3	– Voice Mail along with the First follow-up mailer sent to the leads where we have not been able to initiate the discussion. – Emails which get reverts are dealt accordingly.
4	– Four Call attempts made to reach out to the RPC. – Calls where discussions are started are dealt accordingly. – Contacts where we still are not able to reach RPC, we send a second follow up mailer coping the owner of the lead as a final attempt
5	– Lead for positive responses handed over to the US Salesperson.
Next Step	– Companies where there has been no revert will be used for the drip marketing purposes or carried forward to the next Batch – One follow up email will be sent once a month to companies put into drip marketing campaign.

Figure 7.7 Sample telemarketing campaign

be purely time-dependent or based on specific triggers. In time-based drip marketing, messages are biweekly or monthly. Trigger-based drip marketing is targeted at sales prospects, and the messaging varies based on the stage they are at in the sales cycle. Every stage change triggers a new set of messages. In the sales process, there are long gaps where clients take time to move the process along. Drip marketing is an important tool to keep connected with the client during these gaps. Drip marketing provides several benefits:

- Keeps the brand relevant with current clients, prospects, potential clients, and clients who have dropped out of the sales process (or gone to the competition)
- Provides the sales personnel talking points by referring to the last set of messages
- Informs the receiver about the latest developments or new offerings.

Drip marketing can also be substituted with newsletters that serve the same purpose. For drip marketing to be efficient, the messaging needs to be targeted, the content should be concise and easy to read, and there should be calls to action such as "contact us for more information."

Advertising: While the primary purpose of advertising and sponsorships is brand-building, it is used for direct demand generation as well. Advertising can be online or offline and targeted or generic. Most advertisements, be it online banner ads or billboards at airports, have a means for the reader to connect back with the vendor (for example, a QR code). Some of the common forms of digital advertising include:

Pay-per-click (PPC): This is a form of SEM activity where an advertisement is displayed when specific keywords are searched. The advertiser pays for the ad only if the reader clicks on the link.

Display ads: These are advertisements that appear on targeted websites with messages. These ads are more visually appealing than PPC and used for brand building.

The marketing team works closely with the sales teams to integrate all these elements into a marketing plan. An illustrative list of activities is provided in Figure 7.8.

7.5.5 Enabling the client decision-making process

As outlined in the previous section, the marketing function works closely with the sales team to help a client along the decision-making process. Figure 7.9 provides an illustrative view of the roles played by various functions in a vendor firm, keeping the vendor competitive during the sales process.

MARKETING AND SALES ENABLEMENT

Initiatives	Key Programs
Market Opportunity Analysis & Program Development	• Market planning to identify revenue opportunities in defined geographic regions • Develop target lists & establish coordinated contact strategy for greater impact
Brand Awareness	• Print & digital media • Website & Microsite development & maintenance • Industry specific marketing campaigns • Content Marketing & Thought Leadership / Social Media • Event marketing to drive awareness
Demand Generation	• Targeted lead generation calling campaigns – concept specific • Direct marketing programs (Print & Digital) • Development of Reverse RFPs • SEO & Search Engine Marketing • Assisted sales via the Online Store for low end of the market
Strategic Partnerships & Alliances	• Identify new channel partners • Develop executive referral program • Build relationships with industry influencers
Marketing Communications	• Print & online advertising • Direct mail & Email marketing • Website development (Corporate Website & Microsites) • Collateral development (flyers, case studies, white papers) • Video testimonials – "Voice of the Customer" • Public Relations • Conferences, Events & Sponsorships • Grassroots Marketing

Figure 7.8 Marketing plan activities

Buying Process Stage	Vendor Engagement	Responsibility
Need Recognition	In B2B, pro-actively provide "free consulting" to help prospects recognise their need Provide white-papers This consulting can be packaged as a value added service	Sales, Marketing, Consulting
Need is qualified	Help draw up specifications for the need. Interact with all decisions makers	Sales, Consulting
Search for suppliers/products	Drip-Marketing to ensure that vendor is are top of mind	Marketing
Evaluation of suppliers	Participate in the RFP process Product Demos	Sales, Marketing
Buying Decision	Provide sales collateral that will help in decision making process	Sales, Marketing
Post purchase evaluation	Conduct customer satisfaction surveys	Quality, Operations

Figure 7.9 Role of marketing along the buying process

7.5.6 *Bridging the information gap with a sales toolkit*

This section deals with the knowledge gap between operations teams and senior leadership, on the one hand, and the sales teams, on the other hand. Senior management and operations leadership spend considerable time in strategy formulation and the development and marketing of products and

171

services. They are deeply involved in the entire conceptualisation of service, pricing, value proposition, etc. Once a product or service has been developed, it is transferred to the sales personnel and channel partners, with some basic training and a few sales collaterals. More time is spent on discussing incentives and commissions for the new service than the service itself. It is assumed that sales personnel know how to sell and they do not need much information to start selling. This is the biggest fallacy in the sales of new services.

One of the key marketing roles is to create a detailed training and communication plan and sales toolkit for both existing and new services. Table 7.1 provides a comprehensive checklist for a sales toolkit.

While marketing teams must develop all the collateral provided in this checklist, product demos and prototypes are becoming more important than presentations in the digital world. Digital technologies such as virtual reality, 3-D printing, and computer-aided design have allowed for early-stage prototyping of products and platforms. Product and service demonstrations are becoming a norm, even in the early stages of a sales cycle.

7.6 Industry research and analysis

The marketing team also performs the role of tracking the IT industry and the industries in which its clients operate. While the former is useful for the vendor to develop its internal strategy, the latter is used to build value propositions for its clients. This is an ongoing activity, and the process of collecting and processing data is similar for both purposes.

Step 1: Data collection from various sources, including:

- Industry bodies like the National Association of Software Services Companies (NASSCOM) in India. Similar industry bodies for IT providers would be available in all major countries.
- Industry-specific associations for target industries.
- Global bodies such as the World Bank, IFCI, etc.
- Web search and Google Scholar search.
- Reports from consulting organizations such as Gartner, Euromonitor, etc.
- Traditional sources: Customer surveys, sales team interactions, interactions at conferences and meetings, etc.
- Win–loss analysis.
- Primary market research.

The marketing team needs to set up a structured process for data collection and research. The tools for CRM and knowledge management discussed in the next section are integral to these processes.

MARKETING AND SALES ENABLEMENT

Table 7.1 Components of a sales toolkit

Sales Material	Suggested Stage	Content
Introductory email	Prospecting	Email introducing the company and product
Follow-up mail	Prospecting	Follow-up to earlier mail seeking an appointment
Elevator speech	First meeting/ conferences/ exhibitions	A short introduction used to open face-to-face dialogue
NDA	Initial meetings	Standard mutual non-disclosure agreement (NDA)
About company	Initial meetings	Brochure and presentation about the company, its history, product range, management team, etc.
Qualifying questionnaire	Deal qualification in early meetings	High-level questionnaire to assess prospects needs and qualify prospects as potential clients
About product	Initial meetings	Brochure and presentation— Attachment to "About company". To be sent once a client's product needs are assessed.
FAQs (external)	Ongoing	Available on website and in written form for easing the sales process
Value proposition	Advanced meetings	Why is your company's product better?
Case studies	Advanced meetings	Case studies of other clients for the same or similar products
White papers	Advanced meetings	Technical white papers on products
Product demo	Advanced meetings	Live demonstration of product— onsite or video
Technical documents	Late stage	Detailed product specifications
Implementation guidelines	Late stage	High-level implementation timelines, plans, and dependencies
References	Late stage	Actual calls/meeting with current clients
Pricing	Late stage	Broad pricing guidelines with negotiation ranges and clearly defined hierarchy for approvals for further negotiations
Contract template	Late stage	Sample contract format
Proof of concept	Late stage	A document that outlines how a proof of concept can be created
Website/digital presence	Ongoing	For prospects to seek information

(*Continued*)

Table 7.1 (Continued)

Sales Material	Suggested Stage	Content
Client wins/ PR releases	Ongoing drip marketing	To send to prospects continuously to remain top of mind
Sales rewards	Early stage (internal)	Commission and bonus structure for the sales team
Referral program	Early stage (internal)	Program for sales personnel to bring on channel partners—guidelines and reward structure
Sales targets	Early-stage (internal)	Targets by product/region/sales personnel
FAQs (internal)	Early-stage (internal)	List of potential FAQs from prospects along with responses
Objection handling	Early-stage (internal)	Potential objections that can be raised by prospects and responses

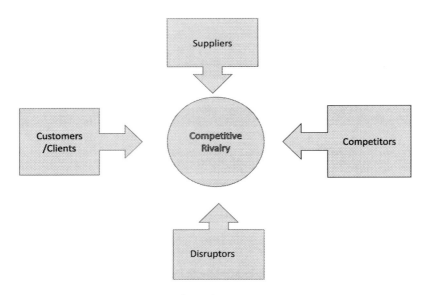

Figure 7.10 Porter's Five Forces (adapted)

Step 2: Analysis of data.

Several factors make up for an external environment. Michael Porter's Five Forces (Porter, 1979) is a well-known framework for industry analysis. Figure 7.10 is an adaptation of the model.

MARKETING AND SALES ENABLEMENT

Some of the questions which help in performing this analysis include:

Customers/Clients

- Who are the clients?
- What are the various industry segments which the clients operate in?
- Which of these segments are growing, and which are not?
- What have been the recent trends related to IT acquisition?
- Are clients expected to consume more or less of the IT vendor's services? What factors will determine this?
- What value propositions are clients seeking?
- How price-sensitive are clients? What is their buying behaviour?
- What factors do clients value in the vendor's products/services?
- Who is their benchmark vendor?

Competitors

- Who are the competitors?
- Are these start-ups or established companies?
- What differentiates the vendor from its competitors?
- What are the company's weaknesses when compared to its competitors?
- Which countries are the vendor's competitors from? Is this expected to change?

Disruptions

- What technology disruptions are expected in the client's industry?
- What business model disruptions are expected?
- Who are the early-stage disruptors in the industry (but possibly not scaled)?
- How will these disruptions change the industry?

Suppliers

- What are the key resources required for the growth of the company?
- Are the right quality and quantity of resources available?
- What steps does the company need to take to overcome any shortfalls?
- What resources are differentiators? (For example, access to specific skills, global delivery locations, etc.)

In most large vendors, marketing departments publish weekly and monthly research reports. One set of reports focuses on the IT industry and its changing landscape and is consumed by senior management. The other reports are specific to the clients and their industries and are disseminated to the marketing, sales, and account management teams. These reports are used to develop client and product strategies.

In addition to determining products and service strategies, the market information discussed in the previous section is used to develop the Features-Advantages-Benefits (FAB) matrix for the vendor's offerings (FAB).

Features are the distinctive attribute of the offering and are quantitative. For example, a vendor may state that they have six operating centres worldwide and 2,000 employees with digital skills.

Advantages are what these features do and how they help. Using the previous example, the vendor's global operations will provide its clients access to skills, scale, and have a "follow the sun" development cycle.

Benefits describe the result of the advantage. For example, access to skills around the globe will help clients increase the speed of the product development cycle and get ahead of their competitors.

Vendor management teams typically focus on features, while operations teams focus on advantages, and senior management on benefits.

7.7 Use of collaborative technology

In Section 7.5.4, we have covered all the necessary tools required for digital marketing. This section focuses on the most widely used IT applications to manage efficient sales, pre-sales, and marketing processes.

CRM: CRM software is the backbone of the sales and marketing process. Several enterprise and cloud-based platforms are available in the market. Oracle Siebel, Sugar CRM, Salesforce, and Zoho are some popular CRM applications in the IT industry. Though modern-day CRMs have multiple features and are being frequently upgraded, the essential CRM features are:

Contact Management: List of all contacts (current and potential clients). The module can manage multiple contacts with an organisation and their roles.

Interaction Tracking: Tracking of all interactions with a client across multiple channels. These could be emails, voice calls, or social media–based interactions.

Lead Management: Tracking of all leads by funnel stage (see Figure 7.2).

Campaign Management: Developing and executing various sales campaigns directly from the CRM.

Salesforce Management: Ability to manage diverse and geographically distributed salesforce, performance monitoring, lead management, and reporting.

Drip Marketing: Automated drip marketing with email integration.

Revenue Forecasting: Forecasting of revenue based on sales pipeline and probability of closure.

MARKETING AND SALES ENABLEMENT

Case Management: This feature is typically required to manage existing clients. All complaints and queries are logged, organised, and tracked using the CRM. This is different from the defect tracking tool used by the operation team of the buyer.

Knowledge base: FAQ, troubleshooting steps, and knowledge base to resolve customer issues.

Reporting: Various sales reports to manage the effectiveness of campaigns, salesforce, and case management.

Most CRMs are modular, and vendors can choose to implement one or more of the modules. Some of the standard modules include sales, marketing, and customer management.

Knowledge Management (KM): KM is a discipline that promotes an integrated approach to all of an enterprise's knowledge assets including (Duhon, 1998):

- Identifying,
- Capturing,
- Evaluating,
- Retrieving, and
- Sharing

While most sales CRMs have a KM module, clients do implement separate KM platforms as well. These platforms have application programming interfaces (APIs) to integrate with the most popular CRMs seamlessly.

In the sales and marketing context, KM plays a vital role in bridging the gap between the product, marketing, and sales teams. These are the repositories of all information required by the sales team in effectively closing a sales deal. Some of the essential features of good KM software include:

- Ability to handle multiple formats (including documents, videos, demos, etc.)
- Searchability
- Version control
- Tagging
- User-based access and easy remote access
- Collaboration.

On a high level, organisation knowledge can be grouped into three categories:

- Facts: project metrics; profitability, estimate vs. actuals (time and cost), bugs (H-M-L); status of the past opportunities
- Information: competition, clients, solutions, processes, frameworks, methodologies
- Harvested assets: solution, proposal, project documents of past projects without mention of the client.

MARKETING AND SALES ENABLEMENT

A detailed breakdown of the organisational knowledge assets would include (but are not limited to):

- Proposal documents
- Documents such as corporate and practice PowerPoints
- Collaterals—brochures, flyers, videos
- White papers/industry point of view
- Case studies/client references
- Project plans
- Business intelligence
- Competitive analysis
- Client analysis
- Code and other programming objects
- Best practices/project lessons learned
- Patents and trademark certificates
- Metrics used for estimation.

In large IT organisations, KM tools play an important role in seamlessly integrating global teams. As mentioned earlier, the KM tools have vast repositories of information about people, process, and technology. Specifically, from a sales and marketing perspective, they provide access to reusable templates, client strategies, deal presentations, pricing strategies, win–loss analysis, etc. Other than using these assets, the sales and bid teams are expected to upload their documents and learnings (after removing client-sensitive information) for future reference.

Proposal and Contract Management Software: Software such as Deal Hub focuses on the request for proposal (RFP), request for quotation (RFQ), and contracting processes. These software have response templates for standard RFPs, features to generate quotes based on client specifications, and managing the contract negotiation interaction process. Like KMs, most standard sales CRMs have modules to manage proposals and contracts. However, these third-party specialist software products can also be integrated back to core CRMs.

7.8 Chapter highlights

- This chapter highlights the importance of the marketing team in an IT organisation and the symbiotic relationship with the sales team.
- Marketing plays a lead role in product management activities.
- While product management has always been critical in a software product company, it has only recently become more important in an IT services company.
- The second critical role of marketing is in demand generation, where it works closely with the sales team to support demand generation through a range of activities.

MARKETING AND SALES ENABLEMENT

- Marketing teams are responsible for brand building, competition tracking, client industry tracking, website management, and other activities integral to the client acquisition and management process.
- Software, including CRM, KM, deal management, and contract management, enable the sales and marketing process.
- These software products are modular and have inbuilt and pre-designed best practices.

7.10 Questions for discussion

1 What are three roles played by marketing in an IT organisation? Describe each of the three roles.
2 How is social media influencing marketing activities? Describe the two most used social media platforms in demand generation.
3 What are some of the key technologies used in the marketing functions of technology companies?
4 What are Features-Advantages-Benefits? Explain with an example from the IT industry.
5 India is home to a large number of IT companies, but they lag behind in branding compared to their global peers such as IBM, Accenture, Oracle, and Cap Gemini. How can you help them in developing their brand globally?

Notes

1 www.ces.tech/
2 www.money2020.com/

7.11 References

Ansoff, H. I. (1957). Strategies for diversification. *Harvard Business Review*, 35(5), 113–124.
Duhon, B. (1998, September). It's all in our heads. *Inform*, 12(8), 8–13.
Miller, R., and Heiman, S. (1985). *Strategic selling* (pp. 97–98). New York: Miller Heiman Associates Inc., Time Warner Books.
Porter, M. E. (1979). How competitive forces shape strategy. In *Readings in strategic management* (pp. 133–143). London: Palgrave Macmillan.
Wind, Y., and Webster, F. E. (1972). On the study of industrial buying behavior: Current practices and future trends. *Industrial Marketing Management*, 1(4), 411–416.

8

LEADING WITH DIGITAL

8.1 Learning objectives

Chapter 8 provides an overview of how the technology industry is evolving rapidly. By the end of the chapter, a reader will be able to:

1   Understand digital transformation and its importance
2   Get an overview of digital technologies influencing businesses
3   Understand the impact of digital technologies on the IT selling process
4   Learn about the newer products and services enabled by digital technologies
5   Understand the changing profiles of both sellers and buyers in the digital world.

8.2 Introduction

The development of steam and gasoline-fired engines and the invention of electricity and telephones have been game-changing events in human history. The Internet evolved 30 years ago, and the world experienced more changes than in all of history combined during this period. Earlier, these events took place decades apart, if not centuries. Now the game-changing events take place only a few years apart. Mobile phones, satellite positioning systems, collaboration tools, and cloud are all examples of interventions that have brought structural changes in modern lives and work.

The world is once again at an inflection point where digital technologies are helping develop new solutions and new frameworks that can transform firm's business models.

This chapter defines digital transformation and then provides an overview of a few of the important digital technologies and associated business models. The chapter also discusses the changes in the IT selling process brought about by greater adoption of digital technologies.

180   DOI: 10.4324/9781003155270-9

8.3 Digital transformation

Digital strategies and digital transformation are occupying a significant mindshare of boards and CXOs of companies. It is therefore important to understand these terms and their impact on a company.

There are several definitions of digital strategies. However, one of the more comprehensive, yet simple, definitions used in academic literature is as follows:

> Organizational strategy formulated and executed by leveraging digital resources to create differential value.
> (Bharadwaj, El Sawy, Pavlou, and Venkatraman, 2013)

Digital transformation is change brought about by adopting digital strategies. Digital transformation started with technology firms and is rapidly being adopted across all industry segments. At that same time, given the vastness of the field, companies are confused about how to transform themselves for the digital age. Digital transformation is not just about implementing technology or solving discrete business issues (Kane, Palmer, Phillips, Kiron, and Buckley, 2015). Digital transformation encompasses strategy changes, business model changes, process changes, and organisational changes.

Intense competition, entry of global players, disruption in business models, and increased customer demands are forcing companies to rethink the role of technology across their operations. To remain competitive in turbulent business environments, companies are looking at digital transformation to provide them with dynamic capabilities.

Senior managers often confuse automation (digitisation) with digitalisation or digital transformation. Digitisation is simply about a manual process being automated, which can be part of the overall digital transformation. On the other hand, digitalisation is about strategy changes enabled by digital technologies. A simple example to understand the difference between the two is given next.

Evolution of Watches: Until the 1980s, watches were primarily analogue. Their primary function was to tell time. However, analogue watches had mechanical moving parts that deteriorated over time. They had limited functionality and were not very accurate. In the 1980s, the entire watch industry was digitised. These digital watches were far more accurate and had no moving parts. Soon they offered other functionality like a stopwatch and dual time. The market for analogue watches eventually shrank, and digital watches gained the majority market share. By the early 2010s, the next wave of watches called "smart watches" started to appear. Using the latest technologies like global positioning system (GPS) and sensors, they offered a lot more than a better way of telling time. In addition to all the features of digital watches, smartwatches could sync with various devices, measure physical activities, and measure health parameters. They stored the data in the cloud and provided analytics on an individual's life. They became the hub of all other devices that an individual owned. The move from digital to smartwatches is a good example of digitalisation.

8.4 Digital technologies

Digital technologies are simply technologies that use microprocessors to process, store, or transmit data. While digital technologies have been widely used since the 1980s, the term is now being used to describe the newer technologies that have emerged in the last decade. There is no clear definition or classification of the newer digital technologies. However, there is broad consensus that these technologies perform three functions in a company.

First, they provide the basic infrastructure on which a company operates. This includes hardware, networking, and storage. The second function is to enable a company and its processes to become more efficient. Enterprise resource planning (ERP) software, accounting software, and process automation are some examples of the second category. Finally, digital technologies allow a company to provide its customers greater value through product or business model innovation. Social media, collaboration tools, portals, and mobile apps are some examples of this category.

Many of the newer digital technologies enable multiple benefits for a company depending on their application. For example, Internet of Things (IoT) can be an integral part of a company's infrastructure and help in enhancing customer value. Similarly, mobile technologies can be both an infrastructural and customer value enabler. Due to the considerable investment in digital technologies, we can observe even faster commoditisation and time-to-market of these technologies (Urbach and Röglinger, 2019). To structure the field of these digital technologies and enablers such as associated business models, we have used a variant of the enterprise architecture model consisting of five layers proposed by Urbach and Röglinger (2019), shown in Figure 8.1. The five layers are infrastructure, data and information, application and analytics, business process, and business model. The technologies discussed in this chapter are not exhaustive but form a large portion of what are considered to be newer digital technologies.

8.4.1 Infrastructure

Network and storage are two crucial elements that enable digital transformation. While digital technologies like artificial intelligence have existed for many decades, it is only the recent advancement in network speeds, storage capacities, and processing power that has made these technologies mainstream. Three "laws" best describe these three phenomena.

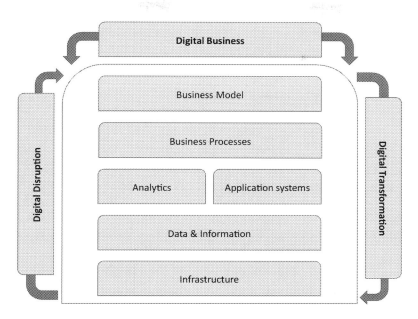

Figure 8.1 Structuring the field of digital technologies
Source: Urbach and Röglinger, 2019

Moore's Law: Gordon Moore, the co-founder of Intel Corporation, stated in 1965 that the number of transistors on a microchip would double about every two years, though the cost of computers will halve (Schaller, 1997). This observation is often referred to as Moore's Law and describes the exponential growth of processing power. The law held true for over 40 years. It is only around 2018 that this exponential growth started to slow down due to thermal limitations, i.e. the ability to dissipate the heat generated by such densely packed microchips effectively.

Butters' Law: According to Gerald Butters, the former head of Lucent's Optical Networking Group at Bell Labs (Roser and Ritchie, 2013), the amount of data coming out of optical fibres will double every nine months. Thus, the cost of transmitting a bit over an optical network will decrease by half every nine months. As the world moved from coppers lines to fibre optics and then to mobile 4G and 5G, this law has made a tremendous impact on industries such as telecom, media, entertainment, and others. As 5G rolls in, the next wave of industries and technologies are likely to get disrupted.

Kryder's Law: Propounded by Mark Kryder of Seagate Technologies (Kryder, 2009), Kryder's Law is the assumption that disk drive density will double every 13 months. Since the introduction of the disk drive in 1956, the density of information it can record has increased from 2,000 bits to 100 billion bits (gigabits), fitted into one square inch. That represents a 50-million-fold increase.

This combination of increasing computing speeds, cheaper storage, and faster transmission has led to greater adoption of existing technologies and the development of several new technologies.

8.4.1.1 Data storage

Data storage is the use of recording media to retain data using computers or other devices. There are many types of storage.

Direct attached storage (DAS) is directly attached to a device and not connected through a network. DAS could also be an internal or external hard drive of a laptop, or a thumb drive attached to a computer.

Network-attached storage (NAS) is another type of storage. There are three basic components associated with NAS. First, NAS needs connectivity to the Internet and a local area network (LAN). Second, it has multiple hard drives attached to the network. Third, the hard drives must be configured in a Redundant Array of Independent Disks (RAID) configuration—hard drives set up to replicate the data in various ways.

Block storage is a technology used to store data files on storage area networks (SANs) or cloud-based storage environments. Block storage breaks up data into blocks and stores those blocks as separate pieces, each with a unique identifier. A hard drive is a common type of block storage.

Another storage option is **object storage**. Object storage has objects rather than files or blocks. By adding comprehensive metadata to the file, this type of storage eliminates the need for the tiered file structures. All files are stored in a flat address space, called a storage pool.

Cloud storage is a service model in which data are transmitted, managed, stored, and backed up on remote storage systems. Users typically access cloud storage through the Internet or a network. Cloud providers typically charge end users a subscription fee based on data stored. The three main cloud-based storage models are public, private, and hybrid. Cloud is covered separately in Chapter 9.

8.4.1.2 Networks

Networking is a vast area but can be broadly classified into wired and wireless networks.

Wired networks use physical cables to transfer data between different devices and computer systems. In a small, wired network, a single router may be used to connect all the computers. More extensive networks often involve multiple routers or switches that connect to each other.

Wireless networks are computer networks that use wireless data connections between network nodes. Examples of wireless networks include cell phone networks, wireless local area networks (WLANs), wireless sensor networks, satellite communication networks, and terrestrial microwave networks. A mobile phone has become the most ubiquitous hardware device used by customers to interact with the Internet and businesses. Therefore, it has become essential for all companies to offer mobile applications, e-commerce, and mobile payments. Incorporating tools such as GPS, QR code scanning, and messaging has allowed several new mobile applications to emerge.

ADVANCEMENTS IN NETWORKS

We have identified three technologies that will form the future of networks.

5G: The fifth generation of telecom networks, also known as 5G, brings improved speed and battery life to smartphones. This technology will also fuel the growth of fixed wireless for residences and offices. 5G speeds will range from 10 to 100 times faster than 4G. 5G will support all communication needs from low-power LANs to wide area networks (WANs), with the right speed and latencies. Beyond speed improvement, 5G is expected to lead to the exponential growth of the IoT-based systems.

Wi-Fi 6: Also called 802.11ax, this technology represents the next-generation protocols and brings a significant improvement in efficiency across all existing Wi-Fi bands. Wi-Fi 6 will enhance the density of devices that can coexist in a small space, further increasing all devices' speed. Wi-Fi 6 is expected to improve almost all wireless users' experience, from office workers to home users. The higher speed, reliability, and higher density will allow Wi-Fi 6 to enable life-safety applications, including remote surgery devices.

Wi-Fi 6 and 5G will coexist as critical wireless technologies for the enterprise.

SDN-WAN: This stands for software-defined networking (SDN) in a wide area network (WAN). Corporate networks have been based around centralised control, routing, and security. All network traffic has been traditionally routed back to the primary data centre, where security applications like firewalls are present. A software-defined WAN eliminates the need for this centralisation by decentralising the rules for info-security. Basically, it decouples the networking hardware from its control mechanism. This allows networks to be more efficient, less expensive, and improves the performance of applications.

8.4.1.3 Internet of Things

In addition to the network and storage, IoT is an integral part of any company's digital infrastructure. The term is used to describe the phenomenon of connecting the Web to physical objects or devices by deploying devices with embedded identification, sensing, and data transmission capabilities. Next, we have briefly described these devices.

DEVICES

These electronic devices contain sensors that actively watch and measure the values of variables they are designed to manage. The data from these sensors are converted to a suitable digital format that can be transmitted to another system. In addition, these devices have actuators that can perform tasks when instructed by another machine.

A device incorporates everything that is deployed away from the control centres at remote and distributed sites. It is a self-sufficient system with a power source and connection to the Internet or an intranet with a suitable protocol. The devices can also perform tasks based on instructions received from a remote-control centre. We have explained different types of sensors next.

Location sensors: The radio signal receivers on the earth attached to a device capture signals from location-sensing satellites. By combining data on the distance and angles of the radio signal from several satellites, the device calculates its location on earth.

Voice recognition: Speech in the form of continuously moving sound waves is captured and sampled at a high rate to be converted to digital format.

Chemical sensing: Chemical sensing is like tasting. To sense or detect a chemical, another chemical is made to react with it. This arrangement can be used to detect toxic leaks from industries.

Health sensors: Simple devices to monitor health parameters like blood sugar and blood pressure that can be used by non-professionals. These provide reasonably precise readings.

8.4.2 Data and information

The enterprise information systems (such as customer relationship management [CRM], payment systems), machines (IoT), and humans (employees and consumers) create data. With the rapid advent of mobile technology and social media, the volume and variety of data are growing rapidly. There are several ways to classify data; we have mentioned a few of them here.

Primary data: These data are collected directly from its source and usually are customized for a specific research or project. Primary data are often managed through structured and unstructured questionnaires explicitly designed for a project. Primary data collection is costly and time-consuming, hence not always recommended.

Secondary data: These are data that have been collected by a third party in the past or are available on any platform but made available for others to use. Industry growth data, gross domestic product (GDP) data, and demographic data based on a census are some examples of secondary data.

Structured data: This type of data consists of numbers and values and can be stored in traditional databases. It describes things in easily measurable terms. Examples include customer satisfaction rating or sales data. Most of the data generated by enterprise IT systems are structured data. The volume of structured data is less, but it is associated with higher quality and lower noise.

Unstructured data: These data do not conform to a pre-defined data model and cannot be stored in existing databases. The social media platforms and connected machines (IoT) are primary sources of unstructured data. The generation of unstructured data in today's world is much higher than structured data, which has created new challenges for organisations. The primary examples of unstructured data are texts in the form of online reviews, comments, descriptions available on social media platforms, and the Web. The unstructured data also contain social media network or relationship data, image, video, and logs from machines.

Due to the emergence of large volumes of unstructured data, the concept of "Big Data" has received significant attention recently. As per Gartner, Big Data involves complex datasets (due to high volume, high variety, and high velocity), which are difficult to store, process, and analyse using traditional data processing tools and applications.

An example of Big Data is data collected on parameters such as weather conditions, wind speed, and resistance of an aircraft on a specific flight path. As these data are collected at short intervals, over thousands of miles, across many flights that use the same flight path, the volume of data collected is vast and continuously growing.

The key characteristics of Big Data are often described by the "5Vs".

Volume: Big Data involves large volumes of data from various sources, including business transactions, smart (IoT) devices, social media, and more.

Velocity: The proliferation of newer data sources like IoT, radiofrequency identification (RFID) tags, smart tags, and QR codes has resulted in data that, in near real time, needs to be analysed and decisions promptly taken.

Variety: As discussed earlier in the section, data come in all types of formats. This includes primary and secondary data, structured data and unstructured data, social media data, etc.

Variability: Data flows and their speeds are changing often and vary greatly.

Veracity: Data come from multiple sources and need to be verified before being used. Data need to be cleaned, deduplicated, and linked across multiple systems. The data quality problems also arise due to the prevalence of fake reviews on social media, the emergence of social bots, and difficulty in pre-processing a large amount of unstructured data.

Next, we have discussed the complexity of pre-processing data before it can be used for model building.

Data processing

The raw data from multiple sources are processed before analysis. Data processing can be divided into two activities: data cleansing and data transformation.

Data cleansing

Once the previous step is completed, the data may be incomplete, contain duplicates, or contain errors. Data cleansing is the process of correcting these errors. Cleansing includes record matching, identifying inaccuracies, and deduplication. The techniques of cleaning and processing of unstructured text data have matured. Effective cleaning and pre-processing also help in feature reduction of text data, which is important for better model building using machine learning techniques.

Data transformation

Data transformation is the process of converting cleansed data from one structure into another format or structure. This transformation can be both manual and automated or a combination. Tools and technologies used for data transformation vary based on the structure, complexity, and volume of the data being transformed. In data transformation, multiple variables may be combined, or continuous data can be converted into categorical variable.

In a traditional data warehouse, pre-processing is done before storing the data for further analysis. The process is expensive and often leads to loss of information. In case of a large volume of unstructured data, raw data is often stored directly in a data lake. The analytical applications perform specific pre-processing (cleaning and transformation) based on their own requirements prior to model building or other analysis.

8.4.3 Applications and algorithm

Some of the key applications and analytical algorithms that form the backbone of a digital organization are described next. The specific technology discussed is blockchain; we have also described the key concepts associated with analytics.

8.4.3.1 Blockchain

Blockchain is a decentralised database in which unrelated parties can share a digital history and reach consensus, without an intermediary. It was first introduced in 2009 with its first application, Bitcoin. Blockchain is in its early stages of implementation but growing rapidly. According to a Gartner study, blockchain-based applications will grow to slightly more than $176 billion in business value by 2025.

Blockchain consists of a series of time-stamped immutable data records that are managed by multiple computers owned by different entities. Each of these blocks of data is secured and networked to each other through cryptography. Each block contains a hash to differentiate it from the previous block. It also includes a timestamp and transaction data. Altering the data in any block requires changing all subsequent blocks. This change requires consensus from a majority of the network, thus preventing tampering by any individual or group. The benefits of using blockchain are highlighted in Figure 8.2.

There are several types of blockchain as outlined in Table 8.1. We have also mentioned consensus mechanisms used for validation in each case.

There was a high interest in public blockchains in the initial years, as they demonstrated complete disintermediation and digitisation of trust. However, in recent years the focus has moved away to "enterprise blockchains". These networks provide an entirely new customer experience and fulfil the unmet needs of the enterprise and end customers.

Enterprise blockchains are like private clouds in the cloud industry. The ring-fencing of technology helps enterprises accomplish their security and control objectives.

Enterprise blockchains offer several advantages:

- Scalability: With a smaller set of nodes and different consensus mechanism, Hyperledger can run up to 4000 TPS versus Ethereum's 7 TPS.
- Trusted members: All the network participants are known, decreasing the risks of network attacks and network takeovers.

Immutability	Transparency	Security	Traceability
Data stored cannot be altered	Business can track every system detail	High level cryptography algorithms	To prevent fraudulent activities

Figure 8.2 Benefits of blockchain

LEADING WITH DIGITAL

Table 8.1 Types of blockchain

Type	Description	Consensus Mechanism	Examples
Public, permissioned	Anyone who meets specific predefined criteria can download the protocol and validate the transactions.	Proof of stake	Sovrin (for digital identities), EOS, and Ripple
Public, permissionless	Anyone can download the protocol and validate the transactions.	Proof of work	Bitcoin and Ethereum networks
Private, permissioned	Only members of the consortium can validate the transactions.	Voting or multi-party consensus	IBM Food Trust, IBM Trade Lens, Hyperledger Fabric
Private, permissionless	Anyone in the private network can participate in the validation of the transactions	Federated Byzantine agreement	Holochain, LTO Network, and Monet

- Privacy: Only trusted members can access and write data to ensure privacy.
- Easier governance and policy enforcement: Rules are easier to change and implement compared to public blockchains.
- No cryptocurrency: No cryptocurrencies are involved, as there is no reward requirement in a network with all the participants known.
- Easier fault intervention: Faults can quickly be fixed through manual intervention since the consensus algorithms offer finality with close to "instant" confirmation time.
- Open to regulatory oversights: Enterprises collaborate with regulators and adhere to new laws such as General Data Protection Regulation (GDPR).

Several factors will encourage the further growth of private and permissioned blockchains.

- Industry collaboration and regulator push: Industry collaboration, solving business problems, and providing a differentiated customer experience are key to the adoption of these blockchains. In addition, push from the regulator also plays a pivotal role in accelerating adoption. In the absence of industry collaboration and regulator push, many blockchains will face "empty room" issues wherein tech is ready, but there are no users.

- Adoption at organisation level: Organisations can create private blockchains for their partners and suppliers and experience enhanced transparency, trust, and lower costs.

As mentioned earlier, blockchain is still in its early stage, and several factors need to be overcome to accelerate its usage.

- Trust and Reliability: Continual vetting of entities running the nodes is required to ensure they are trustworthy and reliable.
- Complexity: Managing the number of networks and managing updates to networks is critical.

Despite these deterrents, there have been large-scale implementations of blockchains because of its benefits in solving real-world problems.

According to a report by PwC (2018), several industries will benefit from blockchain. The largest and fastest impact will be on the financial services industry, followed by manufacturing and energy and utilities. International payments, trade finance, and settlements in capital markets transactions are key applications of blockchain in the financial services industry. Health records and managing land records are some other use cases for blockchain adoption by governments.

8.4.3.2 Analytics

This section covers recent developments in the field of analytics covering Big Data, artificial intelligence (AI) and machine learning (ML).

ARTIFICIAL INTELLIGENCE

The simplest definition of AI is the use of machines to simulate a human mind. Using complex algorithms, AI accelerates day-to-day tasks through automation and improved decision-making (Russell, Norvig, and Davis, 2010).

AI makes it possible for machines to perform human-like tasks by learning from experience and adjusting decision-making to new inputs. AI relies heavily on technologies such as deep learning and natural language processing. Computers can be trained to recognise patterns in data and accomplish specific but complex tasks using these technologies.

AI adoption generally passes through three phases of evolution.

Artificial narrow intelligence (ANI), also known as weak AI, is the basic building block of AI. It is about performing a tightly defined set of tasks. Most use cases of AI today, including Siri and Alexa, are examples of weak AI.

Artificial general intelligence (AGI), also known as strong AI, is the stage where machines will possess the ability to believe and make conclusions like human beings. Currently, there are no examples of strong AI.

Artificial super intelligence (ASI) is the stage where AI will completely mimic human beings.

TYPES OF ARTIFICIAL INTELLIGENCE

AI can be categorised into the following types:

Reactive Machines AI: This basic form of AI allows for a narrow range of predefined tasks. Reactive AI devices cannot form any inferences from past data, and perform activities purely based on the current situation and the available rules available. The IBM chess program is a good example of reactive AI.

Limited Memory AI: This type of AI will make educated and improved decisions by analysing past data available in its memory. This AI comes with temporary memory, which can store earlier experiences that influence future actions. Self-driving automobiles are a good example of this type of AI.

Theory of Mind AI: The theory of mind AI is a much more complex type of AI. These kinds of devices can comprehend human emotions and thoughts and utilise this knowledge in decision-making. The robot Sophia is an early example of theory of mind AI.

Self-aware AI: Self-aware AI involves machines that have human-level consciousness. This form of AI is not currently in existence but would be considered the most advanced form of AI known to man.

The machine learning concept is very tightly coupled with AI.

Machine Learning: ML is a type of AI where a computer system automatically learns from data and previous inputs without being programmed. There are three different categories of ML algorithms.

Supervised learning algorithms build a mathematical model based on a set of data referred to as training data. This data contains both the inputs and the desired outputs. This type of dataset is known as "labelled data", and it is often expensive and time-consuming to label large amounts of data for training. The most widely used supervised learning techniques are regression and multiple types of classification techniques such as logistic regression, decision tree, random forest, and others.

Unsupervised learning algorithms take a set of data that contains only inputs but no classified or labelled output. These algorithms find structure in the data without any external guidance. The most widely used unsupervised learning technique is clustering, which aims to organise unlabelled data items (e.g. data points, objects, images, audio, etc.) into similar groups. To be precise, a clustering solution provides a collection of data items categorised into different groups (clusters) such that a data item within a group is "similar" to data items in the same group but "dissimilar" to data items in other groups. Marketing managers use clustering to identify and define segments in their market. Unsupervised techniques are preferred in few cases, as raw data is cheap, but labelled data requires domain expertise and hence expensive.

Reinforcement learning: In reinforcement learning, there is uncertainty around both input and output variables; the algorithms also try to maximise the notion of cumulative reward. Markov chain and Markov decision processes are examples of reinforcement learning. One of the real-life examples of reinforcement learning is spell check functions in different text editors. Based on a wrongly typed text, the spell check provides a set of different values as a possible suggestion, instead of one single predicted value.

In addition to the categories of machine learning, we have further discussed three important concepts in the domain of AI and analytics.

Deep learning is a subset of machine learning that uses multiple types of information and gets closer to mimicking the human brain. The data can be a combination of voice, text, and visual and numerical data.

Natural language processing (NLP): NLP is a type of AI that use natural language to manage the interaction between computers and humans. NLP gives machines the ability to read, understand, and interpret human languages. NLP is being used extensively in areas such as marketing, finance, and healthcare, among others. Some examples of NLP are sentiment analysis of user-posted comments, and speech recognition, and analysis of clinical documentation. NLP also addresses the need for generating human-like languages from a computer, the application of the chatbot, Alexa (by Amazon).

Expert systems: An expert system is a computer program designed to solve complex problems and provide decision-making ability like a human expert (Jackson, 1986). It offers solutions to queries by combining its knowledge base with reasoning and inference rules. Expert systems were the first successful approach to AI and were developed as far back as 1970. The performance of an expert system is driven by the quality and quantity of knowledge stored in its knowledge base—the greater the knowledge stored in the system, the greater its performance. Expert systems are used extensively in the medical field in areas such as drug discovery and clinical diagnosis. Over the years, expert systems have migrated from a single domain to becoming components in areas such as process automation, where they help solve complex business logic.

8.4.4 Business process

To make the best use of digital technologies and abundance of data, organisations and governments need to automate, integrate, and improve cross-functional work routines spread over departments and the ecosystem (outside the organisational boundary). In the next section, we have described automation. Later, we have also described smart living, which covers process automation across multiple service providers with scope for continuous process improvement.

8.4.4.1 Automation

Process and industrial automation are the building blocks to implement a more advanced form of digital transformation. Automation is justified in several business contexts, a few of which are listed here.

Rote and repetitive tasks: Automation reduces manual work in tasks that need to be done repetitively, with a lower chance of human error. Assembly work on the manufacturing floor, automated inventory management, and billing are examples of repetitive tasks.

Document management: Business processes that range from purchase order and order processing to budget approvals can be automated through workflow software. This software reduces the need for the physical flow of paper.

Decision-making: Some types of decision-making can be automated through the building of rule-based software. An example of this is loan processing. A loan officer can input information collected from the borrower in an automated loan process and provide instant decisions. This process can include significant self-service activity by the customer.

Manual tasks that are risky or may cause injury: Automation such as unmanned trucks, unmanned aerial vehicles (UAVs), and robots can perform and report on many of these tasks that are risky to humans.

Sensor-based tracking and alerts: Companies are leveraging IoT devices such as sensors to achieve end-to-end visibility of business processes that earlier required physical visits. Examples include vehicle tracking and equipment failure tracking.

Digital technologies can be used to automate processes and activities in two contexts: business process and industrial automation in a factory. Many business processes and activities can be either fully or partially automated. Sales, production, and supply chain are typical business processes automated using technologies such as workflows and ERPs. The next generation of process automation is done through robotic process automation (RPA).

RPA refers to the deployment of attended or unattended software to perform predefined structured and repetitive tasks. RPA is currently being used extensively in customer services operations, claims administration, and employee management processes, among others. In the case of industrial automation, computers or robots are used to handle different processes and machinery in a factory to replace human beings.

The benefits of industrial automation are described next.

Improved productivity: Industrial automation helps in reducing manual work in a plant. It also allows plants to run 24/7 with limited human intervention. This leads to an improvement in productivity and other operational efficiencies.

Higher quality: Automation eliminates human error. Further, unlike human beings, robots are not impacted by fatigue, and therefore there is no deterioration in quality.

Increased flexibility: Automation and digital technologies make adding new tasks to an assembly line easier and flexible. With the use of technologies such as digital twins, companies eliminate the need for extensive retraining and expensive downtimes.

Better information accuracy: Automated data collection allows for consistent data collection across a plant. This also helps in improving data accuracy and reducing data collection costs. This provides managers with the data to make the right decisions.

Increased safety: Industrial automation can make the production line safe for employees by deploying robots to handle hazardous tasks.

8.4.4.1 Smart living

In smart living, using IoT (different types of electronic methods and sensors), a large amount of data is collected. The insights generated from these data are used to manage assets, resources, and services efficiently. As the amount of data collected increases over time, the individual business processes can also be improved and better integrated. We have described a few of the emerging areas within the smart living domain in more detail.

Smart home: Also called home automation, this involves installing devices with sensors to automate several things, such as air conditioning temperature settings depending on the presence of people, water temperature, home security with surveillance cameras, smart locks, smoke and fire detection, smart electrical outlets, and smart hubs that enable controlling the smart functions.

This IoT deployment uses a range of short-range wireless communication options to connect these devices.

Smart transportation: Smart transportation incorporates several features, such as a smart navigation system, optimised routing, and real-time location information. This is useful for synchronising traffic lights and providing information on parking space availability. Smart transportation uses location sensors combined with AI algorithms to optimise and predict traffic patterns.

Smart health: Healthcare and systems that are enabled by IT and IoT are termed smart health. A typical example is wearables used by patients that provide live data of critical health parameters to the doctors. Patients recuperating at home can be monitored remotely for heart rate and other parameters. Doctors and nurses use IoT to receive reports and notifications on patients' health and can act accordingly. These IoT-led systems allow hospitals to extend their services to homes and remote locations at lower costs.

8.4.5 Business models

A business model explains how a company creates, offers, and captures value (Chesbrough, 2007).

With increased turbulence in the external environment and shifting consumer preferences, an organisation's business model plays an important role. The right selection of a business model allows it to exploit sustainable market opportunities. Digital technologies allow for firms to adopt novel business models such as platforms. This has been described in the next section.

Platforms

Conceptualising firms as autonomous, independent entities struggling for competitive advantage does not adequately explain present-day business reality. Ecosystem theory visualises firms as part of a broader community instead of limiting partnership options within its supply chain (Mukhopadhyay and Bouwman, 2018). Many large organizations like Amazon, IBM, SAP, Uber, Apple, and Zomato have developed their own ecosystems of partners and complementors; as a leader, they play a critical role in developing and nurturing this ecosystem (Figure 8.3).

Figure 8.3 Ecosystem leader in multi-sided platforms

The ecosystem leader can use a digital platform to facilitate collaboration among multiple complementors in its ecosystem. Though an ecosystem can also be built around a product or service, digital platform–based ecosystems are increasingly dominating the industry. A digital platform can be conceptualised in two different ways. Researchers with an innovation and IT background have defined a digital platform as a software-based system that includes a core module developed by the ecosystem leader and many add-on modules developed by independent complementors (Tiwana, Konsynski, and Bush, 2010). The core module provides essential but restricted and limited functionalities when left alone. But complementors' add-on modules increase the platform value manifold (Mukhopadhyay and Bouwman, 2019). The platform's core is designed to be stable but lean, while the periphery, which is contributed by the complementors, is continuously evolving and rich in functionalities. On the other hand, scholars with an economics background view the platform as an intermediary between two or more groups of customers (Rochet and Tirole, 2003). Without the existence of the platform, the two sets of users cannot interact or interact in a much inferior way.

If we examine the apple iOS platform ecosystem, we can see that the ecosystem leader, Apple provides the core OS capabilities. It also extends these capabilities to the developers or complementors through application programming interfaces (APIs). The Apple developer community brings complementary capabilities; this can be gauged by the fact that the Apple Store has over 1 million mobile applications for consumers primarily offered by independent developers. From the two-sided platform perspective, the Apple app store facilitates efficient interaction between developers and consumers and creates value for the developers, consumers, and the platform ecosystem leader. Social media platforms can be conceptualised as a two-sided platform, where users and advertisers interact. Social media platforms face problems in monetising their huge base, as the users do not find much value in interacting with advertisers.

Many organisations are adopting the platform model for their business. From being a niche phenomenon in a few technology-intensive industries, digital platforms, and their associated ecosystems, are now transforming and impacting all important industries (de Reuver, Sørensen, and Basole, 2018). Digital platform–based ecosystems have become an important source of innovation, as the responsibility of innovation is scattered among multiple players, reducing risk, and increasing the probability of successful innovation. Firms are also competing for market leadership based on their platform strategy and the depth of the ecosystems, instead of their stand-alone strength. With the successful emergence of iOS and Android with related app stores and ecosystems, and the demise of the stand-alone model of Nokia and Blackberry, the mobile device industry can be referred to as an excellent example of the emergence of platform-centric competition.

Professor Cusumano of MIT put it succinctly, "Who wins and who loses these competitions is not simply a matter of who has the best technology or the first product. It is often who has the best platform strategy and the best ecosystem to back it up" (Cusumano, 2010, p. 34).

While in the context of software-based platform ecosystems, complementors are primarily developers, but any independent firms and individuals with a high level of interdependence with the ecosystem leader can bring complementary capabilities and act as a complementor in an ecosystem. For the online food aggregation platform, food suppliers (restaurants and other kitchens) are important partners. They contribute to the focal firm's coherent solution and the associated value proposition. The complementors can have two types of relationships with the ecosystem leader (Kapoor, 2018). Having a strict relationship indicates that the ecosystem leader's offering cannot be consumed without the available offerings of these complementors. A mobile network service provider working on a new technology needs lots of partners (having strict complementarity) who can provide compliant handsets. On the other hand, super-modular partners are not essential for offering the services, but they can increase the value of the focal player's offering many times. Content providers share a super-modular relation with mobile service providers.

8.5 Selling digital

As mentioned at the beginning of this chapter, digital transformation is a strategic transformation enabled by digital technologies. For a successful digital transformation, a company needs to look at every element of its business, including strategy, operations, and business models. Such a change is complex and multi-disciplinary and is led by the chief executive officer (CEO) and top management of a company. All of this makes selling digital solutions a complex task.

Traditional sales professionals who sell technology solutions may not be suitable for digital transformation, as they need to go deeper into helping their customers rethink their strategy. This requires an understanding of the customer's industry landscape, competition, customers, and potential disruptions. Digital is transformative. Therefore, the sales professional is not just advocating business benefits like operational efficiencies or growth but also changing their fundamental business model.

Transformation is also risky, and suppliers need to help customers manage their risk in addition to supporting them with change management processes.

Digital therefore requires consultative selling. Digital suppliers first need to paint a picture of the customer industry's future landscape and then provide their customers with a path to become the disruptors and not the disrupted. The path will involve layers in the digital transformation model, as outlined in Figure 8.1.

The decisions on technologies to be implemented are an outcome of these complex discussions.

Some of the tools used extensively in digital transformation are design thinking for strategy formulation and agile for technology implementation.

Design thinking: The concepts of design thinking have been used in qualitative market research and product design for decades. Its current form is associated with David Kelly, a Stanford professor and founder of the leading design firm IDEO. Since the early 1980s, many companies across multiple industries have successfully applied design principles to strategy and innovation.

Design thinking moves companies away from traditional linear approaches that consider solutions up-front. Instead, design thinking helps companies explore alternative solutions by asking four questions. Where are they today? Where can they all be? How can they all get there? What is the best way? Design thinking is human-centric, with customers and stakeholders co-creating the solutions. It is options focused and allows for multiple possibilities to emerge. Finally, it is iterative and leverages concepts such as rapid prototyping (Figure 8.4).

The design thinking process requires companies to observe what their customers do rather than what they say they do. This helps uncover real issues they never knew existed and leads to innovative digital and non-digital solutions.

Agile development: We have already discussed agile methodology and its advantage over traditional methodology in Chapter 3. In traditional software development frameworks such as the waterfall model, requirements for a project must be agreed up-front. The entire scope of the project is

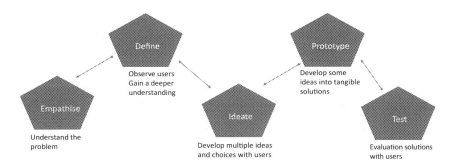

Figure 8.4 Design thinking process
Source: IDEO

planned and timelines agreed between the stakeholders. These methodologies provide a structure to the development process and save the customer time. However, such methods are rigid and do not have the flexibility to adapt to customer and market changes that may happen along the development process. The methodologies have time-to-market lag and have no mechanism for interim feedback. The methods also disconnect the customer from the development process. Agile development overcomes many of the weaknesses of these traditional methodologies.

Agile has existed since the late 1980s but became mainstream only in the 2000s. The increase used of agile development has been driven by rapidly shortening produce life-cycles and a customer need to remain connected with the development process. Agile methods make the following trade-offs:

- Individuals and interactions over processes and tools
- Working software over comprehensive documentation
- Customer collaboration over contract negotiation
- Responding to change over following a plan.

As mentioned before, some of the popular methods used in agile include scrum, extreme programming, and rapid application development.

Collaborate with your ecosystem partners: Selling digital involves multiple IT and technology capabilities and other capabilities such as domain knowledge, customer experience design, innovation at rapid space, and mobile app development. As mentioned in the earlier section, IT companies are unlikely to have competencies in all these areas. They therefore need to develop these competencies by partnerships and being part of ecosystems.

Design a cloud-based solution: IT providers need to focus on developing and delivering solutions based on the cloud instead of an on-premises solution. Chief information officers (CIOs) are moving their computing resources to the cloud to focus more on strategic issues and enabling innovation. This is described in detail in Chapter 9.

8.6 Chapter highlights

- Digital transformation is not all about implementing technology or solving discrete business issues. It encompasses strategy changes, business model changes, process changes, and organisational changes.
- Digital technologies can be broadly classified into four categories: technologies and platforms, intelligence (data and analytics), automation (process and industrial), and network and storage.
- The key digital technologies include blockchain, IoT, and AI.
- Platforms are a group of technologies based on which other technologies, processes, and applications are developed and run.

LEADING WITH DIGITAL

- Data analysis is a process of generating, transforming, and modelling data to discover useful insights to support decision-making. It can be outlined in a six-step process.
- Digitisation is about a manual process being automated. On the other hand, digitalisation, or digital transformation, is about strategy changes enabled by digital technologies. Digitisation is a prerequisite for digitalisation.
- Process automation can be classified into process automation and industrial automation.
- Only the recent advancement in network speeds, storage capacities, and processing power has made digital technologies mainstream.
- Selling digital is much more complex than selling technology solutions. The decision-maker for digital is the CEO, not the CIO/CTO (chief technology officer).
- Design thinking and agile are two critical frameworks for implementing digital.

8.7 Questions for discussion

1 Describe the key characteristics of digital transformation. How is it different from digital technologies?
2 How can digital technologies be classified? Provide examples of each of the classifications.
3 What are the benefits of blockchain technologies? What are the constraints?
4 What are platforms? Why are they proliferating?
5 What are the types of artificial intelligence?
6 What are some key trends expected in the future of networking?
7 What are agile frameworks? Why have they become critical in implementing digital technologies?
8 What is design thinking? What are the five broad steps in design thinking?
9 Please explain a conceptual scenario focusing on problems in a marketing or finance function where blockchain technology can be effectively used. Please explain the primary value created by blockchain technology in this scenario that can be used to justify the investment by the buyer.

8.8 References

Bharadwaj, A., El Sawy, O. A., Pavlou, P. A., and Venkatraman, N. (2013). Digital business strategy: Toward a next generation of insights. *MIS Quarterly*, 471–482.

Chesbrough, H. (2007). Business model innovation: It's not just about technology anymore. *Strategy & Leadership*, 35(6).

Cusumano, M. (2010). Technology strategy and management the evolution of platform thinking. *Communications of the ACM, 53*(1), 32–34. doi:10.1145/1628175

de Reuver, M., Sørensen, C., and Basole, R. C. (2018). The digital platform: A research agenda. *Journal of Information Technology, 33*(2), 124–135.

Jackson, P. (1986). *Introduction to expert systems.* Reading, MA: Addison-Wesley.

Kane, G. C., Palmer, D., Phillips, A. N., Kiron, D., and Buckley, N. (2015). Strategy, not technology, drives digital transformation. *MIT Sloan Management Review and Deloitte University Press, 14*(1–25).

Kapoor, R. (2018). Ecosystems: Broadening the locus of value creation. *Journal of Organization Design, 7*(1), 12.

Kryder, M. H., & Kim, C. S. (2009). After hard drives—What comes next?. *IEEE Transactions on Magnetics, 45*(10), 3406–3413.

Mukhopadhyay, S., and Bouwman, H. (2018). Multi-actor collaboration in platform-based ecosystem: Opportunities and challenges. *Journal of Information Technology Case and Application Research, 20*(2), 47–54.

Mukhopadhyay, S., and Bouwman, H. (2019). Orchestration and governance in digital platform ecosystems: A literature review and trends. *Digital Policy, Regulation and Governance, 21*(4).

PwC. (2018). *PwC's global blockchain survey.* Retrieved from https://www.pwc.com/gx/en/industries/technology/blockchain/blockchain-in-business.html

Rochet, J. C., and Tirole, J. (2003). Platform competition in two-sided markets. *Journal of the European Economic Association, 1*(4), 880–1028.

Roser, M., and Ritchie, H. (2013). Technological progress. In *Our World in Data.* https://ourworldindata.org/

Russell, S. J., Norvig, P., and Davis, E. (2010). *Artificial intelligence: A modern approach* (3rd ed.). Upper Saddle River, NJ: Prentice Hall.

Schaller, R. R. (1997). Moore's law: Past, present and future. *IEEE Spectrum, 34*(6), 52–59.

Tiwana, A., Konsynski, B., and Bush, A. A. (2010). Research commentary—platform evolution: Coevolution of platform architecture, governance, and environmental dynamics. *Information Systems Research, 21*(4), 675–687.

Urbach, N., and Röglinger, M. (2019). Introduction to digitalization cases: How organizations rethink their business for the digital age. In *Digitalization cases* (pp. 1–12). Cham: Springer.

9

SELLING CLOUD TO ENTERPRISES

Learning objectives

This chapter provides an overview of the cloud computing concepts necessary for IT sellers. By the end of this chapter, a reader will be able to:

- Appreciate the benefits of a cloud-based IT solution over an owned IT solution deployment
- Understand the five essential characteristics and three service models and three delivery models of cloud solutions
- Appreciate that the cloud cannot be recommended in all types of scenarios
- Appreciate the barriers of increased cloud adoption by large enterprises
- Develop a client-specific cloud selling strategy by highlighting important and relevant benefits.

9.1 Introduction

Cloud computing offers a paradigm shift in the generation and usage of computing power (McAfee, 2011). Chief information officers (CIOs) can move away from the traditional method of owning IT investment to the new paradigm of accessing IT resources on demand (Weinman, 2012). Though the cloud initially started as a means of reducing capital expenditure (Capex) and IT complexity, firms are increasingly using cloud computing to achieve multiple business objectives. A 2016 survey among CXOs by IBM Institutes of Business Value (IBM, 2016) found that almost 70% of the surveyed companies have used the cloud significantly to achieve the following objectives:

- Expanding into new industries
- Improving the customer experience
- Expanded product/service portfolio
- Creating a new revenue stream.

DOI: 10.4324/9781003155270-10

The emergence of the cloud has also impacted the fortunes of many IT vendors. Many early providers of cloud-based services (like Microsoft and Amazon) could create significant value for themselves. At the same time, failure to adopt cloud has adversely impacted the businesses of several traditional hardware, product, and service vendors.

About half of the cloud computing market is concentrated in North America, while Europe accounts for another quarter (Statista, 2020). But in general, globally, the cloud computing market is growing rapidly. As per recent research (Cisco, 2018), by 2021, 95% of workloads and compute instances will be processed through cloud data centres, compared to only 5% by traditional data centres. As an IT sales professional, it is becoming increasingly critical to understand the nuances of cloud computing terminologies and concepts. This would allow the sales professionals to engage in a meaningful discussion with the clients. Based on the interactions, a roadmap for cloud adoption by large enterprises to achieve cost optimisation, complexity reduction, or competitive advantage can be developed

9.1.1 Defining cloud

As per the National Institute of Standards and Technology (NIST) of United States:

> Cloud computing is a model for enabling ubiquitous, convenient, on-demand network access to a shared pool of configurable computing resources (e.g., networks, servers, storage, applications, and services) that can be rapidly provisioned and released with minimal management effort or service provider interaction.

In a simpler term, cloud can be defined as *renting IT infrastructure and applications on demand over the Internet (instead of having dedicated servers and applications).*

It is easy to confuse virtualisation and cloud computing, as they are frequently used in a similar context. It is best to remember that virtualisation is a technology that allows us to create multiple separate, distinct, and secure environments known as virtual machines (VMs) from a single, physical hardware system. Virtualisation prevents the underutilisation of computing resources by placing several virtual servers on a single physical one. VMs are also much easier to deploy compared to physical servers. It provides redundancy, as copies of VMs can be deployed in separate physical servers.

On the other hand, cloud computing is a service delivery approach, where computing resources are delivered to users on demand over any network. Virtualisation has played an important role in the rapid diffusion of cloud computing, as the cloud infrastructure consists of pools of virtualised resources.

SELLING CLOUD TO ENTERPRISES

9.2 Five key characteristics of the cloud

9.2.1 On-demand self-service

Users can access the right quantity of computing services via the cloud without interventions from the service provider. The computing services provided by the cloud should be fully on-demand so that users have control and agility to meet their evolving needs. This feature allows users to access computing resources for the right amount of time. Cloud service providers have evolved to provide a greater degree of granularity of quantity (Weinman, 2012). As a result, users can access any computing resources for one week, one day, and even one hour. Using the cloud to get access to the right amount of resources at the right time for the right duration helps firms to optimise their resource usage. On-demand self-service limits the chances of unproductive resources. It also tackles the potential problem of capacity constraints that can hurt business growth.

9.2.2 Ubiquitous network access

Cloud computing services are widely available via the network through users' preferred access channels (e.g. laptops, desktops, smartphones, etc.). Responsiveness (latency) of the services should also be within the acceptable limit. In summary, cloud service providers should provide network access in enough places to address location constraints and response-time issues. It is needless to say that networks need to be secured. Network-based access is central to the cloud concept. Without a secure and low-latency system that is accessible from multiple devices, the cloud would not exist.

9.2.3 Resource pooling

Unlike traditional IT deployment, the cloud provides on-demand computing resources (such as storage, memory, processing, network bandwidth, and software) economically by pooling resources. In a variable-demand scenario, developing a shared infrastructure is vital for making available the right amount of resources at the right time. One of the drawbacks of having a shared resource is that resources need to be similar; custom-built resources cannot be allocated to different users.

9.2.4 Rapid elasticity

Successful resource allocation requires elasticity; this indicates resources must be assigned or released accurately and quickly. A retail chain may be using 30 servers in general, but during its specific sale promotion period, it might need 50 servers. After the promotion is over, the demand may come down to 20 servers only. The cloud provider's IT infrastructure should have the ability to absorb significant increases and decreases in demand without service interruption or quality degradation.

9.2.5 Measured service

Following the utility model, cloud computing services are measured and metered. This type of pricing is known as consumption-based pricing, pay-per-use, and linear tariff structure. This measurement allows the service provider (and consumer) to track usage either based on time (number of hours or days the resource is consumed), quantity or volume (gigabytes transferred), number of concurrent users (30 concurrent customer relationship management [CRM] users), or a combination of all these. One of the disadvantages of utility pricing is its inability to consider the cloud provider's possible value addition for a specific customer, as services are treated as commodities. In this model, the cloud providers also bear the financial risk; they would find it difficult to recover their IT infrastructure investment in case of less-than-adequate demand.

9.3 Cloud adoption in large enterprises

The cloud cannot be considered anymore as an emerging IT service delivery model; instead, it has become the preferred IT model for most enterprises. To understand the reasons for the same, we should understand the challenges faced by CIOs before the emergence of the cloud.

9.3.1 What were the problems faced by IT managers/CIOs?

In a traditional IT setup, senior IT managers were too occupied with running data centres with multiple applications. Though IT was increasingly becoming an essential part of a firm's business model, the CIOs had hardly any time for sponsoring innovation or forging stronger partnerships with business leaders. They were too busy executing a large number of operational activities. A few of them are mentioned here:

- **Capacity planning for hardware and software:** It includes estimating yearly demand and provisioning of the same. In spite of spending significant time to estimate demand, there would often be an underutilisation of some assets while over-utilisation (or scarcity) of some other assets.
- **Procurement and installation of these resources:** It involves vendor selection, negotiation, logistics, and project management activities to add or enhance capacity.

SELLING CLOUD TO ENTERPRISES

- **Managing, troubleshooting, and version upgrade of the hardware and software:** One of the IT department's primary activities was to provide access to new users and ensure ongoing support to existing users.
- **Recruiting and managing a team with diversified capability:** This team needs to manage hardware, network equipment, software applications, and service provisioning to end users. Due to rapid advancements in technologies, the stakeholders need to upgrade their skills and capability continuously.
- **High capex expenditure:** Most importantly, CIOs needed to justify a substantial investment annually (as in-house private IT systems are developed on Capex mode). The high investment in IT infrastructure and support leaves limited resources for new application development. In a traditional IT setup, only 11% of the company's IT budget is spent on developing new applications; the rest of the budget is earmarked for support and infrastructure (McAfee, 2011).

9.3.2 Benefits of the cloud

The cloud has allowed IT managers and CIOs to get out of the ongoing orchestration activities required to ensure computing access. The obvious outcomes are increased productivity and a higher scope of IT-enabled innovation. We have explained several important benefits of a cloud-based computing and IT services model.

- **Pay as you go:** Cloud solutions are specifically beneficial for smaller businesses and start-ups; they do not have the capital to build and manage their own IT infrastructure. Their money would often be better utilised for product development, customer acquisition, or market expansion instead of buying servers and software licenses. Using the cloud, they can move from a Capex model to an Operating Expenses (Opex) model and pay for the recurring ongoing expenses.
- **Cost savings:** On-premises resources are dedicated to an organisation; sometimes, even the resources are utilised only by a particular department or location. In cloud-based IT, the resources are not dedicated to specific organisations, and multiple tenants can use it. The same computing resources can be used by a client in India's daytime, while in the United States' daytime (when it is night in India), these could be assigned to US-based clients. Greater efficiencies and economies of scale in cloud-based arrangements lead to cost savings, some of which are passed on to the buyer by the service providers. Though one has to remember, an organisation (with a large computing requirement and

minimal variation in demand) consuming cloud services using a pay-per-use scheme might incur a higher cost.

- **Limited need for long-term capacity estimation:** In the case of start-ups, new services launches are associated with uncertain consumer demand. A successful online product would demand massive capacity expansion, but the probability of a product becoming a best-seller is highly uncertain. Due to the uncertainty, the actual IT usage would be very different from the projected IT capacity. Cloud services follow an elastic on-demand model; services provision is done as per the demand. The users do not need to invest inordinate time and energy in long-term capacity estimation (in an uncertain environment).

- **Quick implementation:** To thrive in a dynamic business environment, enterprises should have the ability to accommodate rapid changes in computing infrastructure capacity. A retail chain would need higher computing capacity during a holiday sale but would have lower use of the resources once the promotion is over. IT managers would go through a long cycle of design–procurement–install–test activities in a typical on-premises IT infrastructure before any new capacity is available for IT users. Service provisioning by cloud providers is instant—no need to go through the design–procure–install process. The enterprises can also save costs by de-provisioning underutilised IT assets, which is not possible in the on-premises model.

- **Higher availability:** The cloud enhances the availability of IT services. A managed cloud platform is generally much more reliable than an in-house IT infrastructure, with fewer instances of downtime or service interruptions. Most tier-1 providers offer 24/7 support and over 99.9% availability. Higher availability of IT services positively impacts the availability of customer-facing or internal business processes. Uninterrupted business services increase revenue and customer satisfaction. Other than increased service availability, the cloud can be used for enforcing data redundancy by storing the same information in multiple locations.

- **Increased focus on business and innovation:** Working with the cloud providers allows the firms to access varied competences related to operating a data centre: IT configuration, problem management, and cybersecurity. Similarly, accessing Software as a Service (SaaS) services allows the firms to access the specialised competencies encoded in the final software product, which is often moderated by the vendor's ability to work with many customers. The cloud enables firms to leverage the cloud providers' domain-specific and technical competencies to achieve their business objectives.

- **Access to the cloud marketplace for ready-to-use apps:** Other than their core cloud service portfolio, the large cloud providers have developed their marketplace, where additional apps developed by partners are available. The marketplace strategy increases engagement with cloud customers and also contributes to developing industry-specific solutions. In 2020, Microsoft Azure launched CXMnow.io for Life Sciences, an omni-channel platform for the industry. The marketplace partners can also provide consultancy and other customisation services, complementing the big three cloud providers' product focus. Amazon has the most evolved marketplace, with 8,500 apps in June 2020. As a relatively new player, Google has the technological capability and is aggressively working to scale up its marketplace.

In addition to these business benefits, the cloud has brought two more transformational changes in our society, requiring serious attention. In his book, *Cloudonomics, The Business Value of Cloud Computing*, Joe Weiman (Weinman, 2012) highlighted these changes.

- **The democratization of IT:** The cloud has helped to democratise ownership and access to IT. While access to on-premises computing and software resources was always available to large enterprises, the cloud has freed smaller companies and start-ups from the burden of owning their own IT infrastructure by large-scale Capex investment. They can easily access technologies and software paying rent on the cloud model; easy access to computing infrastructure has spurred creativity and innovation.
- **Industrialization of IT:** Technology observers have conceptualized the cloud as an information factory (Gilder, 2006). The cloud has led to the industrialization of IT, a limited number of centralised providers having a huge scale. This replaces the earlier tradition of multiple in-house IT units with a limited scale. Taking the conceptualisation further, we can employ many of the best practices in the manufacturing industry. In the manufacturing industry, several prestigious brands (such as Apple and Samsung) focused on design and research and assigned the manufacturing work to specialised manufacturers. As explained before, with cloud, IT organisations can also focus their resources on innovation generation and helping businesses achieve their goal. At the same time, they can depend on cloud providers to manage the operational aspect of the IT. To achieve cost-effectiveness and reduce wastage, manufacturing organisations are using just-in-time manufacturing practices for a long time. Similarly, IT managers can use on-demand resource provisioning capabilities of the cloud to achieve the same.

9.3.3 Scenarios where cloud is not appropriate

Though the cloud has multiple benefits compared to the in-house IT service delivery model, the IT sellers should be aware that there would be many scenarios where the cloud may not provide a better solution. A few of the important scenarios are described next:

When the data growth is flat or not significant: The cloud using its on-demand resource allocation is apt for handling variable and unpredictable capacity requirements, as mentioned in the earlier section. This advantage no longer remains valid in a relatively predictable load; an on-premises IT would provide better control and a cost advantage. But the seller should remember, cost advantage is only one of the factors when deciding to go for the cloud, the buyers in spite of having flat computing resource requirements can opt for the cloud for other reasons.

Security concern: Many companies may not opt for the cloud if the security concern outweighs other benefits. Any compromise in cloud security can result in an extended service outage, data theft, and non-compliance. The responsibility to ensure secure services depends both on the cloud provider and the cloud customer. The major reasons for security breaches are listed next.

- Cloud provider vulnerabilities
- Technology vulnerabilities
- Not defining and implementing appropriate access policies and controls
- Non-compliance with legal and regulatory requirements.

The cloud customer should go for a periodic risk audit, preferably by an external consultant. The risk analysis and assessment can help the cloud customer to improve the existing security framework and implementation. Companies can also decide against storing sensitive data such as customer information, financial transaction information, and design information in the cloud.

Regulations: Recommending cloud solutions should be viewed from the applicable and prevalent regulations of the country and the operating industry. The companies having any operations in Europe or handling European customers' data need to comply with the General Data Protection Regulation (GDPR) framework. The cloud customer (companies using the cloud), irrespective of the cloud providers, need to ensure that 1) the processing of personal data is done in a secured manner, though the activity may be performed by a cloud provider and that 2) data should remain in the European Union or the countries approved by the European Union. More and more countries like the United States and India are bringing their versions of data protection laws, restricting the storage of personal and financial transaction data in any environment.

Legacy applications: IT landscapes of many large IT firms have legacy applications with outdated architecture and programming languages. It would need considerable effort to migrate them to a cloud architecture with modern programming paradigms. These IT applications are stable, and users have developed confidence by using those over the years. The cost of migrating them to the cloud is often higher than the benefits coming out of it. The hybrid cloud configuration allows the on-premises legacy application to coexist with modern applications hosted on the cloud.

Unique customer needs: The cloud is developed on the principle of similar products being available to multiple users. Many of the large enterprises need to follow additional industry-specific and region/country-specific compliance requirements and additional security, including data localisation requirements. Large organisations also do not always follow the standard business processes; thus, their applications are customised to a great extent. Many times, cloud providers do not match their expectations.

Organisations also go slow on cloud adoption due to the **scarcity of skills.** The available skills in cloud computing are in short supply. Technical resources are in great demand who can develop analytics, Internet of Things (IoT), artificial intelligence, and blockchain solutions using cloud IT. Organisations also need senior technical architects and business consultants to get the maximum value out of the initiatives. Often, user organisations go slow on moving to the cloud due to the unavailability of adequate skilled resources at an economical rate.

9.4 Three service models of the cloud

We have discussed the three popular types of cloud service models. Other than the three prevalent cloud services (IaaS, PaaS, and SaaS), XaaS is used as a generalised, collective term that refers to the delivery of any capabilities as a service over the internet.

9.4.1 Infrastructure as a Service (IaaS/raw computing resources)

IaaS gives users access to storage, networking, servers, and other computing resources via the cloud. The user is still responsible for developing and managing their applications, data, and middleware. IaaS provides automated and scalable environments that offer a high degree of control and flexibility. Tech companies have in-house IT expertise, so they prefer this type of cloud service. They opt for IaaS, as they do not want to get into provisioning or managing the computing environment. Sometimes buyers also use IaaS services to handle workload spikes during busy seasons. For example, the Indian retail giant Big Bazar can use IaaS to get extra computing resources on their Independence Day or Republic Day sale. When the sale is over, they can surrender the computing resources.

Amazon is the market leader in the cloud infrastructure services market (IaaS) in 2020, having 32% of the overall market share (Statista, 2020)

9.4.2 Platform as a Service (PaaS/environment ready for software development)

This service is primarily geared towards the developers. Service providers rent out cloud-based platforms for users to develop and deliver applications. In other words, PaaS provides a framework that makes it easier and more efficient to build, customise, and deploy applications.

For example, to develop an analytical application, the cloud service providers would provide hardware, database, and a run-time Python environment. But the users have to build their analytical programs (codes).

PaaS provides benefits by accelerating IT-based solution development, as developers get to work from the beginning without waiting for the development environment's readiness. PaaS also makes it easier for non-IT organisations to get into software development.

9.4.3 Software as a Service (SaaS/ready-to-use software)

SaaS services are the most well-known and matured of the cloud service models. The software application or a suite of applications are hosted, packaged, and delivered by a third party through the Internet (typically on a browser-based interface). By accessing the software application over the Internet, enterprises can offload development, management, and maintenance effort and costs to the vendor(s). One of the most popular SaaS offerings is Salesforce.com's CRM, which acted as an alternative to on-premises CRM (such as Oracle's Siebel). Many of the productivity and collaboration software like Microsoft's Office 365 and multiple Google apps are also offered on the cloud.

The SaaS segment is the largest revenue generator among the three types of cloud services. In 2019, it contributed to overall worldwide revenue of 148.5 billion US dollars, approximately two-thirds of the overall public cloud computing market (Statista, 2020). In SaaS, the largest company by revenue is Microsoft, followed by Salesforce, Adobe, SAP, Oracle, and Google.

The SaaS model of application access has a few advantages over on-premises software installation. The few key benefits of SaaS over on-premises software applications are:

- Using SaaS, one can get more frequent software updates to access bug fixes and new features.
- A single-instance on-premises implementation may suffer from network delay if the application's users are scattered around in many locations.

SaaS providers can provide improved customer experience due to their dispersed nature.

- In SaaS, the payment is based on actual usage, not only based on projection. In an organisation, there are many scenarios where new applications remain underutilised.
- Using SaaS, organisations can ask for legally bound service level agreements (SLAs) to ensure availability and agreed-on performance criteria.

As discussed before, a large organisation may have 1) unique IT application architecture, 2) significant customisation requirements (due to non-standard business processes), or 3) stringent security requirements. As a result, it may not opt for a SaaS-based solution and would prefer on-premises applications or only using the cloud to provision infrastructure.

These three service models of cloud IT and traditional IT are contrasted in Figure 9.1.

Other than the three well-defined services, the concept of Business Process as a Service (BPaaS) has become popular. As per Gartner,[1] BPaaS is the delivery of business process outsourcing (BPO) services sourced from the cloud and constructed for multitenancy. Services are often automated, and where human intervention is required, there is no overtly dedicated labour pool per client. Like other cloud services, the pricing is based on consumption or subscription. As a cloud service, the BPaaS model is accessed via Internet-based technologies. Some of the business processes that can be accessed by BPaaS are insurance claim processing, human resources tax processing, and similar activities.

9.5 Three delivery models of cloud

9.5.1 *Public cloud*

A public cloud is probably the most commonly understood cloud computing option. This is where all the services and supporting infrastructure are managed off-site over the Internet and shared across multiple users (or tenants). The name suggests that these services are available to everybody, the general public, or enterprises. The underlying infrastructure is owned by one of the cloud service providers.

An excellent example of a public cloud at the individual consumer level is an email service like Gmail. Users register for the service through a personal (individual) account but access the same services across the platform through the Internet.

The advantage of using a public cloud is the increased efficiency and subsequent cost-effectiveness from shared resources. Public clouds are typically cheaper than private and hybrid cloud solutions (as well as traditional on-premises computing) because they rely on economies of scale. Users don't

SELLING CLOUD TO ENTERPRISES

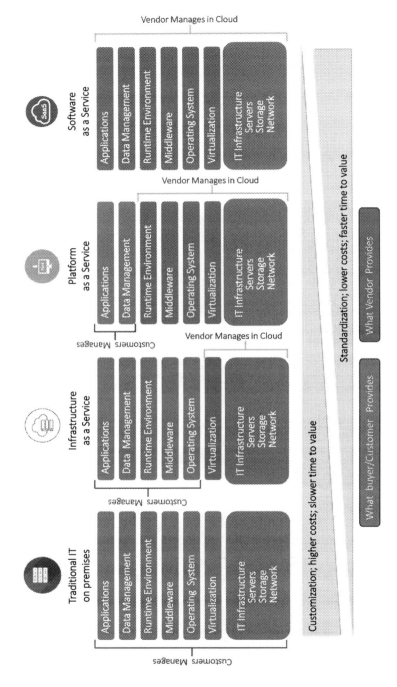

Figure 9.1 Three primary cloud service models

have to pay for services they aren't using and don't have to worry about managing and maintaining the physical infrastructure.

Figure 9.2 shows the public cloud services revenue distribution among three cloud services (IaaS, PaaS, SaaS) (Statista, 2020). SaaS generates the maximum revenue, followed by IaaS.

9.5.2 Private cloud

A private cloud is an on or off-premises cloud infrastructure operated solely for an organisation and managed by the organisation or a third party. A public cloud generally has multiple tenants; a private cloud typically has only one tenant. Private clouds are popular choices for organisations that have high priorities on security and regulatory compliance and, at the same time, want to use the benefits of cloud technologies (such as sharing of resources across the enterprise). Due to the dedicated nature of the infrastructure, a private cloud might not be as cost-effective as a public cloud. Private clouds can reside on-site or off-site. It can have three varieties:

- On-site private cloud managed by the enterprise itself
- On-site private cloud managed by a third-party cloud service provider
- Hosted private cloud: off-premises, dedicated infrastructure managed by the third party.

9.5.3 Hybrid cloud

Organisations find it complicated and expensive to migrate the legacy application into the cloud. But at the same time, they want continued usage of it

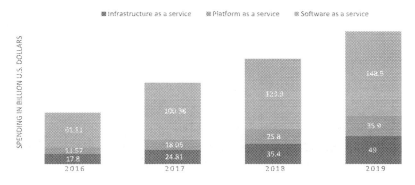

Figure 9.2 Market size of different types of public cloud
Source: Statista

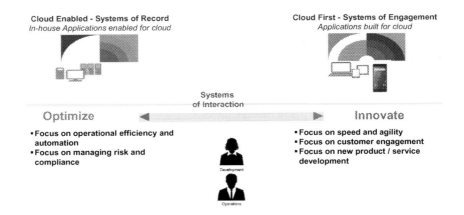

Figure 9.3 Hybrid cloud (co-existence of traditional and cloud IT)

for their business criticality. They develop all new applications on a modern cloud compliant architecture, creating a business case for the coexistence of traditional and cloud IT.

These organisations can use a hybrid cloud environment to combine traditional IT (owned resources) and the cloud (public and private) in varying degrees. Enterprises increasingly prefer this because it allows organisations greater flexibility to meet their IT needs. A buyer has the freedom to choose the optimum mix of its IT requirements (mixing cloud and non-cloud IT).

Generally, the systems of records that contain the data about the customer, products, transactions, sales, and others are not stored in the cloud. The systems of engagement (the front end customer-facing applications) are hosted on the cloud. Systems of interactions ensure that there is enough communication between them (Figure 9.3).

9.5.4 Multi-cloud architecture

Large organisations are also moving to a multi-sourcing arrangement with cloud services being procured from multiple providers, known as multi-cloud architecture.

The multi-cloud architecture includes deploying multiple cloud services/solutions from multiple cloud providers across the enterprise to meet the growing computing needs. The strategy allows organisations to transition between various cloud providers depending on the business needs. On a conceptual level, buyers can choose a particular provider for a specific cloud computing function with minimal intervention from the providers.

The benefits of multi-cloud adoptions are many:

- **Cost Reduction:** Buyers can financially gain by getting different cloud functionalities from different cloud providers. This is achieved primarily because of the competition among the providers. Besides, different providers have achieved efficiency in different types of services.
- **Reduced Risk and Business Continuity:** A multi-sourcing strategy can lead to reduced risk and better business continuity. This is due to reduced dependence on any particular vendor and increased availability and resiliency in case of cloud failure.
- **Increased Productivity, Agility, and Flexibility:** A best-of-breed approach allows selecting the best cloud provider, keeping in mind the business and technical purpose. This is with the assumption that different cloud providers have different strengths and capabilities. Selecting one provider for all purposes led to working with limited features and a longer time in application development.

A survey conducted in 2019 among 2,650 IT decision-makers in multiple global organisations (Statista, 2020) identified the following benefits of hybrid and multi-cloud (Figure 9.4).

9.6 Selling the cloud to enterprises

We start this section by describing multiple challenging business scenarios where the cloud can create significant value (Table 9.1). The cloud sellers should try to focus any of these issues in the context of a potential buyer and start a discussion around it. We have also described the three important types of stakeholders (Table 9.2) who generally form a cloud buying unit and their expectations from cloud.

Keeping in mind the context of an enterprise, the sellers should also provide a roadmap for being cloud-ready. There could be specific applications which would be a no-go area for migrating to the cloud. Similarly, several applications and workloads would be the early candidates for moving to the cloud. A few of them are explained next.

- **Development and test environment:** The journey to the cloud in most companies starts with a cloud-based test system. This speeds up the readiness of the testing environments with multiple configurations and datasets, automated release procedures, and better collaboration between the development, test, and deployment team.
- **New application development:** For new application development, organisations can use IaaS or PaaS instead of an on-premises IT infrastructure. The developers do not need to spend their time managing and

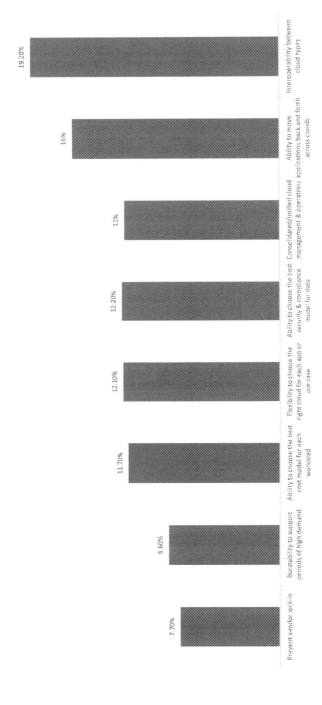

Figure 9.4 Benefits of hybrid and multi-cloud
Source: Statista

SELLING CLOUD TO ENTERPRISES

Table 9.1 Conversation starters in cloud selling

S. No.	Discussion Theme	Definition
1	Application performance	Is the buyer struggling to provide adequate computing performance to all IT users and developers efficiently?
2	Growth of IT computing and data storage	Does the buyer face substantial data growth (structured and unstructured data)? Do computing resource requirements grow at a rapid pace?
3	The total cost of ownership	Does the buyer's CIO have the challenge to reduce cost and, at the same time, implement IT transformation to support business growth?
4	IT management	Does the buyer want to continue with the burden of IT infrastructure, application and data management, maintenance, and technology lifecycle management, or would they prefer to offload that responsibility?
5	Technology	Is the buyer able to proactively keep up with the rapidly changing technology landscape, considering the recent developments in storage, databases, modern application architecture, and deployment?

configuring the development environment. Instead, they can focus more on code development.

- **Enterprise software and CRM:** Many enterprise software (enterprise resource planning [ERP]) modules are available on the cloud; similarly, CRM and other customer-facing applications are being offered over the cloud. A large number of enterprises have migrated to cloud versions, making them obvious choices for cloud migration.

The cloud services (IaaS, PaaS, SaaS) market is dominated by a few large multi-national IT companies such as Amazon, Microsoft, Google, IBM, Oracle, and Siebel. Most of these companies are product-focused (excluding IBM) and need partners who can deliver services essential for making the best use of cloud IT. On the other hand, the revenue and the prospects of the traditional IT service companies (such as Infosys, Accenture, and TCS) would be impacted if they do not play a major role in cloud IT. These companies can partner with cloud providers and offer multiple services that significantly increase the value of the cloud services. To do so, these organisations need significant investment in retraining their employees and

Table 9.2 Key decision-makers and their priorities in cloud buying

	Key Functions in the Buyer's Organisation	Priorities/Interest Area	Corresponding Cloud Value Propositions
1	CIO	• Management and replacement of existing IT hardware and other resources • Limited budget • Limited flexibility with existing IT • Less fund to invest in innovative IT	• Increased flexibility and agility • Focus on managing SLA, mask underlying IT complexity
2	Enterprise Architect	• Challenges of new service deployment using on-premises IT and cloud IT • No ability to deploy the application in one cloud and move to another	• Application efficiency integrating on-premises and cloud IT • Application deployment in multiple clouds
3	CFO	• Ever-increasing Capex • Ongoing depreciation costs of IT investment	• More control of budget (pay for actual utilisation only) • Ensures better return of IT by quicker application development

recruit fresh external talent. The relevant and valuable IT services of cloud IT would be:

- Cloud advisory
- Application modernisation
- Migration of applications and services
- Cloud management and governance.

9.7 Chapter highlights

- Cloud computing offers a paradigm shift from the traditional method of owning computing resources to the new model of using computing resources on rent.
- Multiple studies have found a growing shift towards cloud computing from the traditional on-premises computing model. A Cisco survey (2018) found that by 2021, 95% of all computing workloads would be processed by cloud-based data centres.

SELLING CLOUD TO ENTERPRISES

- Cloud has five key attributes, three types of services (IaaS, PaaS, SaaS), and three models of service delivery (public, private, hybrid).
- SaaS is the most mature cloud services market with a maximum revenue share, while PaaS is the least developed cloud services offering.
- Amazon is the overall leader in the cloud computing market, especially in Iaas, followed by Microsoft. Microsoft leads in the SaaS market, while IBM is the most preferred hybrid cloud vendor due to its strong service portfolio.
- Hybrid cloud offers enterprises the possibility of integrating traditional on-premises IT with cloud-based computing services.
- Large organisations are moving towards a multi-cloud environment to reduce cost and risk and improve agility and flexibility.
- While few product vendors dominate the IaaS, SaaS, and PaaS market, traditional IT services companies can tie up with them and offer services in the area of cloud advisory, application modernisation, application migration, and cloud management.

9.8 Questions for discussion

1 Describe the challenges of an in-house IT infrastructure deployment. What challenges to CIOs face in engaging with an external vendor in managing such an IT infrastructure?
2 Describe the five primary characteristics of the cloud with examples.
3 Identify the market size and the key players in IaaS, PaaS, and SaaS space. Describe the advantages of each service model.
4 Provide a comparative assessment of the cloud services provided by Amazon, Google, IBM, and Microsoft.
5 Identify the key challenges for large enterprises with legacy applications in adopting the cloud.

Note

1 www.gartner.com/en/information-technology/glossary/business-process-as-a-service-bpaas

9.9 References

Cisco. (2018). *Global cloud index projects cloud traffic to represent 95 percent of total data center traffic by 2021*. Retrieved from https://newsroom.cisco.com/press-release-content?type=webcontent&articleId=1908858

Gilder, G. (2006, October). The information factories. *Wired*. Retrieved from www.wired.com/wired/archive/14.10/cloudware.html

IBM. (2016). *IBM institute of business value hybrid cloud survey, 2016*. Retrieved from www.ibm.com/thought-leadership/institute-business-value/

McAfee, A. (2011). What every CEO needs to know about the cloud. *Harvard Business Review*, *89*(11), 124–132.

Statista. (2020). *Cloud computing*. Retrieved from www.statista.com/study/15293/cloud-computing-statista-dossier/

Weinman, J. (2012). *Cloudonomics: The business value of cloud computing*. New York: John Wiley & Sons.

10

CAREERS IN IT: TODAY AND TOMORROW

10.1 Learning objectives

In this chapter, readers will learn the following:

- Globalisation of the IT workforce
- Career paths in IT—business functions and technical functions, including career paths for those with engineering and business degrees
- The concept of the "future of work" and the engagement model of employees with the employers.

10.2 Introduction

In Chapters 8 and 9, we described the key technologies that are changing the IT landscape. A unique set of disparate technologies has given rise to new solutions previously not imagined. With these new areas of technologies and solutions, the roles performed by individuals are also changing.

Of the top 20 jobs in the year 2000, half do not exist anymore. Several of the current roles did not exist five to ten years ago. Roles relating to cloud computing, Internet of Things (IoT), artificial intelligence (AI), and Industry 4.0 started becoming relevant less than a decade ago. Jobs such as search engine optimisation specialist, driverless car engineers, and digital marketing did not exist either.

This chapter discusses career options in the current marketplace, covering both business and technology roles. Today, the jobs are divided based on hardware, software, communication, and security combined with management functions such as business and process consulting, project management, program management, governance, and financial control.

In the second part of the chapter, we discuss the transformative changes in the IT industry and identify future roles and job descriptions.

10.3 The global workforce

As discussed in previous chapters, the IT industry has become truly global. Companies have adopted multiple IT delivery models, including global

DOI: 10.4324/9781003155270-11

223

insourcing and outsourcing. IT suppliers, too, have become global with onshore, near-shore, and offshore operations. This has led to companies locating technology development work around the world, based on an optimum mix of skills availability and cost. The concept of best shoring has emerged as a result of this global reallocation of resources. IT companies have built a network of in-house and outsourced development centres where each centre brings best-in-class talent and technologies to certain value chain elements.

An IT development resourcing pyramid typically consists of many developers and testers at the bottom of the pyramid. Project managers, architects, and business analysts are in the middle of the pyramid. Program and client relationship managers form the top of the pyramid. In a global company, most developers and testers are located at the cheapest location with the maximum skill availability. The higher end of the pyramid is located closer to the country of business operations. As a result, the availability of roles and career progression also follow similar trends. Most entry-level roles are concentrated in low-cost countries, and senior roles, especially those that require interaction with business users, are co-located with the business.

10.4 Routes to IT careers

Engineering degree (bachelor's or master's)

Many streams of engineering degrees make individuals eligible for technical roles in IT companies. While some technologies get covered as part of coursework, companies also provide their employees with extensive training on various technologies. The onboarding process can last as long as six months to a year for fresh graduates, where employees get exposed to various technologies. They then get allocated to projects based on the specific skills they have trained on.

Common engineering degrees for IT roles include:

- Computer science
- Information technology
- Software engineering
- Electronic and communications
- Electrical
- Mechatronics (for automotive-related IT)
- Mechanical/industrial.

For entry-level positions, companies are open to hiring students from all engineering branches, as they have taken advanced quantitative and analytics courses. In addition to engineers, most IT companies hire graduates with degrees in science and mathematics. At entry and junior levels, applicants

CAREERS IN IT: TODAY AND TOMORROW

must go through multiple rounds of written tests and interviews to be accepted. The tests cover quantitative ability, written and comprehension skills, and coding skills.

Master of Business Administration (MBA)

Most MBA programs have specialisation in IT/systems management or sales and marketing. Graduates from these programs are hired into business analyst roles and form the bridge between business users and technical teams. MBAs are also hired in different types of consulting roles. Many MBAs join the different sales and marketing functions of the IT providers.

Diplomas

In countries such as India, several institutes offer bridge programs for IT skills. These range from software coding to network management.

10.5 IT jobs today

Technology is a vast area and spans a range of technologies and roles. These roles traditionally existed in IT provider organisations. As businesses are increasingly becoming technology-driven, these roles are also becoming important in user organisations. Increasingly, user organisations prefer resources who have spent a significant amount of time with IT vendors. As a result of their long association with IT providers, these professionals can collaborate and manage these vendors effectively.

Despite the large number of choices, career paths in IT can be classified into a few broad categories.

Technical Roles: Development and operations are the two primary technical roles in IT based on business deliverables. While development focuses on building technology, operations focus on operating and maintaining the technology on an ongoing basis. Technical roles can also be classified into hardware, software and infrastructure-related roles. They can also be categorised into products and services related roles.

Some of the more common titles in development roles are given in Table 10.1.

Developers usually grow into the role of architects over a period, if they want to remain on a technical path. Architects focus on bringing together different parts of the system together. A technical architect has technical skills and expertise in a specific area and has the breadth of knowledge on how to make an entire system work.

Infrastructure and Operation Management: This is another critical career track in IT services and involves managing the entire technology network. Some of the roles in infrastructure management are listed in Table 10.2.

225

CAREERS IN IT: TODAY AND TOMORROW

Table 10.1 Roles in IT development

Title/Role	*Description*
Architect	While enterprise architects are responsible for the overall architecture encompassing multiple applications, application architects are accountable for the specific software components of the overall solution.
	Other than fulfilling the business requirement, this role is also responsible for the performance, availability, scalability, and usability of the applications and ensuring integration with the other relevant IT systems.
	They also develop an overall IT roadmap, keeping in mind the evolution in the industry and emerging technologies.
Product Specialist	These sets of resources have considerable experience in specific custom off-the-shelf (COTS) software modules. They lead solution architecting, designing, developing, performance tuning, capacity planning, and problem solving involving those product modules. They also guide the infrastructure team for installation, deployment, and systems administration.
Developer	They are responsible for software development and enhancement, as well as bug fixes. The software development can happen in the context of customisation of any COTS module. In many cases, organisations might decide not to use any available product, but develop complete functionality from scratch. Developers, along with the testers, constitute the bulk of resource requirements in IT projects. Many of the software development roles are at the entry level. An experienced developer can become an architect, project manager, or move to the sales profession.
DevOps Engineer	They work with developers, manage software releases, and ensure smooth transitions of software developed in multiple environments.
Quality Assurance Engineer	Their role is to check and report any deviation from the expected outcome of a software. They also evaluate the compliance of process and methodology adopted in projects and help in risk identification and management.
Testing Engineer	They are involved in end-to-end testing. Performance testing is a specialised and sought-after skill used to verify that the developed software can work in a higher load.
	With the advent of automation, manual testing jobs are being rapidly automated.

CAREERS IN IT: TODAY AND TOMORROW

Table 10.2 Infrastructure and operations roles

Title/Role	Description
Operations Manager	Head of overall operations.
Helpdesk Support	Support users of IT systems in case of incidences, problems, and changes. They provide the first level of support to the IT user community.
IT Support Engineer	Provide help and support to individuals or businesses with their IT problems. They monitor the IT infrastructure and work with IT vendors for service restoration. They are also responsible for provisioning and de-provisioning of computing resources to end users.
Cybersecurity Specialist	Protect computer systems and data from attack or falling into the wrong hands. Seen as increasingly crucial by businesses, as cybercrime is increasing.
Cloud Administrator	Manage cloud computing capabilities and subscriptions.
Database Administrator	They manage the databases associated with different applications. Their main activities are 1) estimating data growth and infrastructure planning, 2) data migration, 3) optimisation of database design and associated queries, and 4) developing reports from the data. Due to the rapid advent of social media, the database administrators should be well versed with the nuances of unstructured data.
Computer Hardware and Networking Engineer	Develop hardware requirements and deploy and manage (servers, network equipment, storage). Due to the advent of IaaS cloud services, these jobs are becoming centralised in the environment of cloud providers.

Marketing, Pre-Sales, and Sales: These roles are primarily found in IT vendor organisations and involve managing the marketing and sales processes discussed earlier. While pre-sales roles and some marketing roles are primarily based in offshore locations, sales and marketing roles are located in client geographies. Unlike in the fast-moving consumer goods (FMCG) industry, where sales roles are entry-level positions, most sales and marketing personnel have prior technical backgrounds in the IT industry. They have evolved from technical or consulting roles. This is in sharp contrast with the career progression of sales professions in other industries such as

CAREERS IN IT: TODAY AND TOMORROW

FMCG. In those industries, the sales or marketing people start with the entry-level sales role and move up in the career.

Some of the roles in this track are listed in Table 10.3.

Account and Engagement Management: As discussed extensively in earlier chapters, account management plays a critical role in the IT industry. Account managers require "farming" skills more than the "hunting" skills required by sales personnel. Account managers need a good mix of both technical and relationship skills as they interact with multiple personnel in a customer organisation. In many companies, technical personnel with good communications and interpersonal skills are trained and moved into account management roles.

Some of the typical account management roles are highlighted in Table 10.4.

Business Analytics and Data Management: Given the importance of analytics and its linkages to IT and data management, a number of newer roles are emerging. Table 10.5 provides an overview of the same.

Table 10.3 Marketing and pre-sales roles

Title/Role	Description
Business Intelligence Analyst	Use data to develop insights into a business
Sales Leader	Manage sales function, including onsite and inside sales
Inside Sales	Support outside sales team with lead generation
Sales Support	Provide support to the sales team by developing presentations, analysing customer situations, and developing research on customers
Bid Management Leader	Lead managing the bid management, including coordinating with all the internal and external stakeholders
Solution Architect	Develop high-level architecture, including software and hardware based on client needs

Table 10.4 Account management roles

Title/Role	Description
Client Services	An operational role coordinating with the customer organisation, managing documentation.
Account Managers	Manage a specific set of customers based on the size of the account, location, or industry. Responsible for growing the account.

CAREERS IN IT: TODAY AND TOMORROW

Table 10.5 Business analytics and data management roles

Title/Role	Description
Data Analyst	Identify and curate meaningful data and develop reports and insights.
Data Engineer	Develop data capture, storage, and retrieval infrastructure.
Data Scientist	Conceptualise the use of data. Identify data sources and develop and interpret models to achieve business objectives.

Table 10.6 General management roles

Title/Role	Description
Chief Technology Officer	Overall accountability of all technology planning, deployment, and management in an organisation.
Chief Information Officer	Overall accountability of all information technology planning, deployment, and management in an organisation.
Chief Data Officer	Organization-wide data access and its usage.
Chief Information Security Officer	Securing data from external threats.
Vendor Manager	A vendor manager can lead or be part of the vendor management office in a user organisation. Their overall work can be split into three categories: 1) developing RFIs/RFPs, 2) executing the vendor management process and vendor evaluation, and 3) ongoing relationship management with vendors. They would require a mix of business and IT skills, project management capabilities, and commercial experience.
Program Manager	Manage a significant initiative comprising several projects with a defined business outcome. Program managers also play a critical role in ongoing customer communication. They are also expected to manage the dependencies between multiple projects as well as dependencies originating outside their program.
Project Manager	Manage a project with defined deliverables, cost, and timeline. There is a preference for project managers with PMP or agile certification. Project managers also review the risks on a continuous basis and take corrective actions when required.
Test Manager	Test managers are responsible for planning, designing, and executing overall testing activities in a project and work in close coordination with project and program managers. They also develop overall testing strategy, test cases and data and automation plan.

General Management Roles: Some of the senior and general management roles in the IT industry are listed in Table 10.6.

Consultants: These roles require a background of both business and technology. Consultants work with business groups, whether internal or a

229

client, and provide business strategy and technology roadmaps. All large IT companies nowadays have significant consulting capabilities. The consulting capabilities help them to differentiate from other IT service providers. In many cases, a successful short-term project leads to longer-term and higher value IT assignments. These resources generally have an MBA qualification in addition to their experience of working in different functions and industries.

With the onset of digital technologies, the consultants are going to play a vital role, as many traditional companies are looking at transforming themselves. We have summarised few of the roles available to consulting resources in IT companies in Table 10.7.

Resources in the consulting track also work as business analysts. These analysts are engaged in client interfacing, requirement capture and vetting, technical impact analysis, and developing the service conducting the user acceptance test. In a complex project, their role includes stakeholder management and to increase usage of the new systems by their intended users. Resources with business degrees (MBAs) are preferred for these roles.

The types of roles discussed in this section are not exhaustive and dynamic. Also, there are overlaps between roles and, in some cases, the definitions across companies and sectors vary.

10.6 The future of work

The IT industry is experiencing a structural transformation driven by innovation and business model changes, enabled by newer digital technologies. A quick look at the last two decades would establish that the model of working between two organisations, an organisation and individual, and between two individuals has changed unrecognisably. For person-to-person interactions, from having only phones, technology has resulted in hundreds of apps that allow communication in high-definition video. Hardware and software sales have moved away from one-time purchases to subscription models. Collaboration tools, social media, cloud computing, platforms, and fintech are transforming the ways people and organisations interact. All these changes, in turn, have led to a new breed of technology companies and careers.

The new world is an intermingling of many industries and capabilities. Let us take the example of the automobile industry. In the past, the industry was centred mainly around mechanical and electrical components. Today's connected car is less about the mechanics and more about computing, electronics, sensors, and data analytics. This trend will accelerate even further as automobiles become autonomous.

To develop solutions in the digital world, companies need to bring in many diverse capabilities together. These include design, business modelling,

CAREERS IN IT: TODAY AND TOMORROW

Table 10.7 Consulting roles

Title/Role	Description
Strategy and Organisation Consultant	IT companies are developing competence in core strategy consulting, with mixed success. The large consulting firms like McKinsey and BCG remain the most preferred partners for corporate strategy advisory. Here the key activities would be: • Business strategy for a new venture or expansion • Customer lifecycle management • Change management • Talent and workforce management
Technology and IT Strategy	They generally perform three types of activities. IT strategy–related activities can include cloud strategy, digital transformation roadmap and strategy, and post-merger IT integration planning. Architectural strategy work includes enterprise architecture assessment and design and architecture governance. IT performance assessment work includes IT governance and program management methodology, IT organisation and process assessment, and IT benchmarking.
Operation Strategy	The key activities include process compliance and process maturity assessment, operations and supply chain strategy, risk, and compliance management. IT companies have developed significant expertise in operational consulting over time.
Industry and Domain Strategy	They bring deep industry or domain knowledge, which is complementary to the IT provider's technical and delivery capabilities. Many of them have worked in multiple functional roles in respective industries (such as financial services, retail, chemical, or telecommunication) in senior positions. They are fully aware of the challenges of the specific industry. They work with the technology people to develop solutions that bring out the cost from the business or improve the customer experience or profitability. Many times, they also contribute to developing the IT provider's point of view on the long-term evolution and prospects of a specific industry.

computing, connectivity, sensors, and payments, among others. There is also a greater need for consulting and project and program management skills. The solutions are path-breaking and high-risk and need to be carefully managed.

The "future of work" will have an impact on multiple aspects of people and organisational structure.

Impact on old roles: One of the key impacts of the "future of work" and digital is that several IT and manufacturing roles will be automated. Workflow tools, AI, and robotics are some of the drivers for this automation.

Roles in IT that will get automated include the collection and processing of data and customer service. Accounting and payroll processes, mortgage origination, and customer service through bots and proactive maintenance for hardware are some examples of processes that will get automated. Software coding is also expected to be disrupted. Zero code, low code, and use of AI in coding are expected to reduce the need for large coding teams. Technical support and low-end testing roles are also expected to reduce in numbers.

Creation of new roles: As mentioned earlier in this chapter, a whole set of newer technology roles will emerge, focusing on digital transformation. Some of the roles are included in Table 10.8.

A report published by the World Economic Forum (Ratcheva, Leopold, and Zahidi, 2020) highlights a few of the important technological trends that will dominate the world (Figure 10.1). In another study conducted by McKinsey (Hunt, Layton, and Prince, 2015), more than half of these new global roles (based on these emerging technologies) will be created in five countries, including the United States, China, India, Germany, and the Netherlands.

Impact on the development process: In the past, IT teams worked in silos and were far removed from the end customer. Internal business teams developed new concepts based on market feedback, and these were converted into technical requirements by analysts. The requirements were then provided to program teams, who broke it down into manageable projects. Finally, coding and testing teams were brought in to write the code. In the digital world, this sequence has been turned outside-in. Concepts such as design thinking require end customers to be involved right up-front in the process of product conceptualisation. The entire development cycle is one of co-creation. It involves coders and business users and end customers, all together in one team. This change in process has redefined the concept of development teams. It no longer consists of just technical coders but also involves designers, market researchers, and even experts in consumer psychology. Diversity of teams and co-creation are the hallmarks of successful development teams in digital transformation.

Leveraging a talent ecosystem: Digital has also transformed the way companies source talent. As mentioned earlier, digital requires diverse skills, and some of these are program specific. Companies are moving away for having full-time resources for certain skillsets and instead leveraging a talent ecosystem.

In addition to in-house and outsourced employees, companies are leveraging contract workers, gig workers, and crowdsourcing. Contract workers are provided by third-party staffing agencies and are being typically used for short-term high-volume work. TeamLease in India is one example of such a company. Companies are also open to hiring gig workers for specialised skills. Gig workers are independent contractors who have specialist skills

CAREERS IN IT: TODAY AND TOMORROW

Table 10.8 New-age roles in the IT industry

Title/Role	Description
Advanced Robotics Engineer	Develop, design, and deploy robots for improved precision and speed
Artificial Intelligence Specialist	Understand requirements and develop programs using specialised AI methods
Blockchain Specialist	Design and apply blockchain capabilities
Industry 4.0 Architect	Integrate IoT, AI, cloud, edge computing, etc., to develop solutions
Industry-Specific Application Specialists	Integrate IT and IoT, AI, cloud, and adjacent technologies to develop solutions for specific industries including healthcare, discrete manufacturing, continuous manufacturing, logistics, civil engineering, etc.
Digital Transformation Architect	Transform the business processes and business delivery models leveraging digital technologies. Create digital roadmaps.
Chief Data Officer (CDO)	A CDO is responsible for the organisation's data strategy and governance. The CDO also ensures that the organisation can derive maximum value from the available data.
Chief Marketing Technology Officer (CMTO)	The CMTO coordinates between the marketing and technology departments of an organisation and ensures that the marketing department's IT requirements are properly prioritised and developed and they follow enterprise IT policies (Brinker and McLellan, 2014).

and do not want to be tied down to any organisation. While gig working is getting popular among millennials, it has challenges for both hiring organisations and the workers, as the labour laws in many countries are not clear on the laws applicable to this class of workers. Platforms such as Flexjobs connect gig workers with employers. Platforms have also led to the rise of crowdsourcing of workers. As an example, companies post issues that require complex analytics on platforms such as Kaggle. Teams and individuals from around the world compete to solve these issues for prize money.

Continuous learning: Organisations are having to provide opportunities for continuous learning to their employees to keep pace with the rapid evolution of technologies. In the past, this was based on classroom training using internal or external instructors to conduct training programs. However, the advent of specialised massive open online course (MOOC) platforms has simplified this process. Many organisations are tying up with these platforms to support their continuing education initiatives. Reskilling of employees from legacy technology to digital technologies is another

CAREERS IN IT: TODAY AND TOMORROW

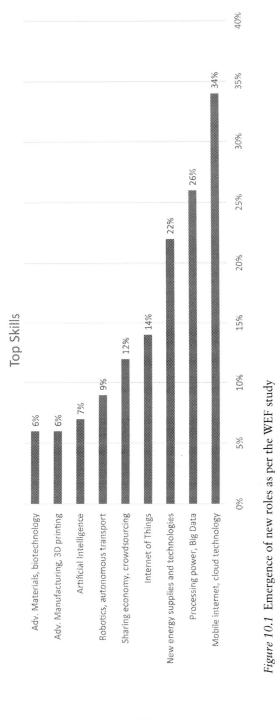

Figure 10.1 Emergence of new roles as per the WEF study

Source: Jobs of tomorrow: mapping opportunity in the new economy. World Economic Forum, Geneva, Switzerland, 2020

CAREERS IN IT: TODAY AND TOMORROW

initiative undertaken by most companies as they embark on their digital journeys.

Workplace shifts: The physical location of where IT work is performed is also changing. The proliferation of collaboration and conferencing tools has enabled remote working and reduced employees' need to be co-located. The COVID-19 crisis accelerated the concept of virtual working and "work from home". The new workplace strategies will reduce the need for centralised office space and increase employees' opportunities to work from the most suitable location, with periodic visits to an office. Concepts such as hot-desking and shared office space are replacing dedicated office spaces.

Focus on diversity: Workplace diversity is an important focus area for most IT companies. Diversity could be across multiple dimensions, including gender, age, education, religion, and sexual orientation. A study by McKinsey has shown that diversity in the workforce is more than a fad. As per the study, diversity has a direct impact on the quality of innovation and business results. As discussed earlier in this chapter, digital tools such as design thinking require diverse skills and thought processes. However, achieving diversity has been challenging as IT companies predominantly hire from a STEM (science, technology, engineering, mathematics) background. Companies have now tied up with educational institutions to encourage diversity in STEM programs and focus on hiring diverse candidates at the entry level.

10.7 Chapter highlights

- The IT industry is dynamic, and the pace of change creates problems for both individuals and the organisations. The rate of change in the technology landscape is too rapid for anyone to plan beyond a few years.
- However, the fundamentals of the IT industry remain the same. The industry focusses on using technology to develop new solutions. These solutions help individuals and businesses develop new capabilities that bring more convenience to people's lives.
- While rapid changes are leading to uncertainties, IT continues to be the most exciting area to be involved in. Everyday IT professionals witness their vision of the future materialise.
- The next set of upcoming skills will be based on a continuously evolving framework that requires IT professionals to update their skills to stay relevant.
- IT professionals also need to be cognizant of the number of changes beyond newer technologies, including redefining work and workplace changes.
- IT organisations focus a lot on acquiring industry and domain knowledge, business consulting capabilities, and research on new technologies. This also creates multiple avenues for professionals in achieving diversity in their careers.

10.8 Questions for discussion

1 How is globalisation impacting the IT industry and careers?
2 Describe the "technical roles" available in the IT industry and provide five examples. Describe "business roles" and provide five examples. How can a technical resource move to a sales and marketing role in the IT industry?
3 How will the changing business models of the IT industry impact the employment framework? Why is having some technical or delivery background considered essential for IT sellers?
4 What is the future of work? What impact is it expected to have on the IT industry? What are a few of the challenges employees in the IT industry face?

10.9 References

Brinker, S., and McLellan, L. (2014). The rise of the chief marketing technologist. *Harvard Business Review*, 92(7), 82–85.

Hunt, V., Layton, D., and Prince, S. (2015). Diversity matters. *McKinsey & Company*, 1(1), 15–29.

Ratcheva, V., Leopold, T. A., and Zahidi, S. (2020). *Jobs of tomorrow: Mapping opportunity in the new economy*. Geneva, Switzerland: World Economic Forum.

Indian Institute of Management Ahmedabad
Institute of Management Technology Ghaziabad   IIMA/MAR0507

RAZORPAY: PROVIDING PAYMENT CONVENIENCE TO DISRUPTORS

"Our mission statement now is 'To Power the Financial Ecosystem for Disruptors'. So, go ahead and disrupt. We have got your back," declared Harshil Mathur, CEO and co-founder, Razorpay, as he concluded his product launch presentation on December 7, 2018. Mathur was speaking at Razorpay FTX, a fintech conference in Bangalore, where Razorpay launched four new products called Flash Checkout, Razorpay Capital, RazorpayX and X Club. Flash Checkout focussed on the payment experience of the end user through personalisation enabled by more than four million saved cards and the payment history of the user. By integrating the Flash Checkout form into their website or app, merchants could reduce their checkout time by 24 seconds and increase the checkout success rate by 15%. Razorpay Capital allowed Small and Medium Enterprises (SMEs) to avail of collateral free loans from bank and Non-Banking Financial Company (NBFC) partners based on a credit score assigned by Razorpay's Alternative Credit Decisioning System. At the time of the official launch, loans worth USD 30 million had already been disbursed through the Razorpay Capital platform with a target to reach

---

Prepared by Divya Ganjoo, PGPX 2017, IIMA, and Professors Saral Mukherjee, Indian Institute of Management, Ahmedabad and Sandip Mukhopadhyay, IMT, Ghaziabad.

Cases of the Indian Institute of Management, Ahmedabad, are prepared as a basis for classroom discussion. They are not designed to present illustrations of either correct or incorrect handling of administrative problems.

© 2019 by the Indian Institute of Management, Ahmedabad and Institute of Management Technology, Ghaziabad. This Case (IIMA/MAR0507) has been reproduced with permission from Indian Institute of Management, Ahmedabad.

Reproduced with permission

USD 100 million by March 2019. RazorpayX was a unified banking product for businesses to manage payments and refunds as well as make disbursals across multiple online/mobile payment methods and multiple bank accounts. Finally, X Club was a networking platform for startups, meant to provide access to learning, mentoring, networking and raising money.

Just four years ago, IIT Roorkee alumni, Shashank Kumar and Harshil Mathur, founded Razorpay from Mathur's family home in Jaipur. What started as a payment gateway for ecommerce was now a portfolio of payment related solutions. The next stage of the journey of this startup depended on how well Razorpay transitioned into being a platform serving the high-growth markets of digital payments and lending.

THE DIGITAL PAYMENT ECOSYSTEM

Payments in India had historically been cash based due to multiple reasons ranging from non-availability of appropriate digital payment options, cultural preference of Indians for cash as well as the fear of being tracked by the tax authorities. Even as more and more Indians were opting for digital shopping, their preferred payment mode still remained cash-on-delivery (COD). Digital payments had the potential to advance the financial inclusion agenda of the government, reduce the leakage in cash-based government subsidy schemes, as well as make India the preferred hub for innovative digital technologies.

Several factors were helping India's march towards a less-cash society. Access to mobile internet had improved while the cost of mobile data had come down significantly, after Reliance Jio launched its 4G mobile service in 2016. Governments and other relevant institutions were promoting the development of digital payment infrastructure through enabling regulations. They had provided multiple incentives for digital payments, while restricting or penalising cash-based transactions. The demonetisation of high-value banknotes in India on November 8, 2016 led to an increase in digital payment adoption and usage. The government promoted the National Payments Corporation of India (NPCI) had developed technical infrastructure for digital payments like the Aadhaar Enabled Payment System (AEPS), National Unified USSD Platform (NUUP), Unified Payment Interface (UPI) and the Bharat Interface for Money (BHIM) application. The government actions and attractiveness of market were successful in stimulating the supply side of the market. The payment landscape in India had seen the entry of multiple categories of players: device manufacturers (e.g., Samsung), large internet companies (e.g., Google, WhatsApp), banks (e.g., State Bank of India, HDFC Bank, ICICI Bank), telecom operators (e.g., Airtel, Vodafone, Reliance Jio), online retailers (e.g., Flipkart, Amazon), digital wallet providers (e.g., PayTM, Mobikwik) as well as global payment gateways (e.g., PayPal, PayU) and home-grown payment gateways (e.g., Razorpay, CCAvenue, BillDesk), etc. With the easy access to capital and the availability of talented resources, innovation in the digital payment space was expected to increase further.

Users had a range of technologies and services available for making digital payments - the popular ones being mobile or electronic wallets, UPI, debit and credit cards, USSD based services (for non-smart phone users) and online banking. Due to the various digital payment methods available and a large number of providers within each digital payment category, a new type of payment aggregator or Payment Service Providers (PSPs) had emerged. PSPs like Razorpay, PayU and PayTM intended to manage the payment and collection processes of merchants and organisations. These PSPs offered their customers a wide range of pre-integrated choices of different digital payment options, saving time, technical complexities and regulatory hurdles involved in integrating with a wide variety of payment products.

Unfortunately, the expansion in supply did not stimulate Indian's demand for digital payments. Though there were a plethora of options and service providers, the Indian economy continued to remain cash-intensive. The currency notes in circulation had grown even after demonetisation, showing the limited effectiveness of demonetisation in pushing digital payments. This situation also raised doubts about the feasibility of achieving the government's target of 30 billion digital transactions during the fiscal year 2018–19. Digital payment providers needed to move beyond providing only payment solutions; they had the potential to provide comprehensive financial solutions for individuals as well as for corporates. They had access to consumer consumption data, thereby providing a unique opportunity to offer relevant deals, coupons and offers to consumers and influence their consumption patterns.

THE FIRM

The foundation for Razorpay was laid at IIT Roorkee's hobbies club. The two co-founders of Razorpay, along with a group of other students, formed the Software Development Section (SDS) – an initiative focussed on developing software solutions for the institute's or students' problems. Their early products ranged from a media player that worked on limited internet bandwidth and a direct connect solution that brought down the institute's internet usage costs. Razorpay, incorporated by Harshil Mathur and Shashank Kumar in 2014, initially focussed on developing a Kickstarter like crowdfunding platform as well as an initiative to automate the fee collection process of educational institutes. While working on these initiatives, they faced a number of challenges with the existing payment gateways systems - significant on-boarding and integration effort, low success rate and non-intuitive reporting. Businesses that wanted to accept online payments needed to deal with high onboarding Turn Around Time (TAT) due to manual KYC (Know Your Customer) and document collection, high payment failure rates, difficulties in integrating various kinds of payment technologies and tedious reconciliation processes. At the same time, the ecommerce industry in India was booming, driven by changing consumer behaviour, increased internet and smartphone penetration and foreign investments. As per one report[1], ecommerce was growing at a CAGR of 43.8% during 2008–13 fueled by Foreign Direct Investment (FDI) of USD 1.3 billion during 2010–13. Seeing these trends, the co-founders decided to sharpen their focus on solving online money movement problems for ecommerce companies. This formed the basis for the concept of Razorpay as a payment solutions provider.

In 2014, both Mathur and Kumar left their jobs at Schlumberger and Microsoft respectively to be full-time entrepreneurs. Razorpay was supported by Startup Oasis, an incubator of RIICO (Rajasthan Industrial Investment Corporation) and IIM Ahmedabad's CIIE (Center for Innovation Incubation and Entrepreneurship). The company became the second India-focussed startup to be selected in the Silicon Valley based tech accelerator Y Combinator's (YC) programme raising a total of USD 2.6 million in the seed funding round from YC and other investors. Between 2015 and 2018, Razorpay raised a total of USD 31.6 million over four rounds of Series A and B funding from investors such as Tiger Global, Matrix Partners, Y Combinator and Mastercard.

Razorpay was growing at a sustained rate (refer to Exhibit 1 for Revenue and Profit/Loss details). By December 2018, the merchant base had grown to more than 170,000 businesses, Razorpay had processed a cumulative USD 1 billion worth of payments and had more than four million saved cards, support for 92 currencies and allowed netbanking through more than 50 banks and nine payment wallets. By 2018, Razorpay had moved its headquarters to Bangalore where it operated out of a two-floor office and had branch offices in Delhi and Mumbai. The employee strength had grown to 350 with the average employee age at 26 years. Employee perks consisted of MacBooks for everyone, free food and snacks, generous insurance coverage and flexible work hours.

Sales and Marketing

Razorpay customers could be broadly divided into two segments, namely (i) startups and SMEs that formed a majority of the customer base and were key to acquisition and growth targets and (ii) established businesses that contributed significantly to the volume of transactions. Clients included large online players such as Flipkart, Swiggy and Yatra, as well as more conventional businesses such as Aditya Birla Capital, Indian Railways Catering and Tourism Corporation (IRCTC) and Airtel. For the large volume customers, error-free robust technological solutions were key, as a difference of even 1 basis point in the error rate could have a direct impact on their top-line, while the smaller customers valued affordable rates, customer support and technical guidance.

Razorpay saw technology as a way to simplify money transactions for various stakeholders. For developers, they focussed on the ease of integration *via* APIs (Application Programming Interface) and extensive documentation in such a way that even a junior developer could integrate that API on his/her own. For end consumers, they ensured that the user experience was seamless with a checkout experience optimised for slow internet connections, and also offered convenient customer support *via* tools such as "Track Refunds". Finance and business teams of merchants benefited from the dashboard that made it simple to generate reports and get visibility into how money and information was moving.

Razorpay primarily operated on a service fee model where it charged a fixed percentage on the transaction amount for every payment transaction made through it. Although the cost of processing a transaction varied, depending on the mode of payment, such as the credit card network, net banking, wallets, etc. (Exhibit 2), Razorpay charged a 2–3% transaction fee for SMEs with an option to negotiate rates for enterprises that had a large volume of payment transactions or had special customisation requests based on customer servicing requirements.

The sales and marketing teams at Razorpay spent time in understanding how money flowed in the target customer's business and how Razorpay products could help simplify those flows. The sales pitch varied between tech and non-tech companies. In tech companies, digital financial transactions were mostly owned by the product arm of the Chief Technology Officer (CTO) office. In non-tech companies, the buying unit could comprise the Information Systems team, Finance team or a separate digital arm of the company. The key influencers when it came to digital payments integrations varied based on the maturity of the business. In early stage startups (about 10% of the market), the purchasing decision could be driven by software developers while in mid or late stage startups, it was usually the Product team. In more mature businesses, decision making processes were complex and varied from company to company. The deeper a client was on the maturity curve, the more complex its money flows and Razorpay could uncover more opportunities to provide higher value through new product features or a combination of services.

The marketing team at Razorpay was divided into SME marketing and Enterprise marketing and was responsible for growth and volumes. The SME marketing team used mass scale targeting to increase awareness among SMEs and ran campaigns primarily on digital media channels to drive traffic to Razorpay's website and encourage self-registrations. The Enterprise marketing team focussed on more established firms, applied different go-to-market techniques based on the specific problems of the target customers and varied the sales pitch based on the product bouquet that catered to that customer. A separate Client Success team focussed on the retention of marquee customers through dedicated managers assigned to address their needs and manage ongoing relationships. The Banking Alliances team, that was part of Razorpay's Business Operations organisation, focussed on growing, maintaining and deepening relationships with banks and NBFCs.

RAZORPAY

Support and Operations

The Support and Operations team handled queries and complaints from merchants and customers and consisted of 65 people across 11 teams. The Customer Support team handled queries and complaints from end consumers, and the Merchant Support team handled issues from the merchants with the enterprise support team providing premium support for key accounts. The Tech and Integration support team supported queries from developers on Razorpay APIs or technical documentation. When a new merchant signed up, the Activations team would perform all the compliance checks before a merchant could start transacting on the platform. To manage the waiting time for activating new merchants, ongoing compliance or checks related to new requests from existing merchants were separated into a different BizOps (Business Operations) team to handle. Disputes (a customer complaint to Razorpay against a merchant) and Chargebacks (a customer complaint to the issuing bank directly) were coordinated with the customer, merchant and acquiring bank by the Disputes and Chargebacks team. The Merchant Risk team would investigate suspicious trends and activities, such as refund rates, disputes and chargeback activities, etc., from a merchant account. If needed, it would suspend the merchant's account from the Razorpay platform and hold onto the merchant's funds for 180 days, the time period within which consumers could raise a dispute or chargeback. Similarly, the Buyer Risk team would watch for patterns suggesting fraud from customer accounts and take necessary actions ranging from blacklisting those accounts to reporting them to the cybercrime cell of the state.

For support and operations, Razorpay hired fresh graduates and trained them in-house. Almost all hires would start off in the Customer Support arm and spend at least a month there before they could move to another team. Early on, Razorpay had a rotation programme where everyone in the company, from founders to developers, was mandated to spend six hours per month in support. As the company grew, controlling the quality of interactions was a challenge and the policy had to be dropped. Instead, processes and regular meetings between different departments and the support team were instituted to capture and cascade the end customer's voice.

With increasing transaction volumes, merchant base and product launches, the support and operations team was now handling more service requests per month (Exhibit 3). However, as a philosophy, the company did not want to house a bulky support team but use automation to reduce activity times or encourage zero-touch support by developing self-service tools for customers. For example, in order to reduce the time that a ticket might spend waiting in the queue before being categorised correctly and routed to the correct team, the team developed a self-serve form on the website where the customer could pre-select a category of complaint. Similarly, when the support team started seeing that the customer queries on refunds were increasing, the support team reached out to product development and created a self-service portal to let the customer track the status of their refunds directly from the form online. More than 90% of the merchants never needed to interact with a sales or customer support person in the process of going live because of the self-service tools and knowledge base on Razorpay's website.

Customers could reach out to the Razorpay support team by submitting a form on their website or *via* email. In addition, merchants had an option to chat with a customer support agent online *via* an option on the merchant dashboard. Enterprise customers could call the support team *via* a "click to call" option on the dashboard. Enterprise customers also had a dedicated Client Success Manager, aligned to the Sales organisation, who maintained a close relationship with the client and was usually the first point of contact for Enterprise customers.

In addition to using automation, gamification was introduced to enhance the engagement and performance of the support teams. Support team members would earn points to compete across four categories on the leaderboard that was visible to everyone in the organisation. Customer satisfaction was measured through a quarterly NPS (Net Promoter Score) survey and CSAT (Customer SATisfaction) survey for every ticket resolved. CSAT was measured on a binary scale (satisfied/not satisfied) with the option to add free-text feedback that the team would review on a monthly basis.

Razorpay's responsiveness to queries and ability to empathise with the customers had helped it gain a lot of momentum with the customers early on. The quality of this support became a USP in Razorpay's sales pitch. However, as more and more products were launched, the urge to address client requests for complex features was accorded higher priority than the concerns of the support team. Without proper tools and systems to keep up with the growth in customer queries with every new product, the support function started to crumble with a corresponding decrease in NPS. Concerned with this, the management team worked on introducing controls and KPIs related to the post-launch maintainability of the products and inculcating support feedback early on into the product development process.

Product Development

Passionate about software development and having faced challenges with the existing complexities of integration of online payments, the founding team consciously focussed on technological superiority and simplicity of integration for developers. With one-line integration code, well documented SDKs (Software Development Kits), APIs and plugins across technology platforms, and developer support, it strived to establish a superior brand image among the developer community that highly valued peer recommendations and support when using new products or technologies.

With rapid expansion in the product portfolio, Razorpay was quick to organise its product development process. Each product had a dedicated product manager that led the development team and a product marketing manager aligned to the marketing organisation. Further, the core product API platform got a product manager of its own. Razorpay's strategy team defined company goals and metrics that then trickled down to the individual product level. The product managers were the custodians of their products and would gather and prioritise inputs on new features, customer pain points and product improvements from various sources including customers, the sales and marketing team, strategy team, support teams and colleagues, in addition to conducting analyses of product metrics and NPS studies. Once the team and various stakeholders reached a consensus on what to build first, the detailed product, design and technical specifications needed to be written and circulated for approvals, before the real development began. The Development team worked on features in time-bound two-week periods called sprints based on the iterative Agile Scrum[2] methodology. Finally, the developed and tested features would be rolled out in phases to certain cohorts or merchants to receive market validation in a risk-controlled manner.

Products

Payment Gateway

The very first product of Razorpay and its biggest revenue generator (Exhibit 4) tackled the core online payment acceptance challenges for merchants. The payment process involved several steps involving different firms as explained in Exhibit 5. Payment failure rates were estimated to reach as high as 25% for some payment methods. Payment mode options, quality of internet connectivity, processing time, effort to pay, wrong or invalid payment information and user interface nuances, were some of the factors that impacted dropouts at the payment stage of an ecommerce transaction. It was technologically complex and effort-intensive to handle returns, refunds, fraud as well as hundreds of edge cases[3] for each payment mode. Payment gateways would ease some of these issues for merchants but integrating with a payment gateway itself was cumbersome as onboarding could take as long as two to three months. There was barely any technical support available, leaving the merchant's already overstretched tech teams struggling for days or weeks trying to overcome integration issues.

Razorpay's pitch to merchants was a seamless payment experience for end customers that would not only make it convenient for them to offer different digital payment options but would also help realise higher conversions and control development and reconciliation costs. Razorpay promised easiest integration, completely online onboarding, a feature filled checkout, PCI DSS compliance[4] and best-in-class performance.

The Razorpay payment gateway featured a toolkit of payment options, a dashboard, checkout button and page, and an array of APIs, plugins and libraries with support for major platforms. It became the first payment gateway in India to offer a fully-online onboarding and activation method with express activation of one hour in some cases. This was enabled *via* a customisable checkout button and a form with all the payment methods, in-built with validations, error handling and retry processes; effectively trimming down weeks of development effort to hours. Alternatively, merchants could choose to use their own checkout forms and only utilise Razorpay's APIs for payment gateway integration. By integrating with Razorpay's payment gateway, the merchant could start accepting payments *via* all major debit and credit cards, more than 50 netbanking options, nine mobile wallets, UPI and Bharat QR. The dashboard allowed the merchant to manage his account, configure payment business rules, access and manage payments, refunds, invoices, etc., download reports and track real-time data on payments, settlements and refunds.

Developer Hub

Razorpay's developer hub was a publicly available self-service portal for developers to help with anything related to Razorpay APIs or integrations. It featured comprehensive technical documentation and developer guides, sample code, API references, software development kits (SDKs), plugins and libraries across all supported platforms and technologies. Developers could also contact Razorpay's help desk or access its online knowledge base for further assistance.

Razorpay's developer resources, responsiveness and product robustness clicked well with the developer community. Word of mouth within the community was a major contributor to inquiries from merchants and large businesses. Razorpay attributed its initial success more to its organic growth through this channel than to any formal marketing or sales efforts.

Razorpay 2.0 suite

Operating as a payment gateway for about two and half years, Razorpay realised that money flows varied by businesses and there were upstream and downstream interactions that went beyond a website's checkout page. These transactions often led to disbursements or offline payments that severely impacted a merchant's or his customer's payment related experiences. These issues or peripheral scenarios deterred scaling up of online payments and represented an underserved opportunity space ripe for innovation. In 2017, Razorpay launched a suite of products under the "Razorpay 2.0" theme, rebranding itself as "a converged payment solution" that allowed merchants to mix and match from various offerings to match their business requirements. Razorpay's Dashboard connected all these products together for the merchant and acted as the online command centre from where the merchant could manage and control his payment operations centrally.

Smart Collect (Razorpay 2.0 product)

Using Smart Collect, businesses could automate account receivables or campaign specific NEFT/RTGS/IMPS[5] collections *via* virtual account numbers. It provided automatic reconciliation of accounts receivables and account level visibility into all incoming payments *via* the dashboard.

Subscriptions (Razorpay 2.0 product)

A common business model for many online businesses was of subscription payments where customers could pay a fee based on a fixed schedule (such as for rentals) or based on how much they consumed over a billing cycle (such as for content-based services). Razorpay subscription automated the recurring payment through credit card, debit card, E-mandate or UPI, taking away the need for a repeated manual action from the customer and thereby increased customer retention rates. The merchant could automate communications related to the subscription status and prompt the next steps to customers *via* webhooks. It also handled edge scenarios such as declined card, retries on failed transaction, change of card, etc. At one point, Subscriptions was the second most revenue generating product for Razorpay.

Payment Links (Razorpay 2.0 product)

Payment Links were web addresses that could be generated on-demand through the Razorpay dashboard or APIs. These links could be sent to the customer *via* SMS or email to allow him to make payments using any of the supported payment methods. It provided a tactical instrument for businesses to maneuver various scenarios such as when a business did not have a website or online app. In one such example, Treebo, an Indian budget hotel chain, saw a 30% drop in no-shows by asking customers, who booked a hotel room with the "pay at hotel" option, to pay in part or full *via* a payment link.

Route (Razorpay 2.0 product)

In certain online marketplaces, the payment received from an end customer had to be split among multiple sellers. In other situations, a firm may have to split a payment made by a customer among multiple vendors. For example, a firm may provide an option to end customers to donate a small amount to a cause while purchasing a product or buy travel insurance while purchasing a flight ticket. "Route" allowed splitting the payment at source in real-time and automated the transfers, settlements and refunds. Traditionally, settlement and reconciliation of multi-vendor payouts needed manual interventions, such as tracking and approvals, and was a pain point for the accounts departments. Using the Razorpay dashboard, the merchant could control the business logic for splitting and settlement as well as track the payouts.

Invoices (Razorpay 2.0 product)

The roll-out of GST in 2016 encouraged online payments but had a lot of merchants grappling with invoicing issues and customer queries. Razorpay "Invoices" was a GST compliant invoice format that merchants could setup from their dashboards and allowed sending of invoices to customers *via* emails or SMS. It also allowed customers to make full or partial payments from the digital invoice.

Responding to specific and sudden requirements of merchants

The demonetisation of high value currency notes in November 2016 took out 86% of the currency by value in circulation and left 12 million mom-and-pop stores unable to handle regular retail transactions. Most of these retail stores only transacted in cash and did not have POS hardware or website or app. The Razorpay team ideated and launched an ePOS App within three days of demonetisation to help such small merchants overcome this situation. A merchant could download the ePOS app on his Android device, get it activated in a few hours' time and start transacting with his cash-crunched customers *via* payment links or wallets in real-time even for offline purchases.

Another such product, eCOD, aimed at disrupting cash-on-delivery (COD) which constituted 60–65%[6] of all e-commerce orders in India. Consumers preferred COD owing to the general lack of trust in the quality of order delivery, avoidance of hassles related to product returns and patchy internet connectivity especially in Tier 2 or Tier 3 cities. eCOD allowed the merchant's delivery executives to accept payments from customers at the time of delivery of goods *via* non-cash methods such as UPI, wallets and payment links.

The Kerala floods of 2018 reportedly affected one-sixth of the population of Kerala and were declared a Level 3 calamity. It was also a time when social media and digital payments played an important role in mobilising people into extending help through donations. The food delivery app Swiggy, a customer of Razorpay, wanted to collect donations for the Kerala floods on its platform and asked Razorpay to quickly set up a page. Although this was a sudden and unplanned activity, the Razorpay team realised that they were in a unique position to help the customer and the community by mobilising the last mile of payment. However, the task was more complex than just setting up a page as it required mandatory segregation of funds, receipt management and compliance with mandates related to

Income Tax exemptions. They quickly got in touch with the Chief Strategist of the Kerala Chief Minister's Relief Fund to understand the nitty-gritty of how to enable transactions. From conception to delivery, they shipped the page out in three hours, creating a strong goodwill with Swiggy while collaborating for a cause and giving back to society.

Reinventing Razorpay: Moving from Products to Platforms

The four new products unveiled at the Razorpay FTX conference were a mix of incremental innovations and fundamental shifts. While Flash Checkout refined an existing product, RazorpayX extended the services to existing customers by offering payment disbursement apart from the existing service of payment acceptance. In contrast, X Club and Razorpay Capital involved a fundamental shift towards developing Razorpay as a platform. With Fintech opportunities in full-bloom in India, Razorpay wanted to diversify beyond pure-play payments, into related business lines in the Fintech universe where Razorpay could leverage the synergies of being a payments player. Diversification of product lines was also becoming a common theme in the payment-tech industry with mobile wallet companies, payment gateways, payment banks, etc., expanding into adjacent sectors such as lend-tech and insure-tech or into additional value-added services such as marketing or logistics. Razorpay's growing proximity to its clients exposed it to the internal workings of its clients' financial operations and allowed it to identify several inefficiencies that it could try and solve.

Flash Checkout

Razorpay added several features to its payment gateway over time to enhance the end user's checkout experience. Flash Checkout focussed on re-designing micro-interactions[7] to reduce the effort that the user had to put in during checkout. Although the Reserve Bank of India had relaxed its rule around two-factor authentication for transactions of less than INR 2,000, banks mandated two-factor authentication as an additional security measure. This meant that, for every online checkout, the user would receive an OTP (one-time password) *via* SMS that he would enter on the merchant's checkout page to complete the payment. However, switching screens back and forth between the checkout page and messaging app and having to enter the OTP created friction with the user as it increased effort, time taken and added distractions to the process. Flash Checkout used a Native OTP feature so that users could enter the OTP within the same payment screen, without leaving the merchant's app/website. In addition, it could preselect a user's preferred payment method based on his payment behaviour across merchants. Customers could utilise their saved cards from the Razorpay network when shopping for the first time with a new merchant.

Affordability was a major factor for Indian consumers. Offers and discounts were a popular way for Indian e-retailers to attract customers. Flash Checkout also allowed merchants to show offers and promotions for popular cards or wallets and incorporate affordability into the checkout process.

RazorpayX

Working with clients enabled Razorpay to realise that digital innovation in corporate banking was often ignored and much of the technology and design was outdated. Financial CRM (Customer Relationship Management) packages used by clients provided fragmented control over money flows and accounting and most corporate dashboards did not provide cohesive insights. Accounting departments got saddled with significantly higher reconciliation issues with the increasing variety of payment channels and scenarios, and spent a lot of time understanding data and deriving usable information.

RazorpayX was Razorpay's version of an AI (Artificial Intelligence) based Digital Banking platform and aimed at providing a major uplift to the way businesses managed and controlled their financial operations. It came with a dashboard, APIs and automations to manage multiple bank accounts, set up payments and refunds, manage and schedule payouts and integrations with other Razorpay products. By creating an account with Razorpay, businesses could enable money flow *via* multiple financial channels (NEFT/RTGS/IMPS, UPI, wallets, cards, etc.[8]) and automate payouts such as salary disbursements.

The financial CRM capabilities built into the product could provide actionable insights such as a client's burn rate, cash left, financial ratios, on-time payments, categorise payment defaulters, etc., based on income, expenses, payments and other accounting data. In effect, it could help startups answer questions like "how much longer can we stay afloat" and "could we arrange more credit". Established businesses, on the other hand, could benefit from the cost and process efficiencies enabled by RazorpayX. By automating payments, payouts and reconciliation efforts across bank accounts, payment methods and receivers, it removed several pain points for their accounting departments.

X Club

X Club was a networking platform to help startups and entrepreneurs meet investors, accelerators, potential partners, mentors and help these startups solve their money flow and capital issues. Having experienced the advantages of having access to an entire community of mentors and fellow entrepreneurs at Y Combinator and the difference it had made to their own entrepreneurship journey, the founders wanted to build a similar platform for Indian startups. The co-founders described it as a "safe space where you can ask difficult questions about running a business". They also looked at it as a platform from where they themselves could learn, and perhaps get to nurture some future success stories.

Razorpay Capital

A large portion of Razorpay's client list comprised inventory-led online businesses. These SMEs struggled with maintaining enough working capital to fulfill orders and manage demand fluctuations. The traditional form of getting access to money was through bank loans but, without enough history or substantial collateral, small merchants found it extremely difficult to find lenders. Banks and NBFCs performed extensive credit worthiness analyses of businesses before lending to them and to decide the terms of lending. The way traditional models worked, all lenders ended up competing for the same pool of SMEs that the models deemed worthy of financing, and this pool formed only a fraction of the overall SME segment. Additionally, it was impossible for one single company to have a direct relationship with the entire SME market, so a common strategy that lenders applied was to partner with loan aggregators or agents who would help source credit takers for a considerable commission. As a result, though there was enough credit and lending appetite in the market, traditional lending systems restricted access to the right audiences. Several startups, providing online peer-to-peer lending solutions and small working capital loans for merchants, were growing well and had raised a lot of funding. The digital lending market was expected to hit USD 1 trillion between 2018 and 2023.

Razorpay Capital was a marketplace offering instant settlements and collateral-free loans to Razorpay's clients. By having access to the transaction history of a merchant, Razorpay had visibility into certain trends and business behaviours, for example, seasonality in sales, financial year end behaviour, refunds and chargebacks/fraud issues, etc., that could be useful as indicators of the credit worthiness of a merchant. This formed the basis for an Alternative Credit Decisioning System, that used transaction history to assign a credit score to a merchant as an input to aid NBFC partners' lending decisions. For merchants that qualified for pre-approved or collateral-free loans, instant access to loans was available with a click of a button from the Razorpay dashboard. With Razorpay being the mediator, merchants could save significant manpower costs and time spent in chasing lenders, managing relationships with individual Banks/NBFCs and figuring out the best interest rates, etc. The lending partner on the other side of the marketplace, would benefit from an additional source of loan generators and quality supply of pre-qualified leads at a fixed cost.

The product allowed a Flexible Repayment model where the merchant could opt for Razorpay to deduct part of his daily settlements towards loan repayments based on his ability to pay on that day. Based on the day's volume compared to the merchant's average transaction volume, the model would automatically know and charge less or more. Another problem that businesses faced was that settlements through a payment gateway happened on a T+2 or T+3 basis[9], so it became hard to manage the float especially during a spike in orders. To help expedite this cycle, Razorpay Capital provided an Instant Settlements or Scheduled Early Settlements option where it took on some additional risk to provide a cash advance by settling their payments on the same day or the next day by 9 a.m.

After a merchant had been transacting for at least three months and hit a steady flow of volume with Razorpay, he would be eligible to apply for Razorpay Capital and would receive an intimation on the Dashboard or *via* the marketing team. If he opted in, he permitted Razorpay to share his credit score with partner NBFCs. Once onboarded, the merchant could apply for pre-approved loans or would be matched with lending partners as well as use instant settlement features. To control the overall experience of the platform, Razorpay also stipulated minimum performance criteria, such as the time to settle a loan, for the lending partners. Over time, they saw Razorpay Capital as an open market for any NBFC or bank to be able to come onboard as long as they met the performance criteria. However, initially they planned to pilot the programme by partnering with only a few NBFCs and banks who valued Razorpay's brand and clientele and had positive internal references from their teams who had worked with Razorpay's payments products. An open marketplace meant that the platform operator needed to handle diverse lenders and their lending practices. For example, NBFCs typically specialised in sectors (Restaurants, Travel etc.) for lending and had different internal standards for the time required to disburse sanctioned loans, different loan repayment schedules as well as different payment instruments.

The choices in scaling up

For Razorpay, the products launched during Razorpay FTX were an important milestone in its growth journey as Razorpay expanded into new product lines like digital lending and unified digital banking operations. So far, Razorpay had positioned itself as a premium, hassle-free and technologically superior digital payments solutions provider for online payment acceptance and disbursal for businesses, mostly startups. Razorpay delivered value to customers on various parameters like ease of integration, developer friendliness, post implementation support, user experience and payment conversion rate. The founders wondered if it was time to review the existing strategy, and if it needed to be modified for the next phase of growth of the firm.

Mathur and Kumar wanted Razorpay to be the most technically advanced and comprehensive platform for digital payments and lending for Indian businesses. However, they sensed that the early signs of commoditisation of the payments ecosystem had started showing and worried that as competitors caught up on features, differentiation based on products would not last long (see Exhibit 6 for a view of how a customer, Rivigo, perceived Razorpay). The founders wondered what they should do to create value for its customers so that Razorpay could continue to command a premium for its products and services. The founders also needed to consider if Razorpay's traditional strength of service convenience could be a differentiator in an already crowded marketplace of digital payments and lending where low price was usually the key purchase criterion.

In the long run, Razorpay wished to become a multi-sided platform on which third party service providers like banks and NBFCs could provide a variety of services to merchants, taking advantage of the analytical capabilities that a platform with rich client transaction history enabled. To attract external complimentary service providers, Razorpay needed to grow the transactions on its platform. As a result, in the short run, Razorpay needed to choose between different options for growth. Should the focus be on growing the revenue or profitability or usage of the platform or something else? This choice was also fundamentally linked to the kind of investor base. Venture capital based funding could allow longer term investments in developing the product suite while Private Equity players needed to provide exits to their clients at higher valuations and hence may have a relatively shorter term focus. A change in the composition of the investor base in terms of the investment horizon during subsequent rounds of funding could alter the metrics used for evaluating growth. Conversely, if the founders believed that Razorpay needed to continue its investments in the product suite rather than show quick results then the firm needed to make choices about the kind of investors that it wanted to attract.

The founders were also deliberating if growth should come from taking a product focus or a solution focus. With product focus, standard products were developed with a large number of features; a few of those features might not be used immediately by most of the customers. This led to a higher initial investment (capex), but also ensured limited ongoing expenses and customisation effort. Razorpay also wanted to invest in different types of products, with the intention of capturing more and varied transactions of the customer.

With a solution focus approach as followed by the multiple competitors of Razorpay, custom solutions were developed for each individual need. This also increased the product-market fit for an increasing diversity of sectors and reduced the necessity of pre-developing a large number of product features and extensions. With a product centric approach, Razorpay had all along been developing standardised APIs which could be used by most of the customers without the need for major tweaks. While the existing product marketing team structure might suffice for a product focussed approach, a solutions focussed approach could call for setting up different SBUs for different industry verticals (e.g., Online Education) or for different product offerings (e.g., Subscriptions). While an SBU structure could allow better design, delivery, sales promotions and customer service, it risked fragmenting the seamless integration of data across different products as Razorpay grew in size, potentially creating data silos. In contrast, a product focus ensured that Razorpay could continue to make expensive but long-term investments in extending the product suite and capture the financial transaction history of merchants across different transaction use cases. While an increase in the volume of transactions and increase in the variety of transactions both ultimately increased revenues, the two paths differed in terms of the richness of the merchant transaction analytics capabilities that could be developed subsequently.

The choice of customer was also important. While Razorpay was focussed on disruptors, the disruptor could be not just startups disrupting the legacy players in an industry but also progressive legacy players in banking, mutual funds and insurance verticals which had created small internal teams to redesign and disrupt the traditional financial services industry. While the needs of these two kinds of disruptors (startups and legacy players) were similar to some extent, there existed a large number of established businesses with a large volume of financial transactions who were not disruptors. While the established businesses represented a growth potential for Razorpay, serving this segment would mean working on offering a different value proposition than what appealed to the startup disruptors. The established businesses had large accounting departments, access to in-house and outsourced IT services teams, better financial stability and cash flows. Such businesses might see little value in entering into a revenue sharing pact with firms like Razorpay for enabling digital financial transactions.

The final growth frontier was the large cash-based economy in India. According to Atul Mehta, Head of Sales, Razorpay, the true competitor of Razorpay was not any specific payment gateway or wallet but the alternative non-digital payment mechanisms including cash. Instead of fighting with competitors (refer to Exhibit 7 for a description of major payment gateways) for an increase in the share of the digital financial transactions market, how could Razorpay be a change agent in enabling a move away from cash towards digital payments? Could Razorpay not just act as a back-end support for disruptors but also present compelling use cases to consumers to wean them away from cash based payments? However, such a gambit might require a move away from its traditional strength in B2B markets towards B2C markets, possibly launching products like digital wallets. Such a move might also mean that Razorpay would have to move away from being agnostic about payment instruments available to consumers on the Razorpay platform and bring Razorpay into direct competition with some of the existing wallet providers. Instead, would it be prudent for Razorpay

RAZORPAY

to stick to the B2B market and be the backend payment service provider? Currently a customer on an ecommerce website might not even notice that the payment was processed through the Razorpay channel. Growing the Razorpay brand in the minds of not just merchants but also end consumers and investors could be the most difficult but promising challenge facing the founders.

Exhibit 1: Revenue and Profit/Loss (INR million)

	2014–15	*2015–16*	*2016–17*	*2017–18*
Total Income	1.07	48.82	258.24	922.22
Revenue from Operations	0.85	7.99	216.37	900.56
Other Income	0.22	40.83	41.87	21.66
Total Expenses	1.48	44.43	265.97	956.68
PBT	-0.41	4.39	-7.73	-127.51
PAT	-0.41	2.87	-5.49	-127.69

Source: Annual Reports

Exhibit 2: Comparison of Payment Gateways pricing (INR)

	Razorpay	*Mobi-kwik*	*PayUBiz (Various plans)*	*Pay-UMoney*	*Paytm*	*Instamojo*	*CCAvenue*
Setup Fees	0		4,900–19,900	0	0	0	0–30,000
AMC	0		2,400–7,400	0	0	0	1,200
NEFT/RTGS/ BankTransfer	2%	1.90%	2.25%–2.95%	2%	1.9–9%	Free	2%
Debit Cards	2%	1.90%	0.75–1%	2%	1.9–9%	2% + INR 3	2%
Visa, MasterCard, RuPay	2%	1.90%	2.25%–2.95%	2%	1.9–9%	2% + INR 3	2%
Wallets	2%	1.90%	2.25–2.95%	2%	0–9%	2% + INR 3	2%
AMEX/Diners/ JCB	3%	2.90%	3–3.70%	3%	1.9–9%		3%
International Cards	3%	2.90%	NA/3–3.25% + INR 6				3%
Multicurrency	3%						4.99%
Wallets supported	8	4	5		1	4	8
NetBanking options	58		45+	50+	50+		53+

Source: Prepared by the authors based on news reports and company websites.

RAZORPAY

Exhibit 3: Number of service tickets handled

	Q1 (Apr-Jun)	Q2 (Jul-Sep)	Q3 (Oct-Dec)	Q4 (Jan-Mar)
2016–17	5,576	8,669	14,884	19,468
2017–18	21,488	24,677	37,830	35,587
2018–19	35,878	43,300	46,400	70,200

Source: Company data

Exhibit 4: Product-wise Percentage Share of Revenue

	2016–17	2017–18	2018–19	2019–20 estimate
Payment Gateway	100	85	70	55
2.0 Products (Payment Links, Subscriptions, Route, Smart Collect)	0	15	30	45
Percentage of Enterprise accounts using more than 1 product	0	25	60	90

Source: Company data

Exhibit 5: Process flow in online checkout

1. Buyer (consumer) clicks the buy/checkout button, selects payment mode, enters payment instrument information (e.g., credit card info) and initiates the payment.
2. The payment gateway/aggregator receives the payment information, encrypts the information and passes it on to the wallet or issuing bank *via* the backend network (e.g., card networks or aggregator partner) as per the selected payment mode.
3. The issuer authorises the payment and sends a success or failure notification to the acquiring bank *via* the network. The acquirer notifies the payment gateway.
4. The payment gateway sends a confirmation to the merchant website.
5. The issuing bank/wallet also sends confirmation to the customer about the transaction.

Source: Prepared by the authors based on news reports and company websites.

Exhibit 6: Customer perspective - Rivigo

Rivigo was a logistics company that operated a unique driver relay model where truck drivers employed by the firm drove company-owned trucks over specific sections of a long route. It also offered a separate Freight Marketplace service to connect individuals or organisations with trucking needs with fleet operators. Typically, a fleet owner insisted on advance payment before a load was picked up at the client site. The client had to pay the advance to the fleet owner through Rivigo's website which used several payment gateways. A payment transaction involved several payment hops involving the client, the client's bank or card or wallet provider, the fleet owner's bank, any intermediary like NPCI if transactions like UPI were involved, Rivigo servers and payment gateway servers. With multi-party involvement, even a 0.5% error rate in one leg of the payment hops could adversely impact the overall reliability of the entire payment transaction. Given the higher average ticket size compared to ecommerce transactions, unreliable payment transactions could cause significant delays in payments leading to vehicle detention and substantial loss in business for fleet owners.

To build in high-availability, speed and robustness into their systems, Rivigo, therefore used multiple payment gateways for accepting payments from the clients which was then passed onto the fleet owners *via* IMPS or NEFT. Rivigo used a dynamic switching algorithm that evaluated the payment gateways' performances on the basis of (i) success rate (how many transactions went through successfully in one go), (ii) turnaround time or TAT (time for the payment gateway to respond with a confirmation of success or failure of transaction so that further disbursements or auto-refunds could be processed), and (iii) Bluff rate (a transaction which was earlier termed as success but later termed as failed or vice versa was called a bluff). The dynamic switching weighed these parameters in real time and diverted exponentially more traffic to the better performing gateway. Rivigo reported that Razorpay received more volume of transactions on an average compared to other competing payment gateways. To stay competitive, payment gateways needed to continuously improve the success rates, speed and reliability of transactions. With a success rate of 75% (that included factors over which payment gateways had no control, e.g., customer change of mind at payment stage), Rivigo felt there was enough scope for further improvement.

Rahul Lodha, VP Engineering at Rivigo, rated Razorpay's support and communication as high-quality. He appreciated Razorpay's being proactive in planning and communicating down-times to Rivigo as well as debugging and identifying root causes for stuck transactions and providing visibility on issue resolution. He praised Razorpay's use of automation, where possible, to enable Rivigo help their customers. For example, Razorpay had provided Rivigo an API that informed that a particular bank payment server might be experiencing high latency or failure rates. Rivigo could then inform their clients of the situation and suggest they use another payment mode.

Lodha also valued the scalability inherent in using a technologically advanced payment gateway. Since the Freight Marketplace vertical of Rivigo was growing in volume, the reconciliation efforts required would have also grown substantially if the payment gateway was of poor quality. Due to the adoption of Razorpay, the finance team at Rivigo did not need to handle payment reconciliations, thereby freeing them up for more pressing business challenges. Also, Rivigo technology team's effort required in resolving issues was reduced due to the debugging facilities such as detailed logs and dashboard provided by Razorpay.

As a technology-based logistics player, Rivigo differentiated itself as a supply chain innovator. It thus valued collaborative innovation efforts. In the Part-truck load business of Rivigo, Razorpay Payment Links helped to remove the use of cash that needed manual reconciliation. Similarly, Rivigo and Razorpay collaborated in brainstorming on ways to reduce the payment failure rates for payments involving NPCI which had a higher failure rate. A potential solution would be to avoid the NPCI network through direct intra-bank transfers but this would have needed Rivigo to have the same bank as the fleet owners and clients. Given Razorpay's placement as a payment mediator, it made sense for Razorpay to offer this service not just for Rivigo but also for its other customers. Razorpay decided to build a solution by tying up with five major banks that carried 85% of digital payments so that customers like Rivigo could provide better payment reliability to their clients.

Source: Prepared by the authors based on interviews with Rivigo.

Exhibit 7: Competitor Profiles (Payment Gateway)

PayU was a global financial services provider headquartered in Netherlands, with a presence in different countries across Asia, Central and Eastern Europe, Latin America, the Middle East and Africa. It was the fintech and epayments division of Naspers Group, a leading global technology investor. PayU enabled merchants to accept digital payments through more than 300 payment methods. As of 2018, the service was available in 17 countries with about 1.2 million payments processed per day. PayU was built through the acquisition of multiple payment gateways and was valued at USD 5 billion in 2018. In 2016, PayU acquired Indian payments services provider Citrus Pay for USD 130 million.

Paytm was founded in 2010 in Noida and initially focussed on prepaid and postpaid mobile, DTH and landline bill payments. It launched Paytm Wallet in 2014 and experienced exponential growth following the demonetisation exercise in November 2016. It was a pioneer in the use of QR based mobile payments in India and in 2018 over 7 million merchants all over

India used Paytm's QR code to accept payments. Valued at over USD 10 billion, Paytm had expanded into offering a variety of services like payments bank, wealth management, ecommerce and gaming. Paytm was available in 10 Indian languages. Major investors included Softbank, SAIF Partners, Alibaba Group and Ant Financial. One97 Communications, the parent company of Paytm, reported revenue of INR 29,874.1 million and a net loss of INR 14,904 million for the year ending March 2018.

BillDesk was a Mumbai based online payment gateway company founded in 2000. It reported revenue of INR 9,290 million and a profit of INR 1,480 million in 2018. Valued at USD 1.8 billion, its investors included Visa, Temasek Holdings, General Electric, Clearstone Venture Partners and TA Associates. The platform was mainly a bill payment system which allowed customers to use net banking or cards.

CCAvenues was founded in 2001 and based in Mumbai. It aimed to provide end-to-end ecommerce solutions and had a base of more than 0.1 million Indian merchants. Its service offerings included payment gateways, invoice payments, subscriptions, automated disbursements and collections, customisable store fronts, sales over social networks and acesss to business loans. In 2017, CCAvenues merged with Infibeam, an Ahmedabad based ecommerce firm, at a valuation of USD 289 million. In Q2FY18, CCAvenues processed 26.6 million transactions worth INR 54,140 million.

PayPal was founded in 1998 and became a wholly owned subsidiary of eBay till it was spun off as a publicly traded company in 2015. In 2017, PayPal reported a profit of USD 1,795 million on a revenue of USD 13,094 million. PayPal was available in more than 200 countries with 277 million registered users. It reported processing four billion payments in 2014. Initially, merchants in India primarily used PayPal to receive funds from foreign customers. PayPal started domestic operations in India from November 2017.

Source: Prepared by the authors based on news reports and company websites.

Discussions on the case:

SCOPE

The case examines the role of service convenience as a value generator in the technology services in the specific context of digital payments. In the contested digital payment market in India, Razorpay wanted to sustain its growth by using technological leadership and service differentiation. To maintain its growth trajectory, Razorpay has launched multiple new products in the digital payment space and also announced a foray into creating a marketplace for digital lending through the launch of Razorpay Capital. The case provides details of the growth of Razorpay and its move from its core strength as a payment gateway to a more platform-centric business model. Razorpay needs to review and decide the different facets of its product and market strategy in view of its pivoting in an evolving market.

The case need to be read with the seminal paper, *Understanding Service Convenience*. (Berry, Seiders, Grewal, 2002).

PRINCIPAL ISSUES

This case can be used to highlight the following issues:

- Differences between product, service and platform-oriented strategy for technology providers
- Multiple stakeholders in the technology buying process and their contrasting priorities
- Concept of value and its importance in technology sales process
- Identifying, positioning and promoting different types of value propositions, identifying a segment that matches the value offering
- Different aspects of service convenience
- Sustaining competitive differentiation in a rapidly growing industry

LEARNING OBJECTIVES

Managing relationships and developing an effective value proposition for the varied enterprise customers is very different from that for retail customers. While sales organizations focusing on enterprises are quite familiar with the concept of cost leadership, they focus less on other aspects of value, particularly on service excellence or convenience. This case introduces participants to different dimensions of service excellence in the digital payment context and how to create an effective value proposition and competitive differentiator. The case also highlights the fact that the value proposition cultivated over time can outlive its utility, as the industry changes and the firm needs to adapt to it.

Suggested Questions for discussions

1 What are the advantages and disadvantages of service focused and product focused business models?
2 What are the benefits for Razorpay to pursue a platform centric business model? What are the main challenges it would face?
3 Identify the different stakeholders and their different priorities in the buyer organization in the context of Razorpay?
4 For a typical customer like Rivigo, how can Razorpay create a compelling value proposition. Your value proposition should have few

compelling themes and how those themes would benefit customer and if possible identify KPI to measure the value creation?

5 What are the challenges Razorpay would face in communicating this value proposition compared to providing a lower-cost solution?

Notes

1 http://indiamicrofinance.com/ecommerce-business-india-2014-2015-report-pdf. html accessed on May 3, 2019.

2 Agile Scrum or Scrum Agile is a time-boxed iterative software development process to build, inspect and ship software incrementally. It incorporates mechanisms for iterative feedback in order to deal with changing or evolving business requirements.

3 Edge cases are the conditions that can occur but occur rarely. In designing products with universal design (i.e. for extremely diverse range of situations, users and abilities), edge cases must be handled to achieve a reasonable level of quality. Examples of edge cases include API designs that can tolerate inputs of malicious nature or at boundary conditions, or designing the checkout experience keeping in mind that network connectivity might drop off in the middle of a mobile payment transaction.

4 Payment Card Industry Data Security Standard. Since Razorpay was PCI DSS certified, merchants did not need to be individually certified to be compliant with security standards for accepting cards.

5 National Electronic Fund Transfer (NEFT), Real Time Gross Settlement (RTGS) and Immediate Payment Service (IMPS) are electronic payment systems that enable users to transfer funds between bank accounts.

6 https://www.livemint.com/Industry/VgOTW8ZS4RaHA5gd7iwM4N/COD-payments-at-ecommerce-firms-back-to-pre-demonetisation.html accessed on May 3, 2019

7 Micro-interaction is a specific moment of interaction in a user interface. For example, a user swiping on a slider is a micro-interaction. In UX, micro-interaction designs are considered extremely important in communicating with the user, gaining their attention and encouraging positive favourable behaviour from the user.

8 National Electronic Fund Transfer (NEFT), Real-time Gross Settlement (RTGS), Immediate Payment Service (IMPS) and United Payment Interface (UPI) were different channels for electronic transfer of funds between bank accounts.

9 T being the date of capture of payment, settlement on T+2/T+3 refers to 2nd/3rd working day after T.

Relevant Readings

Berry, L. L., Seiders, K., and Grewal, D. (2002). Understanding Service Convenience. Journal of Marketing, 66(3), 1–17.

INDEX

Note: **Bold** and *Italic* page numbers refer to **tables** and *figures*.

5G 183, 185
5Vs 187

Aadhaar platform 30
accessibility 33, 143
account management 3, 132, 133, 134, 136, 142, 143, 144, 147, 149, 153, 155, 158, 161, 162, 228
account managers 19, 24, 136, 137, 141, 142, 143, 147, 148, 152, 153, 154, 228
account mining 83
account plans 136, 137, 142, 147, 155
adaptations by seller and buyer 10
advertising 170
agile manifesto 54
agile methodology 54, 55, 56, 199
agile scrum 57
ambidextrous governance 148
analogous estimate 70
analysing 146–147
analytics driven opportunity assessment 92–93
Anderson, J. C. 36, 39, 41
ansoff matrix 139, 140, 160, 161
Application Development and Maintenance (ADM) 18
artificial general intelligence 192
artificial intelligence 1, 19, 182, 191, 192, 201, 211, 223, 233, 249
artificial narrow intelligence 192
artificial super intelligence 192
average revenue per user (ARPU) 42

B2B2C markets 10
Banking, Financial Services and Insurance (BFSI) 11
barriers of cloud 203
best of breed 115
bid management 79, 81, 94, 97, 106, 118, 120, 228
bid process 98, 110, 117, 118
Big Data 28, 69, 92, 101, 187, 191, 234
BillDesk 258
blockchain 1, 19, 24, 118, 188, 189, 191, 200, 201, 211, 233
block storage 184
bottom-up cost estimate 71
brand and image management 159, 243
business analyst 230
business case 33, 41, 42, 44, 59, 88, 93, 216
business intelligence 178, 228
business requirement 18, 116, 117, 124, 226
business-to-business (B2B) markets 5, 6–10; B2B2C markets 10; *vs.* B2C markets 6
business-to-consumer (B2C) markets 5
business value 27–47; Amazon's recommendation system 29–30; changing role, IT 27–29; financial attractiveness of IT solutions, techniques 44–47; global economy, importance 33–36; Government of India's Aadhaar platform 30–31;

INDEX

information technology delivering value 29–31; IT solutions context, value 36–37; IT's role, contrasting perspectives 31–33; net present value 46; opposing view, competitive advantage 32–33; organisational resources and capability, combination 31–32; payback period 47; resource-based view 31–32; return on investment (ROI) 46–47; value propositions 37–44
Butters Law 183
buyer(s): adaptations 10; profiles 22
buyers, IT services 11–12, 109; geography 11
buying behaviour matrix 114
buying IT 108–130

campaign management 61, 176
capability maturity model 54, 150, 151
captives 15
careers 223–236
Carr, N. G. 32
CCAvenues 258
change management 19, 127, 148, 149, 154, 198, 231
channel partners 24, 144, 172
chief digital officer (CDO) 24
chief information officer (CIO) 88
chief marketing officer 158
chief technology officer (CTO) 241
classification algorithm 92
client dissatisfaction 152
client expectations 142, 143
client management 132, 135, 142, 152, 155, 156
client portfolio management 134, 156
client reference 105
client relationship management 132, 133
client relationship strategy 155
client segmentation 135
cloud 184, 203, 204, 205, 206, 207, 208, 209, 210, 211, 212, 213, 214, 215, 216, 217, 218, 219, 220, 221; delivery models 213–217; selling cloud to enterprises 217–220; service models 211–213
cloud adoption 206–211
cloud application market 206, 207, 210–211
cloud benefits 207–209
cloud characteristics: measured service 206; on-demand self-service 205;

rapid elasticity 205–206; resource pooling 205; ubiquitous network access 205
cloud computing 203, 204, 205, 206, 209, 211, 212, 213, 216, 220, 221, 223, 227, 230
cloud selling 203, 219
cloud storage 184
cloud value-proposition 220
collaborative IT 11
collaborative technology 176
communication plan 51, 149, 150, 152, 172
communications 20, 23, 25, 50, 51, 143, 149, 150, 152, 156, 157, 159, 185, 224, 228, 229, 230, 246, 258
confirmatory questions 60
conflict management 126
consultants 53, 60, 83, 121, 122, 123, 163, 211, 229, 230
consulting 2, 3, 18, 81, 82, 83, 112, 115, 223, 225, 227, 230, 231
continuous learning 233
contract closure 110, 120, 128, 129
contract execution 110, 125
contract negotiation 110, 115, 125, 178, 200
contracts types 16
contractual governance 148
contract value 76, 79, 99, 100, 101, 102, 103
contract workers 232
control mechanisms 127–128; types of control 127–128
conversation starters in cloud selling 219
cooperative norms 10
corporate website 167, 168
crowdsourcing 232, 233, 234
cultural differences 147, 152
customer(s) 11–14; needs 22; service loop 144
customer pain points 244
customer personnel, profile 22; culturally diverse 22; healthy scepticism 23; knowledgeable and experienced 22; need for value addition 22–23
customer relationship management (CRM) technologies 133

data analyst 229
data analytics 69, 230
database generation 161

262

INDEX

data cleansing 188
data management 162, 214, 219, 228, 229
data processing 27, 32, 187, 188
data transformation 188
deciders 163
decision-makers 59
decision-making units (DMUs) 37
dedicated teams 15
demand generation 157, 158, 159, 168, 170, 178, 179
demographic data 134, 135, 162, 187
depth interview 59
design thinking 19, 199, 201, 232, 235
development roles 225, 226
digital campaigns 164
digitalisation services 19
digital payment ecosystem 238–239
digital technologies 19, 24, 180, 181, 182, 194, 196, 198, 200, 201, 230, 233, 238
digital transformation 19, 24, 180, 181, 182, 194, 198, 199, 200, 201, 231, 232, 233
digitisation 181
digitised spaces 239, 258
direct attached storage (DAS) 184
diversity 115, 116, 132, 232, 235, 252
drip marketing 169–170, 176

Economic Times 30
Economist, The 30
edge computing 233
effectiveness analysis 146
efficiency analysis 146
effort estimation 69, 70
electronic devices 186
email campaign 166, 169
emotional competence 23
engagement model(s) 14–16, 25, 223; captive unit 15; dedicated teams 15; fixed price 15; scope-based delivery 15; time and material 15
engineering degrees 224
enterprise blockchains 189
enterprise IT 11, 187, 233
escalation matrix 152
estimation 50, 51, 58, 67–73, 69, 70, 71, 72, 73, 76, 77, 154, 208; accuracy 70, 72, **73**; baseline 67; bottom-up cost estimate 71; need 67–68; techniques used in 69–70; top-down approach 70

executive relationship 87
expert judgment 70
expert systems 193
extreme programming 55, 200

fast-moving consumer goods (FMCG) 12
features-advantages-benefits matrix 176
fixed price 15, 99, 100
functional IT 11
fundamental value equation 41
Future of Work, The 230

gatekeepers 138, 163
gig workers 232, 233
global clients 147
global workforce 223
governance 16, 21, 126, 130, 131, 133, 147, 148, 149, 155, 156, 220, 223, 231, 233; structure 147, 148, 149
government business 12

healthcare 11
Heiman, S. 87
high-tech 12
hybrid cloud 211, 213, 215, 216, 221

industrial automation 194, 195, 201
industry associations 162, 167
industry conferences 166
industry research and analysis 158, 172
industry segments 11–12
information exchange 8, 115
information technology (IT) market: understanding 5–26
Infrastructure as a Service (IaaS) 71
infrastructure management 225
in-house training 2
insight IT 11
integrated relationship management 133, 142, 155
intellectual property 12, 15, 31, 112, 158
interdisciplinary subject 1
Internet of Things (IoT) 19, 28, 182, 185–186, 211, 223
investment, drivers 29
IT buying process 1
IT capability acquisition 2
IT careers 3
IT does not matter 32
iterative development approach 55
IT industry landscape 10–11
IT's role in global economy 33–36
IT selling process 180

263

INDEX

IT services types: application development and maintenance (ADM) 18; consulting 18; digital technologies 19; outsourcing 18–19; prime system integration 18

key account planning 137
key accounts 3, 132, 134, 135, 136, 137, 155, 242
key informants 59
knowledge management 3, 99, 104, 172, 177
Kryder's law 183

lead sources 163
legal bonds 10
life sciences 11
listening 144, 146, 155
Logicnet 37, 38
long sales cycles 21; exclusive *vs.* competitive 21; new project *vs.* extension 21; relationship with customer 21; size and complexity, projects 21
loyalty ladder 139, 140

machine learning 1, 28, 92, 188, 191, 192, 193
make or buy decision 111, 113
management information systems (MIS) reports 28
market and situational determinants 8
marketing plan 157, 158, 159, 170
marketing roles 3, 172, 227
marketing support 163
master data management 162
Master of Business Administration (MBA) 225
Master Services Agreement (MSA) 16
McAfee, A. 10, 11
media business 12
methodological competence 23, 24
Miller, R. 87, 88, 163
mobile technology 186
MOOC platforms 233
Moore's Law 183
multi-cloud architecture 216
multi-sided platforms 196

Narayandas, D. 36
Narus, J. A. 36, 39
natural language processing 191, 193

nearshore delivery 17
net present value (NPV) 27, 91
Network-attached storage (NAS) 184
networks 184–185; storage 184
non-tariff barriers 22

object storage 184
offshore delivery 17
offshore development centre (ODC) 15
offshore onsite delivery 18
offsite delivery 18
one-time license fee 13
on-premises IT 208, 210, 217, 220, 221
onshore delivery 17
onsite delivery 17
on-the-job training 2
operational linkages 8
opportunities 81–95
opportunity identification and qualification 79, 80, 81
organisational buying centres (OBC) 37, 38
outsourcing 14, 17, 18, 19, 22, 111, 113, 147, 148, 152, 153, 156, 161

parametric estimate 69–70
partnership 31, 32, 83, 84, 85, 107, 142, 158, 196; with customers 85–86; with other companies 83–85
pay-as-you-go 207
payback period 41, 44, 45, 47
payment milestone 103–104
PayPal 258
Paytm 257–258
PayU 257
personal competence 23
pipeline management 141
plan-driven software project management methodology 52–54
Platform as a Service (PaaS) 212
platform companies 13, 19, 25
platforms 13, 19, 28, 162, 165, 176, 177, 187, 196, 197, 200, 201, 233, 245
Porter's five forces *174*
pre-sales and sales roles 227–228
primary information 59
prime system integration 18
private cloud 215
proactive selling 82, 109
process automation 27, 29, 47, 182, 194, 201

264

INDEX

product companies 12, 13, 15, 25, 83, 158, 167, 168
product management 62, 157, 158, 178
product mix 158
professional competence 23
program 23, 30, 68, 71, 74, 192, 193, 223, 224, 229, 231, 232
project 15, 46, 51, 52, 58, 63, 64, 65, 66, 67, 68, 70, 71, 74, 76, 117, 127, 149, 154, 229; lifecycle 52, 71, 76
project management essentials 50–77; agile methodologies 54–58; customer's pain points, understanding 58–60; estimation 67–73; example 60–61; in-depth interview 59; plan-driven software project management methodology 52–54; primary information 59–60; risk management 63–67; secondary information 58–59; workshop 61–63
project management office (PMO) 149
project phases 52, 76
public cloud 212, 213, 215
PwC 191

Rajala, R. 80
rapid application development. 200
Razorpay 237–260; choices in scaling up 251–254; developer hub 245; digital payment ecosystem 238–239; firm 239–258; Flash Checkout 248–249; invoices 247; Payment Gateway 244–245; Payment Links 246; product development 243–244; Razorpay 2.0 suite 245–246; Razorpay Capital 250–251; RazorpayX 249; reinventing 248; requirements of merchants 247–248; route 246–247; sales and marketing 240–241; subscriptions 246; support and operations 242–243; X Club 249–250
reactive selling 21, 82
recency-frequency-monetary framework 135–136
recommendation systems 29, 30
recording 144, 145, 146, 155, 184
relational constructs 8–10; consequences of 10
relational governance 148
relationship breakdown 8
relationship management 3

relationship termination 153
request for proposals (RFP) 7, 8, 82, 118, 178
request for quotation (RFQ) 178
resolving 144, 146, 155, 257
resource-based view (RBV): capability 31–32; resources 31–32
resourcing pyramid 224
responsiveness 143, 205, 243, 245
retail 12
return on investment (ROI) 91, 112, 149, 167
reverse SLAs 147, 154, 156
RFP/RFI/RFX 82
RFX process 82
risk classification 65
risk exposure matrix 67
risk impact assessment 64, 66
risk management 51, 58, 63–67, 64, 81, 99, 104, 106, 127, 152; essential in proposal phase 63–64; risk classification 65–66; risk exposure on proposal 66–67; risk identification 64–66; risk impact assessment 66–67; risk response planning 67
risk mitigation 50, 112, 132, 133, 152, 155
risk profile 50, 64, 73, 76, 95, 103, 127
risk response planning 64, 67
risk response strategies **68–69**
Rivigo 256–257
roadshows 167
Röglinger, M. 182
role of IT 27, 28, 33

salesforce management 176
sales personnel 8, 23, 82, 159, 166, 169, 170, 172, 228
sales personnel competencies 23; emotional competence 23; methodological competence 23–24; personal competence 23; professional competence 23
sales toolkit 157, 172
same account revenue growth 139
schedule development 73–75
scope-based delivery 15
scope creep 51, 153, 154
scrum 55–57, 78, 200; ceremonies 57
SDN-WAN 185
search engine marketing 165
search engine optimization 165

INDEX

secondary information 39, 58, 59
seller, adaptations 10
sellers, of IT services 12–14; platform companies 13–14; product companies 12–13; services companies 12
selling IT, characteristics 19; high dependency, resources 21; long sales cycles 21; susceptible to non-tariff barriers 22; team-based process 19–21
sensors 181, 186, 194–196, 230, 231
service delivery location: nearshore 17; offshore 17; offshore onsite 18; onshore 17; onsite 17
service level agreements 15, 213
service management standards 150
service providers 11–14
services companies 12, 18, 19, 158, 159, 167, 168, 172, 221
Seshadri, D. V. R. 36
single/multi vendor 108, 111, 114
social media 28, 165, 168, 169, 176, 179, 182, 186–188, 197, 227, 230
Software as a Service (SaaS) 208
software project management 50, 52
software project management methodology: plan-driven 52–54
solution architect 228
solution delivery 106
solution development 66, 76, 79, 97–105, 212; commercial solution 99–104; legal section 104; proposal audit 104; technical solution 98–99; unsuccessful proposals, reasons 104–105
sourcing analysis 110, 128, 129
sourcing strategy 110, 111, 114, 129, 217
Spiezia, V. 33
sponsorships 170
statements of work (SoWs) 147
steering committee 126, 149, 150
structured opportunity assessment 91, 92, 107
subscription-based model 14

talent ecosystem 232
target segment identification 159
team based buying 19–21
team-based process 19–21
technology changes, pace 24; consulting led sales 24; multiple decision makers

24; new and old technologies, blending 24; new engagement models 24; niche vendors, competing 24; sale process, impact 24–25
technology evolution 3
telecom 12
telemarketing 169
time and material 15, 99, 101
top-down approach 70
total cost of ownership (TCO) 37, 109
Töytäri, P. 80
tradeshows 167
traditional manufacturing customers 12
transaction *vs.* relationship-oriented buying behaviour 117
trusted advisor 138, 139
types of buyers 88
types of contracts 16; cost reimbursable (CR) 99–100; fixed price (FP) 100–101; pay per use/transaction 99; shared risk/reward 99; time and material (T&M) 101

unstructured data 187, 188, 219, 227
Urbach, N. 182
user conferences 167
users 19, 28, 54, 65, 88, 124, 163, 184, 185, 197, 199, 205–208, 211–213, 227, 239
utilities 12

value 2, 3, 7, 27, 36–38, 41, 44, 46–48, 79, 80, 91, 95–98, 102, 259; articulation 79, 80; -based selling 1–2, 7, 79–81, 106, 107; delivery 23, 79, 80, 105; equation 41; measurement 79, 80; solutioning 80; theme 96
value proposition 27, 37–44, 47, 48, 80, 83, 85, 95–98, 167, 259; value-based business case, IT investment 42–44
value proposition definition strategy: all benefit 40; most important benefits 40; points of difference 40
Van Rossum, W. 39
vendor 15, 102, 108–110, 114–117, 120–122, 124–126, 129, 130, 149, 153, 160; enablement 125; management 108–110, 113, 115, 129, 130, 143, 147, 149, 153, 156, 229; performance assessment 109,

INDEX

122; selection 106, 108–110, 115, 119–125, 129
visualization 28

waterfall model 52–54, 56, 76, 199
webinars 165–166
Wi-Fi 6 185
winning value proposition 96

wired networks 184
wireless networks 184, 185
work from home 235
workshop 61–63; agreed purpose and outcome of 61–62; facilitation 63; follow-up actions 62; people for attendance 62; process of conducting 62

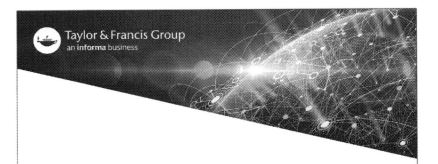

Taylor & Francis eBooks

www.taylorfrancis.com

A single destination for eBooks from Taylor & Francis with increased functionality and an improved user experience to meet the needs of our customers.

90,000+ eBooks of award-winning academic content in Humanities, Social Science, Science, Technology, Engineering, and Medical written by a global network of editors and authors.

TAYLOR & FRANCIS EBOOKS OFFERS:

- A streamlined experience for our library customers
- A single point of discovery for all of our eBook content
- Improved search and discovery of content at both book and chapter level

REQUEST A FREE TRIAL
support@taylorfrancis.com

Printed in the United States
by Baker & Taylor Publisher Services